YEHEZKEL KAUFMANN

CHRISTIANITY AND JUDAISM: TWO COVENANTS

CHRISTIANITY AND JUDAISM

TWO COVENANTS

By

YEHEZKEL KAUFMANN

Translated by

C. W. Efroymson

JERUSALEM
THE MAGNES PRESS, THE HEBREW UNIVERSITY

©

By The Magnes Press
The Hebrew University
Jerusalem 1988

ISBN 965-223-694-2
Printed in Israel

CONTENTS

Translator's Preface   VII

Acknowledgements   XI

Chapter 1 *The Religion of Israel Among the Gentiles*   1

Defeat of Paganism
    Christianity and Paganism: Modern Scholarship   2
    Hellenism and Paganism   7
    Jewish Monotheism Radically Uprooted Paganism   10
Rivalry of Covenants
    Real Basis of Jewish, Christian Moslem Polemics   17
    The View of Jewish Philosophers   26
    Jewish Rejection of Jesus and Muhammad   35

Chapter 2 *Origins of the Christian Church*   46

Jesus the Jew
    Jesus and Jewish Law   49
    Jesus and the Pharisees   60
The Apocalyptic Messiah
    Jesus — Jewish Messiah   71
    John the Baptist   80
    Son of Man, Son of God   84
    Kingdom of Heaven   89
    Faith in Jesus   98
The Messianic King
    Jesus and Jewish Nationalism   105
    Political Implications of Jesus' Thought   108
    Trial of Jesus   119

The Christian Gospel
    Nationalist Elements of Early Christianity   128
    Popular Religion and Jewish Law   134
    Universalist Elements of Christianity and Judaism   147
    The Gentiles   153
    Beginnings of Gentile Christianity   155
    Judaizers   161
    Christianity — Nation versus Church   166

Chapter 3 *Israel's Religious-Racial Identity*   181
    Ethnic Disintegration   181
    Religion's Historical Effect on Judaism   186
    Judaism and Greek Culture   196
    Christianity and Islam — Persecution of the Jews   203

Indexes

Names and Subject   209

Sources   223

TRANSLATOR'S PREFACE

This book is a translation of chapters 7, 8, and 9, volume I, of
Yehezkel Kaufmann's *Golah ve-Nekhar* (*Exile and Estrangement,*
henceforth the *Golah*), Tel-Aviv, 1929–1930, which is a sociologi-
cal-historical study of Jewry's two-millennial existence as a ghetto-
exilic, dispersed people. The three chapters are here numbered 1,
2, and 3 respectively. These chapters, though in some degree a
disgression, are intrinsically related to the essential topic of the
Golah by Kaufmann's basic thesis with respect to Jewish survival. Kaufmann argues (in the *Golah*) that:

1. The natural tendency and fate of dispersed ethnic communities (living among other nations) is to assimilate and be
absorbed into their alien environments.

2. The Jewish diaspora communities, from the time of the
Babylonian exile to the present day, tended, everywhere and always,
quickly to assimilate — linguistically, intellectually — in all aspects of life, excepting only *religion*.

3. Religion, and religion alone, stood as an "iron barrier" [1]
blocking complete assimilation (absorption), holding the scattered
Jewish communities fast as a distinct religious-racial (or "tribal")
entity through the centuries.[2]

The survival, therefore, of Jewish diasporas in pagan as well

1 *Golah ve-Nekhar* [Hebrew], I, 442 and *passim.*
2 Jewish *communities* might disappear gradually through attrition (conversion and apostasy) or suddenly (due to persecutions and banishments); but never by voluntary mass conversion — not even in the
ages of the mighty religious convulsions, which were the defeats of
paganism by Christianity and Islam.

as in Christian and Moslem environments is a spiritual, religious — it may be said, non- or supra-natural phenomenon. It is this fact which ties these three chapters to the rest of the two-volume *Golah*, in which they are embedded and, indeed, to the whole of the author's extensive literary lifework.[3]

Kaufmann's writings divide, according to content, into three major categories, which for all their diversity are united first by certain well-marked characteristics of the author's approach to his subjects and his argumentation; and, more significantly, by their common origin and background and his passionate interest in, and concern with Jewry's existence and fate as a dispersed nation-community.

The three categories are: first, more or less journalistic articles dealing with immediate socio-political problems of the Zionist enterprise in the emerging State of Israel. Here the principal target of Kaufmann's frequently sharp polemic is the lingering Marxist ideology, specifically the doctrines of economic determinism and the class struggle. These, in Kaufmann's view, outworn dogmas polarize the Jewish community. They frighten and alienate the bourgeoisie, making the attainment of social justice — including the Jewish labor movement's justified demands — more difficult, and even imperil the Zionist enterprise.

The second category is biblical criticism and interpretation, of which the magnum opus is the four-volume *History of the Religion of Israel*.[4] It is for his work in this field, to which Kaufmann turned after publication of the *Golah*, that he is best known beyond the bounds of Jewish-Israeli scholarship.

The third category, chronologically the earliest, is socio-historical analysis of the problem of Jewry's existence and fate as a diaspora nation-community, of which the *Golah* is the principal work. This was the focal point of Kaufmann's lifelong interest

3 See Menahem Haran, ed., *Yehezkel Kaufmann Jubilee Volume* [Hebrew and English] (Jerusalem, 1962), pp. *aleph* to *waw*.
4 Haran, Bibliography, item 4.

and concern. In his earliest published articles, dating from his pre-academic years in Odessa, he sharply challenged the Spencerian hypotheses and the "spiritual-center" Zionism of Ahad Ha-Am,[5] a position from which he never deviated.[6]

The major thesis of the *Golah* — the backbone, as it were — is Kaufmann's argument that religion prevented complete assimilation, that is, absorption and disappearance of the Jewish diasporas, both in earlier (pagan) and later (Christian and Moslem) societies. This is the linkage, the tie, which apparently impelled Kaufmann, after publication of the *Golah*, to turn to the study of the origins and evolution of the "religion of Israel," which, again, was his dominant preoccupation from the publication of the *Golah* to his demise in 1963.

This three-chapter excerpt from the *Golah* recounts the story of the defeat of paganism by Christianity and Islam. Judaism, inherently universalist in content and aspiration, was at the moment of Christianity's emergence about to transcend the boundaries of the land and people of its birth and development.

Now, with the triumphant progress of the Christian and, later, Muhammadan covenants, Judaism was confined by virtue of the extraneous circumstances of its birthplace and development, to the Jewish people — a "tribal" religion of universal content. And the Jews — identified, isolated, and held fast by their religion — "a people that shall dwell alone, and shall not be reckoned among the nations."

In the *Golah* Kaufmann is the voice of a twentieth-century Jere-

---

5   Ibid., items 13, 16, et al. A few years after the demise of Yehezkel Kaufmann, the late Mrs. Yom-Tov Hellman, then resident in Jerusalem, recalled that her father, Haiim Baron, an ardent follower of Ahad Ha-Am, summoned Yehezkel Kaufmann, at that time a tutor in his household, into his study, and challenged him, "How dare a very young man, such as yourself, attack this great man?" (or words to that effect). Kaufmann — for all his dependence — firmly stood his ground.
6   Cf. Y. Kaufmann, *Golah ve-Nekhar*, II, ch. 9.

miah. "I know," he said, "that there are in what I write [the *Golah*] words which will be most difficult for our contemporaries to accept, but what shall I do? Other than what I have stated, I cannot say." And in conversation he once remarked. "I wrote that book [the *Golah*] as alarm and warning." [7] Perhaps, like the words of Jeremiah in his day,[8] the cry of Kaufmann is too difficult for twentieth-century ears.

Cross-references in the present volume are to the original Hebrew edition. Quotations from Scripture (the Old Testament) are according to the Jewish Publication Society translation (1916), 1965 edition,[9] with a small number of changes and also, in a few instances, alternative English wording which, in the translator's judgment, were required for clarification. Quotations and citations from the books of the New Testament are according to the American translation of (Smith and) Goodspeed. *The Complete Bible* (Chicago: University of Chicago Press, 1939). Translations of Talmudic and rabbinic writings are, with a few exceptions, according to the various Soncino (English) editions; pseudepigrapha, for the most part, as in R. H. Charles.[10] Rabbinic sources are abbreviated according to Webster's *New Twentieth Century Dictionary,* unabridged (2nd ed., 1966), and *The Random House Dictionary of the English Language,* unabridged (New York, 1967). The letter "f." indicates usually, but not always, the single following page or verse.

C. W. Efroymson

Carmel, Indiana 1987

---

7 I. L. Seeligmann, "Professor Yehezkel Kaufmann," in Haran, 10ff.
8 Jer. 20:9: "Then there is in my heart as it were a burning fire.... And I weary myself to hold it in, but cannot."
9 *The Holy Scriptures,* according to the masoretic text — A new translation.
10 R. H. Charles, ed., *Apocrypha and Pseudepigrapha of the Old Testament* (Oxford, 1913).

ACKNOWLEDGEMENTS

The translator is indebted to numerous scholars, including Dr. Menahem Haran and Dr. H. M. I. Gevaryahu, executors of Yehezkel
Kaufmann's literary estate, for helpful suggestions; and also to
Dr. Peter Slyomovics, Jerusalem, for his detailed and careful re-
view of chapters 7 and 9 of the present volume.

His indebtedness to Jacob Bemporad, Rabbi of Temple Sinai,
Tenafly, New Jersey, is a special chapter. Jacob Bemporad, while
still a student at Hebrew Union College, Cincinnati, introduced
him to the works of Yehezkel Kaufmann, and since then has
guided him in the understanding of Kaufmann's literary legacy.

Above all, the translator is indebted to Mrs. Joseph Russell
(Madelyn Sullivan) Brown, a friendly, generous critic, without
whose constant encouragement and at times insistent yet cheerful
goading, this translation would never have come to fruition.
Mrs. Brown prepared the manuscript of this publication and carefully corrected and reviewed the accuracy and rhetoric of this
translation. She is in every respect the co-author of this translation.

Mr. David Lazar put much time and effort into preparing the
indexes.

According to the decision of the Board of Directors of the
Magnes Press of the Hebrew University, and with much willingness
on his part, Dr. Menahem Haran ushered this translation into print.

ACKNOWLEDGEMENTS

THE RELIGION OF ISRAEL AMONG THE GENTILES

The rationale of Israel's existence and fate in its dispersion in Christian and Moslem, as well as earlier in pagan lands, is implicit and to some degree indicated in the argument of the previous chapter.* The nation Israel succumbed. The Jews were driven from the homeland, and in their diaspora, the *Galuth*, they tended to adopt the alien cultures, the ways of the gentiles. But they were not drawn to the pagan religions; against them they waged unrelenting and, in the end, victorious battle. Paganism was defeated, but it was the two daughter faiths — Christianity and Islam — not Judaism, which reaped the harvest of Israel's victory. Judaism was confined within the bounds of Jewry. This extraordinary phenomenon — that the Jews were not swept along in the mighty religious currents which issued from their midst — that they retained their separate religious identity, not merely in pagan times, but within the monotheistic realms of Christianity and Islam as well — is explored, and its cause elucidated in the foregoing chapter.

Christianity and Islam were new pronouncements, new revelations of the religion of Israel, addressed now to the gentiles. Israel's monotheism was rid of the burden of Jewish defeat and exile, and therewith prepared for acceptance by the nations. Detachment of the religion of Israel from the nation Israel was a precondition of its acceptance beyond Israel. The new revelations, however, conforming as they did to the spirit of the gentiles, could

---

* See *Golah ve-Nekhar*, I, end of Chap. 6.

1

not supplant the earlier revelation of Sinai in Jewish hearts; Jewry could not accept them.

Let us consider a number of circumstances which are requisite to understanding this disjunction: Israel's monotheism severed from the nation Israel.

DEFEAT OF PAGANISM

Christianity and Paganism: Modern Scholarship

Christian scholars have labored these many decades to lay bare the ties which bind Christianity to pagan and, more specifically, to Greek culture. They challenge the traditional view of Christian origins. The roots of Christianity, they argue, are not only of Israel; and the new covenant is not solely the fulfillment and end-purpose of Israel's "old testament." Rather, Christianity is also of the essential spirit of paganism, the blending of Israel's faith with pagan and, more specifically, Hellenistic culture. Greek thought, it is said, influenced early Christianity both directly and by way of Hellenistic Judaism and is, in fact, a second "old testament" alongside that of Israel. Greek philosophy had tended to purify and elevate the popular religion. The Stoa, in particular, developed ethical-religious concepts and world views which transcended tribal and national bonds and aspired to universalism. Prior to the missionaries of Christianity, there were others who traversed lands and seas, preaching the "good tidings" of a refined faith, new concepts of the deity, and therewith the way of redemption for mankind. Mystery cults of eastern origin, promising salvation, the end of man's corruption, access to the divine, renewal and re-birth, tended to supplant the popular idolatries. The pagan world longed for a "redeemer" who would bring renewal, and an end to human corruption. These currents, the religious-moral ferment of the age, prepared the way for the Christian doctrine. Christian missionaries trod the paths of pagan predecessors; the pagan currents of intellectual and religious-moral renewal coalesced in the

Christian message. In their juncture with the monotheism of Israel, Christianity, an amalgam of Jewish faith and pagan culture, was born.[1]

Justified as it is, however, the effort of Christian scholarship to expose the pagan roots of Christianity has gone too far. Christianity is sometimes viewed as basically paganism with a "monotheistic" facade, the pagan component as primary and the Jewish as secondary and extrinsic. Christianity's "warfare" with idolatry was, accordingly, only on the surface; the "defeat" of idolatry-fiction. Some Protestant scholars deny that the triumph of Christianity (i.e., Catholic Christianity) was a victory over idolatry, a view to which Eduard Meyer gives extreme expression. In Meyer's opinion, Christianity is "one of the most distinctly polytheistic religions"; its victory over the rival faiths was "in fact (this cannot be sufficiently stressed) idolatry's triumph over Christianity." [2] Paganism departed by one door and returned by another. By development of "the Son of God" concept, by Mary's elevation to the status of "the Mother of God," and by the cult of "the saints" Christianity became polytheistic. The pagan deities, given new forms, regained the positions from which monotheism had sought to banish them. A popular faith which was wholly idolatrous entrenched itself alongside the official religion with its doctrine of a Trinity which was "one." As in many pagan pantheons, the father-god was shoved aside by "gods" who were more congenial to the human soul, by the "Son," the "Queen of Heaven," the "saints"; these are the "gods" to whom men turn for help in the trials of everyday existence. The "Goddess" Mary is "the Great Mother" of Asia Minor. Mary

1 Numerous Christian scholars, among them Pfleiderer, Kalthoff, Usener, Wendland, Reitzenstein, Harnack, Bossuet, Gunkel, Norden, Zelinski, and many others, have dealt with this problem, both generally and in detail these many years. They are of various assumptions, views, and tendencies, but with the common purpose to discover basic pagan cultural roots of Christianity, and to interpret Christianity in part or altogether as an outgrowth of paganism. Concerning this, see below.
2 Eduard Meyer, *Ursprung und Anfänge des Christentums,* II, 1921, 23 n. 1.

and the "saints" are the gods of the displaced religion, who live on in the hearts of men. Not until the Reformation did this change.[3] A similar phenomenon is to be found in Islam. Although the monotheism of Islam is more insistent and definitive than that of Christianity with its amalgan of "Three" and "One," the popular mind in Islam also retained the older paganism. Saintly cults were common to all Moslem lands, attached particularly to ancient shrines dating back to idolatrous times. The former gods and demons became "saints," and in some localities even the ancient cultic practices survived.

There is at least a modicum of truth in this assessment of the religious revolutions wrought by Islam and, more specifically, by Christianity. Nonetheless, on the whole, it is a bizarre and baseless exaggeration. Popular belief and, in the instance of Christianity, also normative doctrine tend to retain vestiges of idolatry which find refuge in the deeper recesses of men's souls. In thin disguise (in order to survive), they color and bend conscious thought. But even in Christianity, which retained many idolatrous beliefs, these were, after all, no more than tokens of a pagan past. Indeed the need for disguise, the change of form or image, highlights the depth and scope of the religious upheavals which were the victories of monotheism. The traces could survive only in disguise, only insofar as they were not felt to be in contradiction to the new religious insights, and only if their idolatrous origins had been forgotten. It is easy to be misled in these matters by linguistic

3   Ibid., I, 77ff., concerning Marianism. *Cf.* II, 77. Similar views are expressed in works of other scholars, grounded often in a strange mixture of anti-Catholic and anti-Jewish tendencies. Thus Harnack and Chamberlain. Many contemporary Christian scholars, loath to agree that their religion is "Semitic," becalm their "Aryan" misgivings by reasoning that Christianity is basically pagan. O. Spengler, *Der Untergang des Abendlandes,* 1918, establishes a special niche for himself. He says the defeat of Christianity is only on the surface; culture always develops inherently, by growth from within, according to fixed laws; there is no room for external influences. Thus there was never any Protestant attack on Catholicism, only a conflict between "northern idolatry" and the "idolatry of Rome."

4

niceties and definitions which obscure content. Obviously, if the term monotheism is to be applied only to a religion which recognizes only one divine being and whose adherents do not ask intercession of "mediators" and "advocates," then not only in Christianity and Islam, but in Judaism as well, there is a modicum of "polytheism." Judaism also recognized "intermediaries" who were often closer to the people than the awesome and fearful God of monotheism.

The prophet Elijah, in popular faith, mediates between heaven and earth, appearing before men to bring help and blessing. In the Passover service a cup of wine is prepared for him, surely an oblation of wine! There are also prostrations at the graves of the patriarchs and holy men, kindling of candles in their honor, the pilgrimage to "Rabbi Meir the miracle-worker" to ask his aid. All these customs, however, do not lessen in the least the deep-seated conviction that there is no other god besides God. This is the case with Judaism, and it is the same in Christianity and Islam. Even the most benighted Russian peasant who addresses his icon as "god" knows — and proclaims — that there is no god besides God. Mary is called "the Queen of Heaven" by the Russian peasant, but this is only metaphorical. Also, when popular faith ascribes to heavenly beings special powers and broad authority over earthly affairs and daily life, it still recognizes that they are subordinate powers, that their authority is by reason of their proximity to the One, and because they are beloved of Him. Indeed, it was not the worship of "heroes" and "demigods" — pervasive as it was in the ancient world — which was the seal of paganism. Rather, it was the vague consciousness of pagan man that, besides these gods who were so important and determinate in his daily life, there were many more gods like them or even greater, each lord in his domain, and each an independent power. Therein there was no recognition of the "One" who, though hidden and remote in the recess of His holiness, and though He bestowed authority on the "saints" to attend to daily doings of men, was still the omnipotent and only "God."

Thus, in despite of superficial resemblance between the cult of the "saints" and idol worship, there remains the basic difference, namely that the "saints," unlike the "gods" of polytheism, were not symbolic of nature-forces. Consideration of this difference enables us to evaluate the change in popular attitudes wrought by the monotheistic revolutions. Even the most nearly pagan of Christian concepts — the apotheosis of Jesus — did not involve any deification of nature, which is the essence of polytheism. The Christian deity is wholly above and beyond nature; and neither in Moslem nor Christian popular belief was there any reversion to worship of nature-gods. Cultic practices dating from the earlier ages of nature-gods were reinterpreted, and whatever the connections between the old and the new, they were completely forgotten; to their worshipers the "saints" were not transmuted gods of polytheism. Both Christianity and Islam destroyed the idols, culled belief in their divinity from the hearts of men, taught that they were unclean and their cults abomination. Pagan shrines and idols were destroyed, polytheism and all that went with it consigned to the realm of darkness and defilement. This was religious revolution — nations and peoples abandoned their pagan gods. Idolatry, certainly the polytheism of the ages, died.

Nonetheless it was the religion of Israel, Judaism, not the daughter religions which vanquished paganism. That is, Christianity and Islam took over in this respect the essential concept which was begotten within and accepted by Jewry. Moreover, it was this Jewish thought, operating within the two gentile religions, which endowed them with the power to root out idolatry. The sole advantage of the victorious faiths was the non-Jewish form and mode in which the basically Jewish idea operated in them. Novel forms and modes, however, in the actual historical situation, were requisite to the victories. Therein the pagan elements of Christianity were of no value.

This is not the place to consider further the involved question mentioned above, whether and to what degree Christianity can be considered an outgrowth or development of paganism. But even if it is agreed that Christianity was nurtured and fostered by pagan culture, it is clear that the defeat of popular idolatry — the proscription of idol worship and everything connected therewith, the destruction of pagan temples and shrines — was specifically the result of the Jewish element and in no sense an endogenous development within paganism.

Hellenism and Paganism

Nor was the demise of paganism a natural death, a gradual, quiet wasting away; rather, it was in very sense cataclysmic. What went before was condemned; it was false, corrupt! There was nothing within the world of paganism which could have caused this sudden negation of idolatry. Pagan thought and pagan philosophy tended to compromise with popular idolatry, to graft its refined concepts onto the prevailing religions. Proscription or outright rejection of idolatry is not to be found in the writings of Heraclitus, Empedocles, Aristotle, or even of Plato. The pantheon of Hellas was a world of gods in brilliant disarray, filling the mind with vain imaginings; and popular faith, unable to comprehend "divinity," tended to fetishism. Nonetheless even late polytheism, in general, was still revelation, its sanctity unimpaired, and the worship of its gods no defilement. The Stoics compromised with popular beliefs by allegorical interpretation, not unlike Jewish interpretation of scriptural anthropomorphisms. Thus the homilies of Apollonius of Tyana, who has been compared to Paul and even to Jesus. Apollonius, according to legend, wandered from city to city, from temple to temple, from the river Ganges to westerly Cadiz. He taught that men know nothing of the gods, or how they should be worshiped. He opposed sacrifice and preached the transcendent nature of the supreme god. But there were other gods, as well, whom men must know and speak of with reverence.[4]

---

4 See references in E. Norden, *Agnostos Theos*, 1913, 37f. Norden does not observe the basic difference between these preachments (of Apol-

The Epicureans came nearest to negation of idolatry. Yet they also participated in public idol worship when that was required by the state or by social pressure.[5] Some of their philosophic-religious discourse was directed to all mankind, those who dwelt "in darkness"; but popular belief remained oblivious to their esoteric arguments. The only possibility was a faith of exceptional individuals or an intellectual elite which might function alongside the popular creeds and come to terms with them in one way or another.

The mystery faiths also tended to compromise with the cults even when they sought to differentiate themselves. They promised salvation from the terrors of the hereafter and eternal bliss in the bosom of divinity. But there were always restricted fellowships of "the pure" and "the saintly," and certainly they did not seek to displace the cults. Their adherents were qualified by esoteric rites of purification and sanctification for the supreme good, the highest degree of faith. But there was also room for adherents of lesser degree. At the most, certain practices were abolished, for instance, the sacrifices; but there was no proscription of polytheism. That the way of truth and the good is hidden from the children of men, that men walk in darkness was a motif common to the "good tidings" of both the philosophers and the mystery cultists. Polytheisms, however, were not altogether unclean.

The Gnostic doctrines illustrate strikingly the prevailing mood of the mystery cults. Gnosticism was the supreme theological "science," the true knowledge of the deity and the sole way of salvation. Christian Gnosticism opposed polytheism, but because of its pagan roots it did not completely eliminate popular idolatry, and some Gnostics discovered a trace of divinity in paganism. In the Gnostic *Pistis Sophia* the great princes, who were appointed over

lonius and other Greek sages whom he cites) and the Jewish-Christian teaching. Similarities of "style" are important to Norden; and he fails to observe the essential difference.

5 P. Wendland, *Die Hellenistisch-römische Kultur*, 1907, 61, note 2; 63 (references).

the imprisoned rebellious angels, are called Chronos, Ares, Hermes, Aphrodite, and Zeus.[6] According to Hippolytus, the Naasenes (fortune tellers, the Ophites) believed in the sanctity of pagan rites.[7] Basilides taught that idol worship was folly, but his disciples made use of graven images in their divinations and prognostications.[8] More significant, however, with respect of our concern, is the absence of any tendency among the Gnostics to popular proselytism, to preach the faith to the masses. The "gnosis," according to its secret essence, was inherently confined to the chosen few. Men were of two categories: the spiritual (the *pneumati*) and the corporeal (the *hiuli*); or of three: the spiritual, the psychic (*psychi*), and the *hiuli*.

The highest science was "hidden," a mystery, and only the "spiritual" were capable of attaining it and, therewith, "salvation." The *hiuli* were incapable, thus doomed to perdition. Between the two categories, in a variant version, were the psychic, those who were able to acquire a measure of true knowledge. It was forbidden to reveal the highest "science" to corporeal men — and if it were revealed to them, it would be of no avail. Mankind was separated from the beginning, some to eternal life and the others to perdition. The *pneumati* attained knowledge and were saved; the "psychic" could be saved by virtue of the "redeemer." But the *hiuli* were doomed.[9] Therewith the general tendency of pagan religious thought was given its most extreme formulation. But there was no war to the death against popular idolatry; only the wish to found, above it and apart from it, a more profound, or "higher" belief.

Thus it is that the powerful religious movements which inundated the Hellenistic world were characteristically syncretistic, theocrasies

---

6 *Pistis Sophia,* section 136, end. (German translation, Karl Schmidt, 1925, 263f.).

7 R. Liechtenhan, *Die Offenbarung im Gnosticismus,* 1901, 51f., in particular 53.

8 Irenaeus, *Adversus haereses,* I c. 244 (ed. Harvey, 201).

9 See W. Bousset, *Hauptprobleme der Gnosis,* 1907, 260f. (with references).

9

of eastern and western deities. Rituals and customs crisscrossed
national and ethnic boundaries to win converts. They competed,
it is true, but they also coalesced. They did not deny and proscribe,
and the pagan believer was accustomed to accept customs and
deities of various lineage. Even the Persian religion, for all its
endemic zealotry, did not attempt to root out or destroy. It
merged with other beliefs and lived with them in peace. In the
time of the Arsacidae and early years of the Sassanids, Persian
and Greek beliefs commingled; and certainly the Hellenistic world
sensed no revulsion against Persian influence. Ahura Mazda was
equated with Zeus; and Mithras, whose cult was widespread, co-
existed in peace with other gods, and was even joined with them.
The outstanding characteristic of the syncretism which prevailed
in the Greek-Roman world of the period was peaceful competi-
tion. Nor did the animadversions of the philosophers or the yearn-
ings and mysteries of the devotees of eastern lore pose any threat
to the idolatries.[10]

Jewish Monotheism Radically Uprooted Paganism

The idea that idolatry in all its forms was unclean and an abomination which must be destroyed originated within Israel. Its demise

10 Much the same applies to the inner development of heathenism in
Arabia in the period before Muhammad. J. Wellhausen, *Reste arabis-
chen Heidenthums* 1897, endeavors to show that even before Muhammad, Arab belief tended toward monotheism. The term *Allah* served
as a collective noun designating divinity in general, and when the
Arab referred to a particular god he did not refrain from using the
designation *Allah*. Therewith the concept of an all-encompassing
divinity capable of replacing other gods was formed. However, even
if it be assumed that there really was a tendency toward "monotheism"
which was expressed in linguistic usage, that tendency certainly could
not have uprooted the popular polytheism. This collective concept,
Allah, could not displant Lat and his peer-gods or inspire opposition to idol worship. Even the explicit monotheism of the Greek philosophers compromised with idolatry; and, in fact, there is no indication
of any opposition to idolatry among the Arabs prior to Muhammad.

in Israel set the pattern for its exorcism in the Christian and Moslem worlds; that is, Christianity and Islam realized the Jewish proscription among the gentile converts. The destruction of temples and shrines and the hacking to pieces of statues marked the progress of Jewish dogma among the gentiles. Unrelenting opposition to paganism in all its forms was the hallmark of the expansion of the daughter faiths. Christianity and Islam brought essential revolutions in religious lives, decisive breaks separating pagan past from monotheistic present and future. A new era was born: that which had been was proscribed and reviled only, however, insofar as the Jewish component operated with in new religions. The novel element in the acceptance of Jesus-Paul and Muhammad among the gentiles was not the appearance of a "prophet" or "savior." Paganism also had its "prophets" and "saviors." The revolutionary innovation was that Jesus-Paul and Mohammad preached the monotheistic religion of Israel among the peoples and therewith the destruction of paganism. This is particularly evident and unequivocal in Islam.

The one new tenet, which Muhammad taught the Arabs and which transformed their religious life, was the doctrine of God's unity; that Allah, the God of Israel's patriarchs and prophets, is one, and that He alone is to be worshiped. But the dominant force in Christianity also, for all the seemingly primary belief in the "Son of God," was monotheism, the belief in the Father, the revolutionary idea. The change in the spiritual outlook of the peoples to die and thus redeem, that man must be baptized in His name was not the cult of "the Son": that the Son was sent from on high to be saved. This doctrine of itself was not incompatible with paganism; it certainly did not imply the demise of popular idolatry. The radical change in religious thought was the Jewish world view, the rejection of polytheism, which implied a novel concept of man and the world. Jesus was not the son of Chronos or Zeus, not of pagan provenance. He was unrelated to the gods of any pantheon. He was the "Son" of the God of Israel, the God of Abraham, Isaac, and Jacob. Christianity rejected the Gnostic doc-

11

trine that Jesus was the "hidden God," the "stranger-God," hitherto unknown, in which doctrine pagan genealogy was implicit. The gospel of "the Son" rejected every pagan deity, all the gods of the gentiles in the name of the God of Israel. Were it not for this rejection, Jesus would have become a pagan "redeemer." Belief in him would have combined with and fulfilled paganism somewhat after the manner of Mithra. Moreover, it is not true that Mithra would have overcome paganism had it not been for Jesus (Renan). The religions of Jesus and of Mithra were utterly unlike; Mithra sought admittance into the company of other gods and, at most, primacy among them. Whereas Mithra contended for his own right, Jesus waged battle in the name of "his Father." The Christian message denied all paganism and proclaimed the unity of Israel's God. It was this denial, the Jewish component in the Christian good news of "the Father," not of "the Son," which radically challenged and changed the religious life of the Greek-Roman world. It can therefore be said that, so far as the defeat of paganism is concerned, the half-idolatrous elevation of Jesus to the status of the "Son of God" was immaterial. The monotheistic revolution would have come about if Jesus had remained the "son of man," the "servant of God," or "His son" in the Jewish sense of the term as in the gospels, and also if he had been thought a messenger-prophet such as Muhammad.

The importance of distinguishing carefully between what is essential and what is secondary is evident if we compare the historical evolution of Christianity with that of Islam. Thus, we observe that the Christian message in the pagan world was qualitatively and essentially different from the "gospels" of the Greek "theologians" (*theologoi*) and from the preachments of the mystery-prophets and others who promised "redemption" in the ancient world. The pagan moralists reproached their hearers for a "sin" which was other than the "sin-evil" (*kakotis*) of the Christian evangelists. The latter condemned all paganism, polytheism as such, idolatry in all its manifestations. They did not essay to reveal any occult mystery or highest "science." For them, that was not a way of redemption from the world's corruption, the evil incarnate in nature. "Sin," first and foremost the sin of idolatry, was the source of evil, the root of all evil. Christianity, as it transcended the bounds of Israel into the gentile world, conscious of the special mission which was incumbent upon it, molded its message and challenged all paganism. This was the beginning of the good tidings to the gentiles. It is expressed in Paul's address to the Athenians (Acts 17:16f.) — and it is immaterial whether the specific words are of Paul or of Luke, author of the Acts. Jesus' message to the Jews was his call to return-repent so that a chosen remnant of Israel, the righteous of his generation, might be saved from the judgment of Gehenna. The "kingdom of heaven" was announced for those who were "called," the few who, in addition to the commandments of Israel's Torah, practiced piety and righteousness and withdrew from the world to devote themselves wholly to their Father in heaven. This Christianity in its earliest years was distinctly sectarian, requiring extreme piety and abstinence. In Israel it was a "mystery" move-ment, a sectarian doctrine, bearer of the secret of "the kingdom of heaven." [11]

When, however, it went forth to the pagan world, its perspective changed; it was possessed of a new mission: to root out idolatry. It is true that, according to Paul, Jew and gentile alike were steeped in sin, and Jesus was sent to save the elect both of Israel and the peoples. This, however, was the doctrine in principle. In the fact, Christianity confronted — among the gentiles — a sin which was nonexistent in Israel, the sin of idolatry (together with its temple prostitution rites). In his address to the Athenians, Paul dubs the age prior to Jesus as one of "ignorance," *agnoias*, an age when men worshiped their own handiwork and knew not God. Now God orders all men to "return in repentance," for the day of judg-ment is nigh. Repentance is to turn from the service of idols, from "ignorance." The same theme appears in the Epistle to the Ro-mans, chapter 1, even though the general content of the letter is, on

11 See below, ch. 2.

the surface, the argument that Israel, recipient of the Torah, is not privileged beyond other peoples. God's wrath is manifest against the evil of all men in that they do not acknowledge Him. Even though they could have known Him by virtue of their native intelligence, they pursued vanity. They preferred idols, the images of men and beasts, to the glory of God, for which sin God had consigned them to the rule of sin and evil lusts. Evil came to the world in the wake of sinful false worship: pagan adultery and oppression, envy, murder, deceit, cruelty, hatred, and all iniquity. Christianity would root out the basic, the source, and therewith all evil. It undertook the mission of Judaism in the gentile world, wherewith its basic character changed. The essential difference in Christianity, as it emerged from the bounds of Israel, was not the abolition of the ritual commandments, not its "universality" and its rupture of the Jewish "barrier" rather, in this new popular mission which, in the nature of things, pervaded the whole of the Christian movement. At this point Christianity ceased to be the faith of the few "who were the eunuchs for the sake of the kingdom of heaven." Its task became the eradication of idolatry from the hearts of men. It is as though Christianity, in breaking the bounds of Israel, returned to Judaism. It was no longer the inheritance of the righteous few, the pious of its generation. It took over the popular mission of Judaism, the battle against paganism.

Certainly the sectarian-ascetic component, characteristic of Christianity in its beginnings, was not done away with. Christian monks and priests were inspired with the ideal of castration for the sake of heaven. But that was not the element which enabled Christianity to win peoples. If there had been only asceticism, Christianity would have remained the religion of individuals or esoteric fellowships. The tendency of Christianity, its theoretical goal, was in fact in the beginning the formation of esoteric, "mystery" sodalities, congregations of the "elect," saints or holy men, who would be saved by the grace of God on the day of judgment, which was nigh. The other tendency, however, which was implicit was of broader moment. Its wider mission came to the fore with its progress into the gentile world; and therein Christianity burst the bounds of its earlier Jewish sectarianism. This was, moreover, also Christianity's essential monotheism, its negation of idolatry. In this there was the tendency to popular-public preachment; it was a doctrine for all men.

Therewith Christianity took over the mission of Judaism. Judaism had never aspired to be the faith of a sect. Its basic concept, monotheism and the negation of idolatry, was exoteric, popular. Monotheism was not a faith only for the select few, those possessed of occult "science," the "pneumatics," or "eunuchs for the sake of heaven." Judaism aspired to be the faith of mankind, men, women and children. Idolatry has no place; it must be expunged, lock, stock and barrel. Therein Judaism differed from all the "mystery" cults of the Hellenistic world; and that popular mission, to eradicate idolatry wherever it was to be found, Christianity accepted. Christianity also was not content to save the few, the "elect," those endowed with "grace." To the pagan world, Christianity also was an hostile, destructive force, misanthropic, and its adherents worthy to be persecuted without mercy. Like Judaism, Christianity was a popular faith, its basic tenet inherited from Judaism: the absolute negation of idolatry, its mission to eradicate all idolatry, including its "mystery" refinements. In its expansion, Christianity emerged from the generality of mystery faiths. It abandoned its earlier sectarianism and undertook to realize the age-old goal of Judaism, the elemental-popular mission which preceded the gospel of the "kingdom of heaven." Therewith — and only therewith — could it become a religion of the peoples, of nations.

Thus it is that the secret of Christian success was not its mysteries, not that it preached the good news of a "redeemer" whose figure in this respect bore some resemblance to that of the pagan "redeemers." Rather it was its legacy from Israel, the popular moment, nonmysterious and nonsectarian, the absolute negation of idolatry which was latent in Christianity. Indeed, Christianity won Germanic and Slavic tribes, peoples unacquainted with the mystery longings of the Hellenic-Mediterranean world, untouched by the decadent end-of-paganism clime. The situation was much the same with Islam. The religion of Islam, however, was nonsectarian and nonmysterious from the beginning; also, it offered no redeeming "Son of God." The common feature of the two "daughter religions" was their battle with idolatry, that they sought to supplant it with the faith of Israel. Both of them fought for the God of Israel, and only thereby disinherited idolatry.

The warfare of Christianity and Islam against paganism was, therefore, in fact Israel's challenge to idolatry, Israel's faith and Israel's God against the gods of the gentiles. Christianity and Islam denied the divinity of the pagan deities. God had revealed himself only in Israel's history and Israel's scriptures. Idolatry was stupidity or the handiwork of Satan. The Lord, the God of Israel, was engaged in battle against the gods of the gentiles, God's divine presence, transcendent, above all and the cause of all, is divine providence, the God who speaks to man and probes the secret recesses of his heart. He, the God of Israel, is absolute and omnipotent, source of all being, and only in Him and His grace, not in any pagan or esoteric "wisdom," is their salvation. He made His will known in ancient days, revealed Himself, and worked wonders in the sight of the assembled multitude. Israel was "witness" to His deeds. In Israel's God there is the promise of everlasting salvation for all mankind; by faith in Him and fulfillment of His statutes and ordinances. No dark barrier of "secrets" revealed only to the chosen few stands between God and man; He is the God of all men, loving the downcast, the meek, the "humble," the "poor of spirit." The Lord, God of Israel, does not call upon man to help Him in battle against the forces of evil. No kingdom of darkness and evil contends with Him for rule over man and the world; this God is omnipotent. Sin alone separates man from God, from His salvation. Sin is to contravene God's will and command, His law which is given to man. Both in Islam and Christianity there was, it is true, an element of determinism. In Christianity, in particular, the doctrine of grace: that some were destined afore-

16

time to salvation and others to damnation by divine decree — this the pagan ingredient in Christianity. Nonetheless, in the popular mind it was the Jewish doctrine of "return," repentance, which was decisive; this the promise that man's fate was delivered into his own will. Man could obtain salvation by making God's will his own. By accepting the law of the God of Israel, man entered into covenant with the omnipotent God who is nigh unto all who call upon Him. The gods of the gentiles could not withstand the challenge of this God of Israel.

Christianity and Islam implanted the faith of Israel among the nations. The two were new forms of Jewish faith. In order to understand this extraordinary event, that Judaism itself was unable to win acceptance precisely when it took on new forms, we now elaborate the nature of the difference between Judaism and the two daughter religions.

RIVALRY OF COVENANTS

Real Basis of Jewish, Christian and Moslem Polemics

In the course of time many diverse beliefs and practices would divide Judaism from Christianity and Islam; and especially from the former. Christianity's doctrine of the "Son of God," the problem of God's unity, infringed the first principle of Jewish faith — "the Lord is one." Nonetheless, the differences in doctrine (and even those in cultic practices) were not the source and cause of separation of the faiths from Judaism. Christian scholarship has occupied itself through the ages with the differences between Christianity and Judaism, and to explain the separation in terms of different beliefs, world-views, and religious attitudes. Judaism is said to be a religion of fear and of law, its God a dreaded sovereign-king. Christianity, on the other hand, is a religion of love and grace, its God a merciful, loving father. Judaism is ritualistic and concerned with "physical" purity; Christianity is a religion of

17

faith demanding spiritual and moral virtue. Judaism is community oriented, societal; Christianity individual-personal. Judaism is impersonal law and covenantal-national. Christianity is personal, universalistic, human. The core concept of Judaism is the abstract "Law" (Torah); that of Christianity, sanctification of the man-God, Jesus. Judaism affirms man's life in this world; it is optimistic and calls for moral-ethical action of the individual and society. Christianity is pessimistic, ascetic, preaching mortification of the flesh. Judaism teaches the doctrine of absolute monotheism; Christianity beclouds the issue with its doctrine of the Trinity and, especially, with the apotheosis of Jesus. Thus and more: Rationalist authors in particular, both Jewish and Christian, have tried to explain the differences in speculative terms, metaphysical, philosophical-religious. Indeed, the two religions are set apart by a world of divergent beliefs and opinions, both religious and speculative.

Nonetheless, the question remains: Are these and similar differences the historic cause of the rift, the root cause of the schism? Churches which become — or are from the start — distinct spheres and entities, each following its separate course, are conditioned naturally to develop diverse beliefs and tenets. But this does not mean that these differences are the original source of their separation. Within Judaism (as also in Christianity and Islam) there are various trends and currents, so different one from the other that it is difficult to determine which beliefs or views are the original cause of the separation of faiths. Judaism could accommodate a degree of "love," "individualism," tendencies to asceticism, the concepts of distinction between God and His presence (Shekinah), a "logos" or "son." Philosophic Judaism on the one hand, and on the other cabalistic and Hasidic Judaism, bear witness to the breadth of variation within Judaism.

The separation of Christianity from Judaism goes back to the days of Jesus himself — Jesus whom the best of Christian scholars describe as "Jewish" and not "Christian"; who, for all his call for "love" and ethical purity, continued to observe the whole of the Law and commandments.[12] And, indeed, what novel speculative-theoretical insights or moral principles — as opposed to Judaism — did Muhammad teach?

In fact, the original basis of the separations was neither speculative-theoretical nor moralistic-pragmatic; rather, the question of divine provenance, authority. This was the argument of the early church fathers, those whose writings determined the separations; an argument by which they sought — in vain — to "rationalize."

The facts, as in other matters, are particularly clear and uninvolved with respect to Islam. Muhammad did not propound new beliefs or opinions. His innovations, as compared to Judaism and Christianity, are not founded on any well-defined concepts or ideas (except for his arguments against the "Son of God" tenet, and his surprising statement that the Jews venerate Ezra as son of God). He combines various beliefs and opinions which he chanced upon. Even his attitude to the Pentateuch was not fixed from the beginning, and he might have accepted it without any alteration. He observed the Day of Atonement, told his followers to pray toward Jerusalem, and even continued to fulfill much of the Law. The essential problem was whether he was God's emissary. This, and not the doctrines which he pronounced, was the first question both for him and for his earliest followers. He himself feared lest he was possessed of a demon.

His wife, Khadijah, gave the answer, not by rational argument, but — when he beheld the angel — by placing him at her knees and revealing her countenance. The angel disappeared lest he be put to shame before a woman. Muhammad's opponents demanded that he produce a sign. The Jews did not reject his teachings, his beliefs; they did not believe in his mission, that he was sent or that there was reference to him in "scriptures."

Similarly, with respect to Jesus, the inevitable question which agitated the crowds when they beheld his "signs" was: Who is he?. This was also the first query of his disciples and apparently also

12 See below ch. 2.

19

of Jesus himself (Mark 8:27f.; Matt. 16:13f.; Luke 9:18f.). Who is this man who heals the sick? Who pardons sinners? He and his disciples believed that he did everything by "the Holy Spirit." But his opponents said that it is "by Beelzebub, the prince of the demons" (Mark 3:22; Matt. 12:24; 9:34). The same question — who is he? — and nothing concerning his teachings and beliefs — was asked in the trial before the Sanhedrin (Mark 14:61 and parallels). Healing of the sick, exorcism of demons, and revival of the dead were the earliest "signs" of Christianity.

Christian apologetics of the period of the "apostles" centered in the problem of the new religion's divine impulse; and the decisive proofs were miracles and signs, never rational arguments. The resurrection of Jesus from the dead and the witness thereof by the women and the apostles were the beginnings of the movement. The apostles also wrought *gevuroth* and "miracles" in order to authenticate their message. Thus, also, proof texts from the Jewish Scriptures were important in their argumentation.

All the gospels insist on the correspondence of the events of Jesus' life with "Scripture." The essential was whether Jesus was the messiah foretold of the prophets. Paul, when he preached in the synagogues, cited "Scripture" to prove that Jesus was the. messiah — but the Jews disagreed.

The development of Christianity as a sect within Judaism was conditioned by this dispute, but it was also the beginning of the definitive schism which followed. The differences between the two faiths sharpened with the degree of divine authority ascribed to Jesus, and the source of his authority. Paul's nullification of the Law broadened the gap in that he made the abolition of the Law dependent on Jesus, but even that innovation was not, of itself, a cause of separation. Paul's idea could have led to abrogation of certain practices within Judaism without abrogation of the whole of the Law; and Paul continued to observe various commandments, and not just by compulsion or to avoid controversy (Acts 18:18; 20:16). Moreover, the gentile church divested itself of Jewish practices only gradually; and piecemeal annulment was not of itself impossible within Judaism. The abolition of the sacrifices and the commandments which were dependent on the land of Israel are witness to the extent to which Jewish observance was subject to change. Written law was altered more than once by the oral Law; and the very concept of the ultimate abrogation of the Law was not wholly alien to Judaism.[13] The issue was, again, a question specifically of authority. The "Torah" concept as congealed in the Judaism of the second Temple was a "Law" of eternal validity. There was no possibility of a prophetic revision of the commandments, for a new prophetic Law; nor for the explicit abrogation of any commandment as though by divine will. Moreover, the scenarios of "the time to come" when the commandments would be abrogated, had already been determined. The oral law was, in theory, implicit in the written law; it was elucidation by inference and ancient tradition. Jewry, therefore, could not believe that Jesus was the "end of the Law." Nonetheless, the essential was the question of Jesus' divine authority, which in Paul's formulation was extensive and intensive to the point of a complete break with Jewish belief. In any case the problem of Jesus, which was the origin of the break with Judaism, was not with regard to religious innovations or annulment of commandments. Jesus did not annul; he cautioned that even "the slightest of these commands" must be observed (Matt. 5:19). Nor was he rejected because of any neologisms which expounders have tried to discover in his words. He was not rejected because he "had overcome his Judaism from within," an "overcoming" discovered by the extraordinary subtlety of contemporary scholarship. Jesus' disciples were unaware of it. They remained devout Jews, and Jesus certainly could not have been rejected because of an "inner" victory.[14] In Jesus' lifetime there was no question of his attitude to the Law; and in general the nature of his opinions and doctrines was not the central problem. As with Muhammad, so with Jesus,

13 Niddah, 61b.
14 See below, ch. 2.

the question was whether he was sent of God. Was he, indeed, vested with "authority"?

In Jewish-Christian-Islamic polemics, also, the matter of divine authenticity was always basic and decisive. There was no essential theoretical or metaphysical difference of opinion between Jews and Moslems. Muhammad's prophetic authenticity was the core and focus of the many disputations concerning scriptural exegesis and evaluation of historic events and cultic practices. Judaism could find no fault with the monotheism of Islam. There was, of course, the opinion that the Moslem cult of the Ka'bah stone at Mecca was idolatrous. But this was a side issue, and the dispute went on in despite of Maimonides' opinion that "the Moslems are not idol worshipers, neither in speech nor thought. Their prayer is to God alone, and that in manner which is without fault." [15]

Jewish polemic centered in the argument that Muhammad was not a prophet, that his doctrine was not divinely ordained, that he was not authorized to alter the statutes of the Pentateuch and to institute new commandments. Muhammad was "deranged," "stupid," a prophetic fool, despicable. He was lecherous, a woman-chaser, and unworthy of divine inspiration. He invented his new religion on his own in order to magnify himself and because he sought rule and submission.[16] Jewish polemicists argued that there is no indication in Scripture of Muhammad's prophetic calling, and countered the charges that the Jews had falsified Scripture and deleted the references to Muhammad. In addition, they ridiculed the Koran and its commandments.[17]

Jewish-Christian polemics on the other hand comprised also, as stated earlier, religious-metaphysical questions. Polytheistic ten-

---

15 Maimonides, *Responsa* (Hebrew), ed. J. Blau, II, Jerusalem, 1986, no. 448. Jewish scholarship has agreed with Maimonides in this respect.
16 Maimonides, *Epistle to Yemen*, ed. Abraham S. Halkin. New York, 1952, iv.
17 Cf. Moritz Steinschneider, *Polemische und apologetische Literatur*, 1877. Appendix 7, *Jüdische Polemik gegen den Islam*, 244ff. (Classification of the various themes of Jewish-Moslem polemic.)

dencies gave occasion to animadversions concerning the Christian concept of divinity. Jewish disputants dwelt on the irrationality of the doctrine of the Trinity, and ridiculed the doctrine of the miraculous birth of Jesus. The statements of the Jew Trypho are a very early example of this argumentation. The doctrine of a being so close to God, a "Son" alongside the Father-God was blasphemy and revilement.[18] Christianity's belief in the "Messiah" is trust in man, and it also is blasphemy and revilement.[19] That God had begotten a being in human form is impossible, and contrary to reason.[20] The belief that Jesus was born of a virgin is pagan nonsense, which Christianity inherited from Greek mythology — the myth of Perseus, begotten of Zeus, born to the virgin Danaë.[21] Thus it is that the Jewish argumentation was always rationalistic, directed in particular against the doctrines of the Trinity and the legend of the birth of Jesus.[22]

18 Justin Martyr, *Dialogue with Trypho the Jew*, chaps. 55f., 66f.
19 Ibid., ch. 8.
20 Ibid., chaps. 38f., 68f.
21 Ibid., ch. 67 et al.
22 Cf., the satirical tract of Profiat Duran, *Be Not Like Thy Fathers* (Hebrew), published by Isaac Akrish, Constantinople, 1570, which is typical of this argumentation. Duran argues in the name of reason, "its analogue and proofs," and of logic and its limits. Nachmanides in his disputation, at Barcelona, 1262, says that our, that is the Jews', essential argument is not the matter of the messiah; rather, the essence of the argument and disagreement between Jews and Christians is not what they say regarding the nature of the godhead. But what you [Christians] believe, the essential of your belief is contrary to reason, to the nature of things, and not foretold by the prophets. And it cannot be interpreted as a miracle that the creator of heaven and earth and everything therein impregnated a Jewish woman, "that the embryo developed for nine months, was born, and grew." All this is incomprehensible and "the words are in vain." See M. Steinschneider, ed., *Disputations of the Ramban* (Hebrew), 1860, 12. He concludes with arguments against the interpretation of the Trinity as "wisdom, desire, and power." Saadia, in his *Beliefs and Opinions* [English translation, 1948], also points out the contradictory nature of the Trinitarian doctrine (second essay, ch. 4f.), but he realizes that therewith the matter is not resolved (ch. 7, et al.). For the most part, the Jewish polemics centered on the miracle stories and citations from Scripture.

Popular polemics also attacked the dogmas of the "Son" and the "Mother" with ridicule and by rational argument: "for God cannot have a son, since He has no wife," etc. There was, of course, this fundamental difference; and it alone could be considered decisive and the core of contention between Jews and Christians.[23]

For all this, however, the historical basis of separation lay elsewhere. The earliest disputations and controversy go back to the period before the dogma of the Trinity and the apotheosis of Jesus, and also before the legend of his conception by the Holy Spirit. In the time of the apostles, it was only the messiahship of Jesus which was in question, that is, whether in his life history the messianic prophecies of Scripture were realized; whether he was to be accepted as the anticipated messiah. There was as yet no Trinity doctrine, and the appellation "Son of God" was understood in Jewish sense. No controversy concerning the "Son of God" concept, as such, is reported in the New Testament, and no difference in dogma separated the Christian sectarians from Judaism; rather, only the problem of Jesus, his authority and identity. Moreover, the separation continues to this day between Judaism and that liberal Christianity which accepts neither the Trinity and the divinity of Jesus nor the legends and miracles of the New Testament, and retains only the "moral-ethical" heritage. Similarly, we observe that the separation between Islam and Judaism is not due to any essential doctrinal-metaphysical divergence.

In fact, the alpha and omega of the Jewish polemic against both Christianity and Islam was always denial of Jesus' and Muhammad's divine or prophetic calling. Inauthenticity was assumed beforehand and reaffirmed retroactively, and the argumentation was intended only to bolster and clarify what was assumed in advance. If the two faiths are counterfeit, "human handiwork," it goes without saying that they are not of God, rather only the outward resemblance of His handiwork,[24] and their taints and defects are

23 As stated by Nachmanides.
24 Maimonides, *Epistle to Yemen.*

to be exposed by reasoned evaluation. The basic assumption, however, was accepted in advance and thus, in the eyes of their opponents, Jewish polemicists proved nothing. Those tenets of the
Christian dogma which appeared to defy reason offered ready
targets for disparagement and derision. In all three religions, however, there were more or less irrational beliefs which had to be
"interpreted." Even an anthropomorphism of the Pentateuch and
the Jewish legendry-folklore, "which introduce confused opinions,"
so also the miracles of Christianity and Islam can after all be explained away — as indeed was the way of their scholars. Jewish
mysticism in its time absorbed many pagan elements and even
found room for a kind of Trinitarianism which was perhaps cruder
and more pagan than that of Roman Catholic Christianity. But
to the cabalists "Jesus and his troublemakers were dead dogs, loath-
some, evil-smelling," etc.[25] The basic differences which separate are
not abstract beliefs or metaphysical propositions concerning divinity
and the world. Religious sancta and traditions are characteristically
connected with divine revelation and profusion of holiness. The
unifying element of a religion, which distinguishes it from other
religions, is first of all its specific, particular symbolism and the
belief in the sanctity of its tradition and insignia. Its content may
change but, so long as the continuity of belief in the holiness of
its sancta is not broken, it retains its distinctive character, and its
further development is determined by its particular norms.

Moses is authentic, his Torah is truth; but Muhammad is "mad,"
a "fool," Jesus a "mamzer" who wrought miracles by unclean
spirits — these are the popular prejudices which underlay and
preceded the theoretical concepts of the learned disputants through
the centuries. The historian may describe and explicate the disputa-
tion-phenomena in their successive stages by reference to these
judgments of Jesus and Muhammad and their sources. Jewry did
not acknowledge Jesus or Muhammad as bearers of divine revela-

25 M. Steinschneider, *Polemische und apologetische Literatur* 362, from
a manuscript of the "Zohar."

tion and symbols of holiness during their lifetimes or shortly thereafter. In consequence, everything connected with them as religious
symbols, irrespective of theoretical or ethical content, remained
alien to Judaism. The confrontations were not with respect to philosophical, metaphysical or moral opinions and beliefs; they concerned sacramental symbols, the bearers of revelation. The origins
of schism, dispute, etc. were not theoretical or philosophic, not
opinions; rather belief, belief born not of speculations and "proofs"
but deeply imbedded within the hearts of believers, emotions of
devotion and veneration to which the children of men are given.

The View of Jewish Philosophers

Religions obviously have their particular structures and patterns,
wherewith they incorporate and symbolize their varying ideational
content. The historical beginning of Judaism was the pronouncement of an unique and unprecedented idea: The concept of a
supreme God above and apart from nature, by virtue of which
idea it would eventually defeat idolatry. This was, in fact, the de-
termining factor in Israel's warfare against paganism. The victories
of Christianity and Islam over paganism were victories of the
Jewish concept. The conflict among the three faiths was wholly
unlike that between Judaism and idolatry. Christianity and Islam
also acknowledged Israel's God. But Judaism was more than an
abstract idea; it included an array of symbols and concretizations
of the one supreme God. Judaism not only taught the reality of
the one God but considered itself the vehicle and product of His
revelation, given of Him. Its scriptures, customs, and institutions
were divinely ordained and forever sacred, of unique and absolute
value. Recognition of God's unity, of His supreme holiness, which
arose in the soul of Israel in relation to Israel's faith, and which
issued from the beginning of its religious idea was bound up with
the historic crystallization of this idea. There could be no divine
revelation, no sacred inspiration other than that which was rooted
in Israel's Torah, which came of its spirit and its arcane treasures.

Jews did not reject the teachings of Christianity and Islam as such, rather Jesus and Muhammad as vehicles, as recipients of divine revelation; and therewith everything connected with their persons. God had covenanted with the people Israel and with mankind in ancient times, and given His Law. The covenant was once and forever, not to be altered; there could be no "new testament," no new Law. The contention of Judaism, Christianity, and Islam was a battle of covenants.

After the defeat of polytheism, Judaism was increasingly cons-. cious of its prophetic fundament and based its claim to unique sanctity on the special circumstance of Sinaitic revelation. The basic doctrines of the three faiths and of their philosophies were the same. The reference of each covenant was history, tradition; never reason, argument.

Saadia Gaon lists "the trustworthy legend," that is, the tradition of the fathers, as a "fourth source" of knowledge (beyond sense perception, native intelligence, and reason) and thinks that revelation "quickly" supplied confirmation required, by the popular mind, of the beliefs which for others are verified by the longer route of reason.[26] In fact, however, "trustworthy legend" is the basis and source, the distinguishing and differentiating element of Jewish religion. "Legend" bears witness to the revelation of the Torah. It is guaranty of permanent validity, and therewith implies the invalidity of all other "Toroth" (teachings, laws).[27] Judah Halevi explicit distinguishes between Israel's Law and the "speculations" of the philosophers. His "Jew" opens his argument with the statement: "We believe in the God of Abraham, Isaac and Jacob, in Him who brought forth the children of Israel with signs and wonders." [28]

---

26 Saadia, Preface, 5, 6, parable of the weigher of wealth and the assessor.
27 Ibid., part 3, ch. 6f.
28 *Kuzari*, part 1, 11f.; and, in particular, the response of the Kuzari: "Now shouldst thou, O Jew, have said that thou believest in the Creator of the world, its Governor and Guide...?" (English translation, Hartwig Hirschfeld, New York, 1946.)

Torah is validated by the miracles and wonders and great visions performed in sight of all Israel at Sinai (and not by logical argument). The deliverance from Egypt, not the creation, is the origin of the religion of Israel. The truth of the Torah is authenticated in that Israel went forth from Egypt, stood at Sinai, and witnessed the sublime wonders "with their own eyes" and thereafter by utterly reliable "tradition." [29] Thus the truth of Israel's Torah is specific personal witness which is unique; revelation valid forever at Sinai, to the whole nation at one time, not to an individual. The miracles performed publicly confirm it. They cannot be considered the result of necromancy, calculation, or fantasy.[30] Finally, that both Christianity and Islam derived from and depended upon Jewish Scripture and affirmed it is proof of its preeminence.[31]

Maimonides also based the continuing validity of the Law on provenance and tradition rather than rational argument. He considered that philosophy which was at variance with the Torah as tinged with antagonism and envy of Israel and its Law.[32] To be sure, true philosophy does not contradict Torah. But reason can and ought to prove only that the Torah also includes the first principles which are confirmed by human thought. At the least, however, there is nothing in Torah which is contrary to reason. Philosophy, therefore, can only confirm the possibility of the

---

29 Ibid., part 1, 25. "The continuous tradition which is as the vision itself."

30 Ibid., part 1, 81f.

31 Ibid., part 1, 4f. Halevi mentions Jesus' statement that he did not come to abrogate any commandment of the Torah. This statement was used by other Jewish polemicists. Cf. conclusion of the tract, *Be Not Like Thy Fathers* (above, note 22). See also *Refutation of Christianity* of Simon ben Zemah Duran, printed in the collection, *Milhemet Hobah* (Hebrew), Constantinople, 1710. M. Mendelssohn, in his *Jerusalem,* also refers to Jesus' observance of the commandments according to the Pharisaic interpretation. (See below.)

32 Maimonides, *Epistle to Yemen*, iii. Maimonides lists among the classes, which rose up to thwart the divine will and to destroy Israel, the polemicists and sages such as "the Edomites, the Persians and the Greeks" who sought to contradict faith and to abrogate Torah.

Torah; Torah, however, is not established by speculation or reason but by tradition and acceptance. Also, the very basis of Israelite faith, the doctrine of creation, is not to be proven by logic; that principle is confirmed by tradition. Maimonides argued that preexistence of the world could not be verified, and that the problem could not be decided by logic. If the idea of preexistence were established, "the Law would be destroyed altogether," since this concept "destroys the Law in its essence. It denies every miracle, and obliterates all the hopes and threats which the Law holds out." If, however, creation is confirmed, the miracles and the Law are possible (or "admissible"). Since, then, there is no proof of preexistence, we can understand the sacred texts literally and say, "The Law has given us knowledge of a matter the grasp of which is not within our power, and the miracle attests to the validity of our argument." [33] Thus, the authority of Torah begins with the possibility of miracles and visions which are supernatural; and they, that is the biblical narratives and the tradition in which they are incorporate, are positive witness to the divine source of the Law.

The Law, therefore, is divinely revealed, beyond the order of nature. Maimonides, like Judah Halevi, bases its unique sanctity specifically on the tradition of Sinaitic revelation and formulates the Jewish belief in its unique preeminence with exceptional clarity. The event of Sinai is *sui generis* and testimony to the truth of Torah, without parallel in any other religion. Sinai is "a pillar at the center of faith, and the proof of its authenticity." The Mosaic lore is not accepted because of the signs and miracles attributed to Moses. Indeed, miracle workers are subject to skepticism and distrust, and Israel did not believe in Moses, rather in the theophany of Sinai. There, at Sinai, Israel — not others who might have reported the signs and wonders — they themselves beheld

33 *Guide to the Perplexed*, part 2, ch. 25; see also ch. 16: Since the preexistence of the world cannot be proven, we adhere to the doctrine of creation "because of prophecy, which explains things which exceed the power of speculation."

29

the fire and lightning, heard the sounds, and drew near the Mount. They heard the voice: "Moses, Moses, speak to them these words!" That experience alone is proof of Moses' prophetic calling. We know that it is true, flawless, because it is said: "Lo, I come unto thee in a thick cloud, that the people may hear when I speak to thee, and may also believe thee forever." The implication is clear: Without this Sinaitic revelation, Israel would not have believed "forever." [34] With this assurance, Israel could not accept any future prophet who, relying on signs and miracles, would annul the Mosaic prophecy. Moses' prophecy was attested not by signs; rather, because "we had beheld it with our eyes and heard it with our ears even as he heard." All Israel for all time, those unto whom Moses was sent, were eye and ear witnesses to his prophecy.[35]

Such is the evidence on which Maimonides based the absolute and unique truth of the revelation of Sinai and, further, also the corollary that the teaching is forever, never to be supplanted. Indeed, this also is stated explicitly in Torah: "All this word which I command ... thou shalt not add thereto, nor diminish from it" (Deut. 13:1). No prophet has authority to change anything "from now on," wherefore if someone, whether of Israel or of the gentiles, should arise and perform signs and miracles and say that he was sent of the Lord to add or to abrogate a commandment, or that the Law was given not for all generations, but only for a limited time, behold, he is a false prophet — "and his death [shall be] by strangulation." [36] Israel, therefore, must hold fast to its Torah. Christianity and Islam are new religions, "not of the

---

34 Maimonides, *Mishneh Torah*, Madda', Hilkhot Yesodey haTorah, 8, 1.
35 Ibid., 2–3. Elsewhere (*Guide to the Perplexed*, part 2, ch. 33) Maimonides says that at Sinai "not everything that reached Moses also reached all Israel. Speech was addressed to Moses alone." But here he does not merely expound the written text. In the sequence, he says that Israel also heard the sounds of the first two commandments and all Israel beheld the great vision (spectacle), the fire, the lightning, thunder.
36 Maimonides, *Mishneh Torah*, ibid., ch. 9, 1.

Law of the Lord," thus untrue. The signs and wonders, wherewith their believers attempt to prove their authenticity, thus "human handiwork" which cannot decide between the faiths, because the authenticity, permanence, and uniqueness are attested, not by signs and wonders, but by the theophany of Sinai, seen and heard by the people Israel.[37]

37 Maimonides, *Epistle to Yemen.* The covenant entered into at Sinai is a "great, incomparable and unique historical event." Never before or since has a wohle nation witnessed a revelation from God or beheld His splendor. The purpose of all this was to confirm us in faith "so that nothing can cause us to stumble," and "to reach a degree of certainty which will sustain us in these trying times of fierce persecution and absolute tyranny." And the reason wherefore Israel will not accept any new law is that "our" ancestors "witnessed Moses ... holding a colloquy with the divinity.... He assured us that no other law remained in heaven that would subsequently be revealed, nor would there be another Divine dispensation.... We pledged *ourselves* and obligated ourselves to God, to abide by His Law, we, our children and our children's children until the end of time.... Any prophet, therefore, no matter what his descent, be he priest, Levite or Amalekite, even if he asserts that only one of the precepts of Torah of Moses our teacher is void.... Such a one we would declare a false prophet and we would execute him if we had jurisdiction over him. We would take no notice of the miracles that he might perform ... Inasmuch as we do not believe in Moses because of his miracles.... Our ... faith in Moses is due to the fact that we as well as our fathers heard the Divine discourse on Sinai...." Again, in the *Guide to the Perplexed*, part 2, ch. 39, Maimonides bases the authority of Torah on the prophetic uniqueness of Moses: For "nothing similar to the call addressed to us by Moses our Master has been made before him by any one of those we know who lived in the time between Adam and him, nor was a similar call ... made to one of our prophets after him. Correspondingly it is a fundamental principle of our Law that there will never be another Law ..." See also (end of) ch. 40, an oblique reference to Muhammad's sexual life. In opposition to Christianity, *Mishneh Torah*, Hilkhot Melakhim, 11, 3, the messiah will not perform miracles and signs, nor resurrect the dead. He will be a mighty king and subdue peoples, but he will not change the Law, "for the Law, its statutes and ordinances are forever." In Hilkhot Teshuvah (Repentance), 9, 2, Maimonides says that the messiah will be wiser than Solomon and almost as great a prophet as Moses. Joseph Albo, *Book of Principles* (Hebrew), part 3, ch. 14f., disputes Maimonides' opinion

31

It is significant that this greatest of Jewish rationalists removed the basis of contention among the three monotheistic faiths from the realm of beliefs and opinions. This may be because he was concerned primarily with Islam. For him the ratio — man's logic — held the balance in matters of belief. If logic contradicted religious faith, logic prevailed. Concepts, "first principles," and opinions were, indeed, not wholly unrelated to religious belief, yet independent. The two were distinct spheres. Man could attain "that knowledge of the Creator which was proper to him," spiritual improvement and "good character" even without knowledge of Torah or observation of its commandments.[38]

The goal of true religion is not to impart "concepts," rather to found the "holy congregation." It provides instruction which contributes to the perfectibility of men and removes obstacles to their improvement. Therewith, men become more virtuous and more knowledgeable — the masses according to their comprehension and individuals according to their attainments.[39] True religion also expounds correct opinions, but their source is elsewhere, specifically the human intellect. Thus religion, even though bound thereto, is not a product of the intellect. Its root is not human reason, but prophecy, special divine revelation, inspiration beyond the bounds of nature, a specific manifestation of Deity. "Ideas," are therefore not its essence, since these can be acquired naturally — without divine intervention — by human reason. Certainly a religion which contradicts reason cannot be true, and obviously religions can be classified on this basis. Nonetheless, Maimonides himself resorts — perhaps more than necessary — to exegesis and

that there is reference to the "immutability" and uniqueness of the Torah in the Torah itself (Deut. 13f.). This Albo opines (only) as dogma "derived" from the mission of the "messenger." Thus, if ever any one should prophesy contrary of the Mosaic Law, he is not to be accepted — unless, indeed, his mission should be "verified" in the presence of six hundred thousand (ibid., ch. 20).

38 Maimonides, letter to Hasdai Halevi Hasephardi, *Responsa and Letters of the Rambam* (Hebrew), ed. E.L. Lichtenberg, Leipzig, 1859, II, p. 23a.

39 Maimonides, *Epistle to Yemen,* and *passim* in writings of Maimonides

midrash in order to validate the "truth" of Jewish beliefs. He is, in fact, aware that the same method — exegesis, etc. — can be used for other religions and also that their scholars are given to this methodology even more than he is.[40] It follows that scholarly protagonists of different, at any rate the monotheistic religions, do not argue about philosophic principles. The wellspring of religion is prophecy, revelation and, in particular, historic witness of revelation; again, in substance, tradition. Maimonides argues the timeless validity of Israel's Law, and therewith the less than divine origin of other religions; this on the basis of the theophany of Sinai (or the ascent of Moses). That the religious basis of the "higher congregation" is better suited to its purpose (compared to other religions) is derived from the precedent assumption of its uniquely divine source.

Moses Mendelssohn, eighteenth-century father of the Jewish enlightenment, held similar views. Mendelssohn thought that religion also included a speculative element; but ideology was not the essence of positive, that is, revealed religion. The source of the "eternal verities" was the human intellect, the birthright of all men, including those to whom true religion had not been revealed.[41] God did not reveal the "eternal verities" to mankind with signs and wonders; rather, He implanted them in their souls. There was no need to reveal these truths, the "religion of mankind" (*Menschenreligion*), at Sinai. Indeed, it was not necessary to reveal them by signs and wonders, since they could be verified by logical proof.[42] Judaism is a revealed constitution, not a revealed religion, and thus other than Christianity, which seeks to impose beliefs and opinions on its adherents. Admittedly, religion also includes the verities: that there is a God; the facts of His existence, His essence, omnipotence, omniscience; providence, reward and punishment. These truths, however, were not revealed at a given moment in

---

40 Maimonides, *Guide to the Perplexed*, part 2, ch. 25, referring to the "figurative" interpretation of miracles by "the Islamic allegorists."
41 M. Mendelssohn, *Jerusalem*, published in 1783, part 2, 40f.
42 Ibid., 48f., 112f., et al.

time to a particular people and in miraculous circumstances.[43]
The Law vouchsafed to Israel at Sinai contains, in addition to
speculative truth, other elements which were validated by the
voices and lightnings. Thus, together with the truths of the *Menschenreligion,* the Torah comprises historic truths, creation, the patriarchs, the nation Israel, which required confirmation by signs-
wonders, and, in particular, statutes and ordinances, confirmed
"solemnly, publicly, in uniquely miraculous manner" by God, and
thus "incumbent forever on the people Israel in all its generations." [44] Israel, therefore, can be freed from the obligation of
Torah only if the "Supreme Legislator" were to reveal His new
Law "with those very same voices, that identical publicity and
pronouncement, and beyond any doubt or misgivings" in which
Israel's Torah was originally given. Only a new Sinaitic theophany
could abrogate the obligation imposed on Israel at Sinai. Until that
event Israel must bear the divinely placed yoke.[45]

To Mendelssohn, therefore, Judaism is a special and specific
revelation of the divine will for Israel. Though he is not explicit
about it, it is clear that, in his opinion, other religions (even
though they may also be grounded in divine "providence"),[46]
because they were not revealed with voices and lightnings do not
attain to that extreme eminence which is of the religion of Israel.
Mendelssohn, the "enlightened" sage, does not consider opinions
(the "verities") the marrow of positive religion. Thus, also, differences of opinion are not the root cause of different religions.
Even if all mankind were to believe in the principles of the

43 Ibid., 48, 112f.
44 Ibid., 111f. Thus Mendelssohn does not base Judaism solely on sta-
    tutes; rather, also on "beliefs," historic events. Therewith he negates,
    without being aware of it, his entire conceptual framework of "historic
    truths." See also 38f., 48, 50, et al.
45 Ibid., 127f. Mendelssohn argues (129 f) that the Christians must also
    acknowledge Israel's obligation to observe the commandments; this
    because of Jesus' specific command and his personal observance of all
    the mitzvoth.
46 Ibid., 42f.

Menschenreligion, the differentiation due to the various revelations, on which the religions are based, would remain. It is specifically in the disjunction between the contents of the positive religions and the "eternal verities" that the well-grounded perception that religion is other than a matter of speculative truths finds expression. Only contemporary liberal theology, Jewish and Christian, wrought (speculatively) confusion and sought to explain the differences as ideational and ethical. In fact, there is also in this endeavor recognition of another basis of differentiation, that of distinctive forms of worship, prayer, burial.

Thus, the origin of the separation of the two newer faiths from Judaism was rival miracles — exorcisms, visions, resurrection, reinterpretation of scriptural passages, and not different philosophies or ethical views. It was in both instances, therefore, the authenticity of theophany, revelation, not theories and doctrines which separated the religions. Why — it was asked — did the Jews reject the *toroth* of Jesus and Muhammad? Muhammad did not announce a new law for Israel. As stated above, he was disposed at first to maintain Jewish Law. And Jesus — for all his tendency to extremism — demanded nothing which was wholly alien to Jewish thought. Jewry certainly did not reject the teaching of Jesus; the source of his teaching was Israel's lore. No Jew could find heresy in his demand that one love *also* his enemy, or his call for social justice, or his preachment of the terrors of the day of judgment. The question was always authenticity of the prophet, not his doctrines. Why did the gentiles accept Jesus and Muhammad, and why were they rejected by Jewry? With the answer to this question, the "mystery" of the schisms in Israel's monotheism is solved. Differences of theoretical or speculative doctrine become subordinate, relatively insignificant.

Jewish Rejection of Jesus and Muhammad

The major stumbling block which has tripped scholars concerned with the problem of Jewish rejection of Jesus (and Muhammad) is the manner in which it has been formulated. The problem is widespread in relation particularly to Christianity. This is the formulation — why did the Jews reject Jesus — due partly to Christian influence, Christian and also Jewish scholars have accepted even from earliest times. From the beginning, Christian scholars could not understand the phenomenon, so strange from their point of view, that Israel did not accept the Messiah who was sent to them by God. Paul, in particular, was troubled by the problem. Israel, so it was assumed, ought to have accepted Jesus.

In fact, however, the extraordinary phenomenon was not Jewish rejection, but gentile acceptance of Jesus and Muhammad. The fate of Jesus (and Muhammad) was, in fact, no different from that of many other "prophets," "seers" and "redeemers" in Israel and among other peoples and tongues. The rejections are no "problem." During Jesus' lifetime, the populace was drawn to him and believed that he was the "messiah." Jews heard his reproaches and parables and beheld his miracles — and many believed. When, astride an ass, he entered Jerusalem, they shouted "Hosanna," and when he was crucified, they despaired. Similar events occurred both before and after Jesus. After his crucifixion, his very enthusiastic followers continued to believe in him, as was the case with other "messiahs." But for the people as a whole, he was now only another "false messiah." Thus, Israel's "rejection" of Jesus implied that belief in the crucified messiah could be the faith only of a sect, one among other sects. Certainly Jesus' followers were harassed. This, however, was the usual lot of sectarians; the pietists (Hasidim) also were persecuted in their time. The Jewish-Christians remained within the congregation of Israel, and when Jacob ("James the Just," the brother of Jesus) was killed, the Pharisees were outraged.[47] So far, in the natural course of events, Jesus might have founded a sect of the faithful within Israel, even as other founders of sects in Israel and among the gentile peoples. Thus Muhammad — to whom Gabriel spoke and who was called to be Allah's prophet — and among whose followers were Jews.

47 Josephus, *Antiquities,* 20:9:1.

That the Jews as a whole did not accept Jesus is not surprising. Belief in Jesus spread slowly, and from the beginning he was subject to ridicule. The problem is not why Jewry did not believe, but why Jesus and Muhammad found acceptance among the gentiles — why they became more than founders of sects.

First of all it is clear that the mission, the roles which Jesus and Muhammad might have performed (if all Israel had accepted them), would have been completely different from that which was theirs among the gentiles. Within Israel, they would have been links in the long chain of prophecy reaching back to antiquity, continuation of ancient tradition, at the most instituting reform — new commandments in the given religion. Muhammad's mission, in his words, was to eradicate idolatry. In Israel, idolatry had long since been eradicated; Muhammad could have been a "prophet," another prophet — not more. And if all Israel had believed that the crucified Jesus was the "messiah," that would not have meant revolutionary change in Jewish religion. Jesus' "name" would have been linked with the anticipated messiah, and possibly with a number of new rituals such as obtained among the Jewish-Christians.

Among the gentiles, Jesus and Muhammad were the end of idolatry. Their task was not to bring reform of a Law and a tradition which had long been accepted and observed. Their message was a completely new religion, the religion of Israel, therewith the demise of popular idolatry. They did battle against the gods of the gentiles in the name of the God of Israel, the God revealed in Israel, against idolatry and for a radically new religious concept, a new divinity hitherto unknown. Muhammad sought only to destroy idol worship in the name of the God of Abraham; and, in fact, that was the essential accomplishment also of Christianity. Christian "love," Christian asceticism and communism, its cults of poverty and celibacy were honored more in the breach than in practice. The practical consequence of Christianity was the destruction of paganism (which of itself brought about a certain change in morality). The essential accomplishment, however — the elimination of idolatry — could not be wrought by Jesus or Muhammad within Israel.

Jesus and Muhammad did not overcome paganism, therefore, as new "prophets," rather as bearers of monotheism, the religion of Israel. They conveyed to the pagan world an hitherto unknown universe of beliefs and opinions which revolutionized lives: this the very specific power of their message among the gentiles, the impact of the monotheism which they preached. Their victories over idolatry among the nations is qualitatively similar to that which had occurred within Israel in antiquity.

Here, therefore, is the answer to our question: Jesus' and Muhammad's historic role, the implanting of monotheism among the gentiles, was completely different from what it might have been in Jewry; and for this reason their influence within and outside Israel was so diverse. Beyond Israel, the conquest of idolatry was linked to their names; they became prophets to the nations. In Israel, this conquest had been decided once and for all in ancient times; theirs was not the role of founders of a new religion for Israel. We may say that, rather than that they fought for monotheism, monotheism fought for them in the gentile world. It was not "Jesus, the Son of God" who won the world (as Zelinski says), but Jesus the herald of the God of Israel to the gentiles. Muhammad was no "Son of God," and he also "won the world." The power both of Jesus and Muhammad lay in the fact that through them the God of Israel prevailed in pagan lands. There, as His prophets, they pronounced new revelations, the word of God Almighty, the God of Israel.

It was no doctrine, therefore, which caused Israel to "reject" Jesus and Muhammad; rather, the nature of the historic task which, by virtue of the objective religious conditions respectively in Israel and pagan environments, they could and could not fulfill. In Israel's religious life, there was nothing to prepare the nation as a whole to believe in the mission first of Jesus and, even less so, of Muhammad. The specific development which prepared the gentiles to accept the faith of Israel was symbolized for them in Jesus and Muhammad. This, of course, was absent in Israel. It was, moreover, precisely this fact, that Jesus and Muhammad were not accepted in Israel, that they and thus their messages were detached, separated from the Jewish nation, which enabled them to implant Israel's faith in alien quarters. With recognition that their calling was to spread the religion of Israel among the gentiles, we become aware of the linkage between Israel's rejection and gentile acceptance.

The gentiles were able to accept the religion of Israel only after its severance from the political destiny of the Jewish nation. Thus, the two phenomena of rejection and acceptance are inherently bound together. Jesus and Muhammad were not recognized in Israel as prophets because monotheism was already Israel's faith; specific religious practices were established, and there was no need of "new covenants." For the gentiles, on the other hand, Jesus and Muhammad were heralds of monotheism. The new faith, which displaced paganism, was stamped with their personalities. Jesus and Muhammad were prepared for their role as protagonists of the religion of Israel in the gentile world by their ejection from Israel. In them, the faith of Israel was symbolized in forms apart from the people Israel.

These three phenomena — Israel's rejection of Jesus and Muhammad, gentile acceptance, and the spread of the faith of Israel among the nations — are, therefore, not unrelated. The basic fact is the battle of Israel's faith against the paganism of the gentiles, and it was in this battle that Jesus and Muhammad functioned as prophets to the gentiles. They were qualified for their roles since in them the faith of Israel was detached from the nation Israel — the detachment which, because of the nation's political fate, was prerequisite to the acceptance of its religion by the gentiles. Nonetheless, the essence of these events was the specific vehicles of the new revelations. Whereas Israel did not recognize them as prophets, covenants with the God of Israel were made in their names for the gentiles. The new revelation of Israel's God was in each case the essential; Israel's faith could be detached from the nation Israel only by means of a new revelation. In the triseciton — one covenant into three — Israel's faith conquered paganism. It was Judaism which was given to the gentiles in the creeds of Jesus and Muhammad. The historic advantage of the two new religions was that they proffered the religion of Israel in the guise of revelations unencumbered with the nation Israel. It was not any innovation, either in dotcrine or rites and practices, rather only the new form which was the essential in the separation. Neither were the innovations in beliefs-tenets or intellectual precepts a factor of separation. Here, again, the situation is particularly unambiguous with respect to Islam. Conceptually, Islam taught nothing new; its novelty was the new prophet, the culmination-prophet. Muhammad did not abrogate the commandments in the manner of Paul. He annulled only some commandments and substituted others which were adapted to the time and circumstances. It is usually maintained that he conformed monotheism to the spirit of the Arab peoples and their life style, which in fact he did. But the adjustments which he instituted were not determinant. Indeed, Islam also won non-Arabic nations, to whose spirits and customs Muhammad's innovations were certainly not conformed. It was of no consequence to non-Arabic peoples whether they bowed in worship toward Mecca or Jerusalem, or whether they made pilgrimages to the sands of Arabia or to the land of Israel, or whether they observed Arab or Israelite commandments. And, unlike Paul, Muhammad did not lessen the burden of the Law. He added numerous rites and prayers and difficult prohibitions such as that of alcoholic beverages.

Indeed, the same is true of Christianity. The church fathers list the advantages of Christianity as opposed to Judaism: Christianity is a refined religion, of "belief" without "works," of "love" without "fear," of the ethical without "ritualism." And even if it is assumed that there is a measure of truth in all this, it still is no solution to the problem. Can it be imagined that the pagan peoples were prepared to accept only a faith which was wholly "belief," "love," and "ethics" without any admixture of "ritualism"? Can it be imagined that the German barbarian and the Slavic savage could accept the religion of Israel only after it was purged of all its "dross" and based wholly on faith, love and morality? Islam and Christianity itself are proof that this is not the case. The pagan peoples did not accept "the refined faith" of liberal Protestantism; rather, Catholic Christianity with all its commandments. They accepted and observed the Christian rites, but not its "love" and "ethics." The Christian innovations of the earliest days were not such as to enable it to win nations. Its preachments — poverty, humility, celibacy, "love" — are sectarian, not of this world. The extension of popular Jewish ethics, which the early sectarian Jewish Christianity preached, demanded too much; it never took root. The abrogation of the commandments, except for circumcision, was no advantage; and Christianity won whole peoples only after it instituted new "commandments" of its own. Christianity and Islam were superior to Judaism in one respect only: They were new revelations of the religion of Israel unencumbered with the fate of the exiled Jewish nation.

In summary, Christianity and Islam defeated paganism and won peoples not by virtue of any intellectual or ethical idea or concept which distinguished them from Judaism. Their victories were due to the fundamental principle — absolute monotheism — inherited from Judaism. The schisms were differences of covenants, of revelations. And inasmuch as Judaism could not win peoples because of its exilic impediment, the significance of the covenants turned the scales. In them, Israel's faith could be detached from the nation Israel and its exilic fate, and win acceptance of the gentiles.

Thus, the origin of the detachment of Israel's religion from the nation Israel was not the birth of a new religious concept whereby Christianity and Islam might have been better equipped than Judaism to win pagan peoples, but the emergence of new historic heralds of the religion of Israel who were no longer of the Jewish community.

This implies that it was not any universalist outlook beyond that of Judaism which fitted the new covenants to win converts among the gentiles. It was not because they were free of any "na-

41

tionalistic limitation" or "narrowness" in which Judaism allegedly persisted. In that respect, Judaism as a religion was no different from the two daughter faiths. The very separation of Israel's religion from the people Israel was realization of the universalism which was inherent in Judaism. In that Jewry had created the institution of religious conversion, it annulled the bond between religion and race. Therewith, it created an objective basis for the separation of Israel's faith from the nation Israel. By virtue of religious conversion, Judaism had become a self-subsistent entity, no longer tied to Jewish nationhood. Its symbolic link to an Israel of converts was free of ethnic limitation. Therein Jewish and Christian conversion was identical: Jewish religion apart from Jewry had become possible, of which possiblity the Samaritan, the Christian, and the Moslem faiths are successive stages.

The Samaritans were rejected by the Jewish community. But they accepted the Law of Israel and became — from their point of view — another "Israel." By accepting Jewish revelation, the Samaritans approached the status of Jews racially; attachment to Israel "of the flesh" was still considered essential. Samaritanism was the product of the perplexities of the age which created religious conversion.

Christianity — born of the subsequent age of Jewish proselytization — conversion, accepted the concept "Israel" shorn of all but religious qualification. Islam, coming later, was without any connection with "Israel." In the time of Muhammad, there were already two "peoples" to whom "Scripture" had been vouchsafed. Even though Islam claimed descent from Abraham, the "ancient proselyte" of Judaism, "Israel" was no longer symbol of Jewish conversion.

The historic separation from contemporary exilic Jewry, not a more universalistic tendency, was the determinant. It seems obvious that if Christianity, even in the formulation of Paul, had become the faith of Israel, that is Israel "of the flesh," it would not have spread more than Judaism. If Jesus and everything connected with him had remained or become "Jewish," if "the hope of Israel" had been pronounced in his name, if Jewry had believed that he would return and restore "the kingdom" to Israel as the disciples anticipated, if Jerusalem had dedicated itself to him — if all these things and more — had occurred and conversion to Christianity had been conversion to Judaism, Christianity would not have been accepted by the gentiles. Christian ethics, abrogation of "ritualism," "individualism," "universalism" would have been of no avail. The advantage of Christianity was not a breach of "nationalism" and "the nationalistic limitation"; rather only actual separation from historical Israel, the Jewish people; the fact that Christianity did not become the religion of the Jewish nation. Paul expressed his authentic feeling characteristically when he said that Israel's "rebellion" had worked out to the advantage of the gentiles. It was that "rebellion" whereby the "Israel" of Christianity became an abstract idea. By Israel's "rebellion," Christianity was prepared to become the religion of the gentiles. Christianity succeeded not because it denied "Israel," rather because the people Israel denied it, whereby the tie to Jewry was severed.

The course of the separation of Israel's religion from the people Israel, this phenomenon of the acceptance by alien peoples of Israel's teaching in new revelations wholly without connection with the nation Israel (and even accompanied by rancor and hostility to Israel "of the flesh"), is most direct and evident in Islam. Islam was born of the soil of Israel belief. But from the beginning it was unconnected with the nation Israel. Muhammad was not a Jew, and the movement which he roused had nothing to do with Israel's messianic hope. Muhammad was not "sent" to Israel but to his own people to teach them worship of the one God and to eradicate their idolatry. He was a prophet, neither missionary nor reformer, and he came neither to teach nor to reform and alter a religion which already existed. His religion is no more than another formulation of the religion of Israel; yet he did not bring the faith of Israel — or of Christianity — as such to his people. He thought he was sent to establish a third "nation," on the model of the two "nations" of the earlier Scriptures, that is, the Jews and the

Christians. He was sent by Allah to the Arabs, in which thought detachment from the nation Israel was implicit. The Arab people did not receive their faith from Israel. Islam is neither "judaizing" nor attachment to "Israel," even in the metaphorical sense of Christianity. Through Muhammad, Allah covenants with the Arab nation as he had covenanted earlier with Israel through Moses; and also with the Christian "people" (Muhammad considered the Christians a "people") through Jesus, the son of Mary. And even if Mohammad had accepted Israel's Torah without change, if he had conquered Jerusalem, built the Temple, and reinstituted the sacrifice as prescribed in the Pentateuch, this idea of itself — that a new prophet, similar to Moses, had been sent, would have sufficed to break any bond of this new covenant with the nation Israel. Muhammad was himself the focus of the movement and its herald, himself the "sign," and in no sense realization of Israel's messianic destiny. Therein, the revelation which was realized in Israel was a new non-Jewish symbolism; Israel's Torah was given anew, this time to the nations through a prophet sent to them. Unlike Christianity, it was given without connection with the nation Israel, with its political destiny, its exile, and its messianic expectation.

As against this, the development of Christianity is complex indeed. In its beginning, Christianity was a Jewish-messianic movement. It was created of that very element which inhibited the expansion of Judaism. Jesus was a Jewish "messiah," the "king of the Jews," whose mission was the salvation of "the lost sheep of Israel's house" (Matt. 10:6 et al.); and he ordered the apostles not to proclaim the good news to the gentiles. Moreover, even if the Jewish cast of the messianic intentions of Jesus himself questioned, Christianity was in its origin certainly a "messianic" movement. Jesus' disciples thought that he was come to restore "the kingdom for Israel" (Acts 1:6); and when Christianity began to win gentile converts, it was still messianic and Jesus its "messiah," *Christus*, "the redeemer of Israel." When Paul journeyed from city to city and founded gentile-Christian congregations, he preached the "redeemer" raised by God for Israel from the seed of David "as he promised" (Acts 13:22f.). This, he said, was "the promise that God made to our forefathers ... the promise in the hope of seeing which fulfilled our twelve tribes serve God zealously..." (Acts 26:6–7), and it was because of that hope, he said, that he had to wear "this chain" (Acts 28:20).

Thus, Christianity was grounded in the Jewish messianic belief. It required much transformation in order, detached from Israel, to be prepared as a new covenant bearing the Torah of Israel given now to the gentiles. This development, the evolution of a gentile religion from a Jewish national movement, an overwhelmingly significant historical phenomenon, is the subject of chapter 2.

ORIGINS OF THE CHRISTIAN CHURCH

The early expansion of Christianity was tied in with the emergence of a new "congregation of Israel." These were "God-fearing" gentiles who remained apart from Jewry, sharing neither its hopes nor, in the nature of things, the stigma of exile which obstructed the spread of Judaism among the nations. The phenomenon of another "Israel" was of itself not without precedent, the Samaritan church being an earlier instance. But the Samaritans evolved before the age of religious conversion and, in the course of their judaizing, came to think of themselves as racially of Israel. Thus, their fate was conjoined with that of exiled Israel. On the other hand, the new gentile congregation which came into being during the lifetime of Paul, the apostle to the gentiles, evolved by way of the institution of religious conversion which was a creation of the Jewry of the second Temple. These Christians considered themselves a congregation of "proselytes"; children of Abraham by the spirit, grafted onto the "congregation of Israel." [1] Nonetheless, they were mindful that

---

1 Cf. Eph. 2:12: The gentiles were formerly "aliens to the commonwealth [or from the kingdom, or from the rights] of Israel." The "barrier" had been breached by the messiah, and the gentiles given a portion in Israel. Cf. Rom. 11:17f.: the metaphor of the grafting of the "wild olive shoot" on the good olive tree, and ibid., 4:16-17, concerning the seed of Abraham, who is father to them also "who share the faith of Abraham ... as the Scripture says, 'I have made you the father of many nations.' " Cf. the exegesis of R. Judah, Jerusalem Talmud,

they were not Jews, and hostile to Jewry even from the start. In this way, they could suppress the exilic-messianic component of Jewish religion and think of themselves as bearers of a new covenant which was not Jewish. They were a new kind of "Israel" unburdened with the exilic disgrace of Jewry.

The gentile church was born in the midst of acrimonious debate among the founders of Christianity, that is between Peter, James, and Paul and their followers; and its development is connected with Paul's doctrine of the abolition of the Law. The earliest gentile Christians followed Paul, and it was their Christianity which would win converts in the Graeco-Roman world. What, then, was the significance of the Law, and why was the abolition decisive? The usual explanation is well known, and has already been considered in some measure; the end of the Law meant doing away with Jewish ritualism, that is, the ceremonial commandments, and emphasis of the ethical component of the religion of Israel. Further, with the annulment of the Law the nationalistic restriction of the old religion was done away with; Christianity became a higher, ethical faith, universalistic, embracing all manking. In this way, Paul expounded and crystallized the essence of Jesus' teachings, even though he drew conclusions from those teachings which Jesus had not imagined. Jesus was, in fact, "nationalistic" and did not intend to abolish the Law and the commandments. He did stress, however, the moral aspect of faith; he interpreted the Law with "inner freedom," disregarded some commandments, and opposed the Pharisees and their ways. Revolutionary change, therefore, even though Jesus was not conscious of it, was implicit in his message. Then came Paul who "revealed Christianity" by explicating and expounding what was latent in Jesus' teachings, thereby, according to the prevalent explanation, preparing Christianity for conquest of the world. This exposition is confused in every detail.

In fact, the spread of Christianity was not due to lack of rituals.

Bikurim 1:4; and Gal., ch. 3f., and other passages in the Epistles of Paul: The believers are "the seed of Abraham."

Christianity won converts with its new Catholic ritual, which for all its difference from Jewish ceremonial law, was still a "ritualism." Thus, it is not to be assumed that the end of the Mosaic Law was of decisive importance in that it meant the abrogation of a set of customs and commandments. Moreover, Paul based the abolition of the Law, as will be seen in the following, on the absolute significance of the sacrifice of God's son, and not on the priority of the ethical. Paul was, in fact, the originator of the Catholic ritual, and his teaching in this respect is unrelated to the moral demands of Jesus and his strictures against the Pharisees. After all that has been said in the foregoing chapters,[2] it should be evident that the abrogation of the commandments did not mean removal of a "nationalistic restriction" or that Pauline Christianity was more universalistic than contemporary Judaism. The direction and thrust of the historic forces and events which we have described in the preceding chapters were quite different from those imagined by Christian scholars.

The significance of the annulment of the Law was not that it marked the priority of the ethical over the ritual, but that the sacrifice of Jesus thereby became an event of divine salvation overshadowing the revelation of the Law at Sinai. A symbolism of the covenant was created whereby the new Christian would be detached from the congregation of Israel. Moreover, the doctrine of the redemptive sacrifice accorded well with the spiritual attitudes of the gentile judaizers, and facilitated the evolution of a predominantly gentile Christian church. A new protagonist of the faith but not of the nation Israel came into being: the gentile church, heir of the religion of Israel given in a "new testament," and with destiny unencumbered with the fate of exilic Jewry.

The markedly apocalyptic element in the new religion also played its part in the separation of the gentile church from Israel and its development in Jesus' name. Thus, the vehicle was created whereby the religion of Israel would go forth to conquer the world. Pagan

2 Y. Kaufmann, *Golah ve-Nekhar*, I, chs. 6 and 7.

nations succumbed little by little by means of this Judaism which was symbolized in the covenant, a fact which neither Jesus nor his disciples nor Paul foresaw or thought possible. Pauline Christianity was not rooted in the ethical teachings of Jesus, and was not the product of Jesus' quarrels with "the Pharisees." It grew out of the legendary, mythological appreciation of the person of Jesus, which prevailed among the earliest followers and was accepted in the end by Jesus himself.

These views will be expounded in the following.

JESUS THE JEW

Jesus and Jewish Law

It is the opinion of Geiger, Graetz, and other Jewish scholars — and also many more liberal Christian scholars — that Jesus was wholly Jewish in outlook. Jesus did not intend to break with tradition, or to found a new religion; and certainly he did not imagine that he was founding a religion of the gentiles.[3] This view is, how-

---

3 Cf. J. Wellhausen, *Israelitische und jüdische Geschichte*, 1st ed., 1894, last chapter, concerning the gospels. Wellhausen altered this chapter in succeeding editions but held fast to his opinion that Jesus did not "abjure Judaism." He stood within the Law, as did the Pharisees. Cf. J. Wellhausen, *Einleitung in die drei ersten Evangelien*, 1905, 113: "Jesus was not a Christian, but a Jew," and did not seek to found a new religion. E. Meyer, *Ursprung und Anfänge des Christentums*, 3 vols., 1921; last chapter of II, 420f. Jesus did not want to violate the Law, and did not intend to found a new religion. Similarly, A. Harnack, *Die Mission und Ausbreitung des Christentums*, 4th ed., 1923, I, 39f.: Jesus' views were grounded in Jewish pietism as expounded by the Pharisees; he dispatched no apostles to the gentiles, etc. (See below concerning the gyrations of these scholars to resolve their bafflement, and their consequent discovery in Jesus' words of a kernel of negation of "nationalism." whereby they relate the "fruit" to the seed.) Jewish tradition, both popular and scholarly, held the same view. H. Graetz, *Geschichte der Juden*, II, 1; *Sinai et Golgotha*, 1867, and A. Geiger, *Das Judentum und seine Geschichte*, 1865, part I, 108–48, consider Jesus a follower either of the Essenes or the Pharisees who never attacked Jewish belief. In popular tradition, Jesus was indeed a

ever, incompatible with orthodox Christianity, and it is difficult
for Christian theologians to accept its implications. If Jesus was
"a Jew and not a Christian," and wholly devoted to Torah, why

sinner in Israel, a sorcerer who had dealings with tainted powers. But
he did not deny the Law or intend to found a new religion. In the
Talmud, various transgressions are ascribed to Jesus: (1) sorcery
(Sanhedrin 43a), licentiousness (ibid., 107b); Sotah 47b; Jer. Talmud,
Hagigah 2: 2; (2) effrontery and disrespect for the sages (tractate
Kalah; Gittin 56–57, et al.). Similarly, Jesus seduced Israel and led
astray (Sanhedrin 43a), and was even an idolater ("He ... put up a
brick and worshipped it" (Sanhedrin 107b, Sotah 47b, Jer. Hagigah,
2:2). Cf. R.T. Herford, *Christianity in Talmud and Midrash*, 1903,
51f. (scientific edition of Talmudic sources); J. Klausner, *Jesus of
Nazareth*, 1922 (Hebrew), 8f. Also, Jesus "made himself a god," *Yalkut
Shimoni*, Warsaw, 1875 (Hebrew); Balak, end of paragraph 768, cited
by Adolf Jellinek in the *Beth ha-Midrash* (Hebrew), 1858–78, V,
207–208; see also *Yalkut*, Balak 23, *remez* (allusion) 771, concerning
the verse. "And he took up his parable" (Num. 23:7). Jewish tradition
was influenced, of course, by Christianity's deification of Jesus. Nonetheless in most sources Jesus, though a "sinner of Israel," is a loyal
Jew (Gittin 56–57). In the *Life of Jesus* (*Toledoth Yeshu*), Jesus was
a bastard who made bold to teach the "ineffable name" in the Temple.
He performed miracles and said that he was the messiah and the son
of God. Christianity was founded not by Jesus but by Simon Cephas
of the "sages of Israel," who endowed the nations with good laws
so that they would not molest Israel. Cf. "The Story of Simon Cephas"
in *Ozar Midrashim* (Hebrew), ed. by J.D. Eisenstein, New York,
1919, 557f. The opinion that Jesus did not intend to deny the Law,
and that he was not the founder of Christianity, is current in Jewish
polemic writings; thus, in particular, the tract, "Refutation of Christian Belief" (Hebrew) of Simon bar Zemah Duran, published in the
anthology *Milhemet Hobah*, Constantinople, 1710. Duran exploits the
narratives of the gospels with much acuity, though without critical
discrimination, and draws the historically correct conclusion that Jesus
certainly "did not wish to deny the Law, and to make himself divine;
his error was that he thought he was the messiah, and when he was
put to death he no longer believed that. The development of this idea
was a series of errors, sophistications, which Jesus neither required
nor imagined ..." (56b). Not only did Jesus not intend to abolish
the Law, he piously sought to add fences to it to strengthen and
reinforce it (54a). John the Baptist was "saintly to the point of folly"
(46a), and the extreme ethical injunctions of Jesus were the "piety
of folly" (54a, 63b).

was he condemned to die? And if Jesus was faithful to the Law, what support or basis is there in the teachings of Jesus for Pauline Christianity? Since Rousseau and Reimarus, some Christian scholars have held the view (which is basically Jewish) that Jesus was condemned as a false messiah; but this opinion, though correct, has not gained general acceptance. It is difficult even for non-orthodox Christians to agree that Jesus was condemned as a "Jewish messiah." Most Christian scholars are inclined to deny the politically messianic aspect of Jesus' life altogether. And those who do not deny the explicit statements of the gospels and perforce acknowledge Jesus' "messianic" claims still try to purge them of political tinge and to think of them as wholly "spiritual."[4] Christian scholarship, in sum, explicates Jesus' fate as determined by his opposition to contemporary Jewish doctrine: Jesus was indeed, in beliefs and opinions, a Pharisaic Jew, and did not intend to break with Jewish practice. But opposition to Judaism was implicit in his teachings even though he was unconscious of that. He opposed the Pharisaic concept of the ceremonial laws; he made morality the supreme criterion and on that basis did not hesitate to annul Pentateuchal commandments. Therewith, he challenged the moribund ethic of Pharisees and priests, and attained to "inner freedom" from the Law; he overcame his Jewishness and thus laid the groundwork for the removal of the nationalistic limitation. The Pharisees "sensed" that Jesus had gone beyond the precincts of Jewry, and plotted his death.[5]

---

4 J. Wellhausen, *Einleitung*, 93, admits a grain of truth in H.S. Reimarus' opinion that Jesus considered himself the "messiah," but thinks that Jesus did not aspire to restore the "kingdom of the house of David" or to realize "patriotic desiderata." Jesus sought religious renewal, the release of Israel not from the gentile bondage, but from the yoke of the priests and Pharisees; and to this end claimed "inner" messianic authority. Eduard Meyer, *Ursprung*, 1921, I, 164, et al., disagrees with Bousset and his followers who reject the documentary evidence of Jesus' messianism. But Meyer thinks that Jesus and his companions were unconcerned with politics.

5 E. Meyer, II, 425–32, and cf. note 4 above. J. Klausner, *Jesus of*

In fact, however, Jesus had no intention of abrogating Jewish doctrine or practice. He said in so many words that he "came" to "enforce" the Law and the "prophets" (Matt. 5:17–18), and that "not one dotting of an i or crossing of a t will be dropped from the Law until it is all observed," till heaven and earth shall pass (ibid., 18–19, cf. Luke 16:17). Further, neither in his words nor deeds — viewed objectively — is there anything which is contrary to Jewish belief or any indication of "inner freedom" from the Law. In his attitude to the Law and in his appreciation of the moral (as opposed to the ritualistic) commandments and even in his disputations with the Pharisees, there is nothing — either conscious or otherwise — of rejection of the Law as it was understood in his lifetime. In these respects, Jesus did not teach anything which was new and original with him.

Jesus was a teacher of the Law "like one who had authority and not like their scribes" (Matt. 7:29). He held himself to be a unique being, the "Son of God," beyond all mankind, endowed with "authority" such as given to no man; which concept will be explicated in the following. But his authority was not to enact new statutes, a new Law; he was "redeemer," not a lawgiver. The Law in his day had become eternal, coeval with the creation; and its abrogation was inconceivable. Jesus was sure that it was God's word, valid forever, unchangeable. Precisely because he believed himself sent of God he could not lift a finger against the "Law"; a kingdom is not divided against itself! The will of God had been revealed through "Moses and the prophets" (Luke 16:31); and, significantly, Jesus, for all that he considered himself the Son of God, never used the prophetic formula: "Thus saith the Lord," or similar phrases.

Jesus had been given "authority" to teach the Jews the right way, to combat Satan. But he thought of himself as fulfilling the Law and the prophets, as elucidating their final purpose and teach-

Nazareth (Hebrew), 402–441, attempts from a Jewish-nationalist standpoint to find points of conflict between Jesus and Jewry.

ing the saintly and also the more worldly of his time what they must do to attain the "kingdom of heaven," and not as the revealer of a new Law. His position with respect to the Law was, in fact, precisely that of the Pharisaic teachers and expounders; the Law was the unchanging fundament on which they based tenets and judgments, even when they interpreted in their own ways. Jesus stated his attitude explicitly: "Do not suppose that I have come to do away with the Law or the Prophets. I have not come to do away with them, but to enforce them" (Matt. 5:17–18).

This statement, however, that he had not come to destroy, implies a very audacious claim, unlike any which had ever been heard in Israel. Jesus was speaking to disciples who looked to him as a higher, an heavenly being; they might have "thought" that he came to destroy the Law and the prophets. The Law and the prophets however — so he said — would endure forever; his "authority" was not over the Law and the prophets, rather fulfillment and elucidation of the Law, guidance and moral precept according to the intent and spirit of the Law. The "I" of the Sermon on the Mount is the "I" of the expositor and preacher who attaches his thoughts to what "hath been said." And yet, there is another note in his words, that of authority, of the ruler of the kingdom of heaven about to come, of the universal judge whose advent is nigh. Jesus might caution that the Law and commandments are to be observed, and concerning piety, sobriety, and humility, but he speaks as one to whom special power is granted, not only to admonish, but also to judge and to set the world aright. Nonetheless, he does not think of his role other than as fulfillment of the Law and the prophets.

In all the accounts of Jesus' disputations with the Pharisees over points of the Law, Jesus never cites a prophetic word which was revealed to him, or claims "authority" to alter Pentateuchal statutes. He either explicates the texts according to the expository system of the Pharisees or cites the intent and spirit of the Law.[6]

6 Re the plucking of the heads of wheat on the Sabbath, see the reference

He teaches the resurrection of the dead not as a prophet who speaks in the name of God; rather, he expounds Torah in this sense in the manner of the Pharisees.[7] Man obtains immortality by the Law and the commandments,[8] and Jesus, like his contemporaries, is concerned with the problem: What is the essence of the Law and the prophets; and on what are the commandments based?[9] He observes the Law and the commandments, and stands fast against the temptations of Satan.[10] In the Sermon on the Mount, Jesus speaks as though adding to what was said "by them of old time," and as though amending statutes of the Law. Yet what he demands is simply rigorous pietism, the conduct required of the righteous if they accept his teaching as "fulfillment" of the Law and the prophets. With respect to divorce, Jesus seems to countermand Torah in that he forbids divorce unconditionally (Mark 10:2–12; Luke 16:18) and says that marriage to a divorced woman is adultery (ibid.; Matt. 5:32). In this, however, Jesus interprets Gen. 2:24 (Matt. 19:4f.; Mark 10:6f.), and cites passages of Scripture in juxtaposition. The writ of divorcement, he says, was prescribed by Moses because of Israel's "hardness of heart"; which is not unlike the sages' explanation of the Law of the "woman of goodly form" (Deut. 21:11f.).[11] Jesus' exegesis of Gen.

to David, Matt. 12:1–4; Mark 2:23–28; Luke 6:1–5, and the inference from minor to major, Matt. 12:5–7; concerning healing on the Sabbath, see Matt. 12:11f.; Luke 13:15–17, 14:5; cf. Mark 3:4. In the matter of vows, Jesus refers to the commandment to honor parents, Matt. 15:3–5; Mark 7:10–12; and concerning oaths, again inference minor to major, Matt. 23:16–21. Cf. J. Klausner, 292–93, 343–44.

7 Matt. 22:31–32, and parallel passages. Cf. Sanhedrin 90b: "which the Lord swore unto your fathers to give unto them" (Deut. 11:9) — (to give) "you" is not said, but "to give them"; thus, resurrection is proved from the Torah (see Sanhedrin, 92a).

8 Matt. 19:17–18; Mark 10:17f.; Luke 18:18f.

9 Matt. 22:35–40, and parallels; ibid., 7:12. In this also, Jesus follows the Pharisaic method (see below).

10 Matt. 4:1–11; Luke 4:1–13.

11 Kidushin 21b: The statute was given only in order to restrain the evil instinct. Cf. J. Klausner, 397. Klausner here refers to Maimonides'

2:24 is typically rabbinic, and might well have been preserved in the midrashic writings; in particular, there is no hint of "inner release" from the Law. There was, in fact, an ancient Jewish sect which, though faithful to the Law, on the basis of exegesis similar to that of Jesus, required monogamy, even though the Law allowed more than one wife.[12]

Only scholars who are unaware of the nature of the oral law can imagine that the homiletic expositions of Jesus were the product of his special "inner freedom" and private beliefs. Jesus' innovations are modest, indeed, compared to those whereby scholars of the oral law conformed the statutes of the Pentateuch to the evolving religious and moral consciousness of succeeding generations. Pharisaic Jewry, for all its annulment of individual statutes, believed always that the Law was valid eternally; and in this respect Jesus was altogether a Pharisee. Jesus expounded the Law in accord with his ethical and spiritual views, and believed that not a single "jot" of the Law would ever be annulled. His doctrine of the Law cannot, therefore, have been the wellspring of Pauline Christianity.

Jesus's disciples remained faithful to the Law, and opposed

---

exposition of the reasons for the sacrificial order. According to Matt. 5:31–32, 19:3f., Jesus forbade divorce except because of adultery, which is the position also of the school of Shammai (Gittin 9, 10). In Mark and Luke, divorce is forbidden unconditionally; and this, it seems, was Jesus' view (cf. the exposition of Gen. 2:24, which is cited also in Matthew: Jesus' statement concerning the divorced woman. Jesus was not pronouncing a rule; rather, he expounded Torah, drawing the extreme pietistic implications, which Christianity then characteristically interpreted as command. Cf. Gittin 90b, statements of R. Johanan and R. Elazar, in condemnation of divorce.

12 S. Schechter, *Documents of Jewish Sectaries*, I, *Fragments of a Zadokite Work*, Cambridge, 1910, 4–5. "Belial" ensnared Israel and directed their faces to fornication, wealth, pollution of the sanctuary "by fornication, the taking of two wives at the same time. But the foundation of creation is: male and female created He them. And when they entered the Ark, they entered two by two." This exposition is surprisingly similar to that of Jesus. Re Essene doctrine concerning sacrifice, marriage, and servitude, see Josephus, *Antiquities* 18:1:5.

Paul and his views. Moreover Paul, as Graetz shows, did not rest his case on what Jesus had said; he states in so many words that Jesus was "made subject to law" (Gal. 4:4f.). The idea that the Law was valid forever and unconditionally prevailed in the early Christian church to the point that Paul considered himself subject to the Law, and believed in its absolute uniqueness. It would not be supplanted by another law; its end would come with the age of grace, and even then "any man who lets himself be circumcised" would be "under obligation to obey the whole Law" (ibid., 5:3). To the early Christian, the "Old Testament" was the only written law, and the sole source of proof texts for the validity of Christian tenets. The Christian tradition, including Jesus' teachings, was a kind of "oral law," of which the precise language and texts were not themselves sacred; they were definitively compiled and canonized as a new "written law" only in the course of generations. Pauline Christianity, therefore, also believed in the sanctity of the Torah, and did not interpret Jesus' homiletic exegeses to mean that the Law included anything which was not the word of God. The basis of Paul's abrogation of the Law is elsewhere; it is neither explicit nor implicit in Jesus' teachings. And just as the disciples did not sense any diminution of the Law when Jesus contrasted his extreme pietistic demands with what was taught "by them of old times," so also the Pharisees. They could not hold him an apostate because of his exegeses of the Law.[13]

---

13 Cf. S. Duran, (note 3, above). Jesus' intent in the Sermon on the Mount was only "to build a fence for the Law"; Jesus pushed piety to the extreme and erected defenses to reinforce and strengthen the Law. In Duran's opinion, this is the "piety of folly" (54a). It is not in the nature of "fulfillment"; the result cannot "properly be termed Torah," since the body politic would be destroyed if it were "practiced" (63b). This is the usual rabbinic judgment concerning such ethical extremism; Jesus' teachings are "piety of folly" and not revolutionary or denial of the Law. On the contrary, they are of the category of "fences" or defenses of the Law, with which rabbinic writings abound. This was certainly the impression which Jesus' preachments made on Jews of his day who were not given to extreme piety. The Jew Trypho of Justin Martyr's *Dialogue with Trypho the Jew,*

Christian scholars, for the most part, regard Jesus' moral teachings, that is, the doctrine of the primacy of the ethical, as a revolution in ethics; he differed from the Pharisees in his emphasis on right conduct. He castigated and reproved the Pharisees because they scrupulously attended to the ceremonial and neglected the ethical commandments. Pharisees were scrupulous in tithing and "let the weightier matters of the Law go — justice, mercy, and integrity" (Matt. 23:23f.; cf. Luke 11:39f.). To Jesus, righteous conduct and commitment were the essential: "Therefore, you must always treat other people as you would like to have them treat you, for this sums up the Law and the Prophets" (Matt. 7:12; cf. Luke 6:31). The commandments incumbent on men are: "You shall not murder, You shall not commit adultery, You shall not steal, You shall not bear false witness, Honor your father and mother and, You shall love your neighbor as you do yourself" (Matt. 19:18–19; cf. Mark 10:19; Luke 18:20). The greatest command of the Law is, "You must love the Lord your God with your whole heart... (the) second like it: You must love your neighbor as you do yourself. These two commandments sum up the whole of the Law and the Prophets" (Matt. 22:35–40; Mark 12:28–31; cf. Luke 10:25–28). Christian theologians find in this primacy of the moral and spiritual the essence of Jesus' religious revolution, and the precedent for Paul's abrogation of the Law. Jesus opposed the Pharisees and, in the spirit of Israel's ancient prophets, proclaimed a new doctrine of what God requires of men.[14]

In fact, the doctrine of the primacy of the moral was not new. The concept had long been accepted in Jewry, and is to be found

ch. 8, says that he has read the gospels and found in them twenty-two commandments "so great and wonderful," beyond what any creature can do.

14 H. Weinel, "Prophetie und Offenbarung," in *Neutestamentliche Apokryphen,* ed. E. Hennecke, 1923, 292, inadvertently nails down the fact: Hosea's contention with his contemporaries ("For I desire mercy, and not sacrifice," 6:6) is "the struggle of Jesus with the Pharisees for the essential of God's will."

throughout the literature of the period of the second Temple and thereafter; and to opine that Jesus' quarrel with the Pharisees concerned the primacy of the moral is to misread the facts. The Gospels bear witness that Jesus and the Pharisees alike taught that the essence of the Torah is the love of God and of man (Mark 12:32f. and the parallel passages). Hillel told the gentile who wanted to convert: "What is hateful to thee, do not unto thy fellow — this is the whole of the Law" (Shabbat, 31a); and Akiba said: "Thou shalt love thy neighbor as thyself — this is the supreme commandment of the Law" (Bereshit Rabbah 24). There was, in sum, no difference between Jesus and the Pharisees with respect to the primacy of the ethical. Inded, the rabbis went even further than Jesus, basing the whole of the Law on the love of man — philanthropy. Jesus, on the other hand, warned against neglect of even "one of the slightest of these commands" (Matt. 5:19), and himself observed the whole of the Law and demanded that his followers do the same. His immediate disciples — those who heard his words — obeyed him in this, and tenaciously opposed the innovations of Paul.

This same idea is prominent in the censures of Jesus. His is not a new dispensation but accepted prophetic doctrine which, however, tended to be honored in the breach, and into which Jesus now breathed new life. The novelty of his admonitions was that he applied the ancient prophetic rejection of sacrifice without repentance also to the new piety of the ceremonial law. He was not content to assert that the essential of the Law is ethical conduct; he went on to challenge the sanctimonious piety of those who imagined that in strict performance of ritual commandments their duty was done. Nor did he merely give utterance to his thought; he expressed it forcefully with that same note of bitterness which was characteristic of the prophets and also of the Jewish apocryphal literature of the period. Like the Ethiopian Enoch (94f.), Jesus prefaced castigation with the stock phrase: "Woe to..." This moreover was not a mere literary flourish; it was severe, personal denunciation. Jesus' was an age of unbounded devotion to the

Torah and its commandments, the beginning period of the Talmudic literature when every word and letter of the Law was sacrosanct; and it required much courage and religious and moral assurance to cast even the slightest doubt on the meticulous observance of the Law. Jesus' censure, therefore, reveals a strong, original and vital character. Nonetheless, for all the pathos of his denunciations, there is no suggestion that the Law is abrogated. Indeed, he censured in the name of the Law. The doctrine of the primacy of the ethical, which postexilic Jewry inherited from the prophets, did not imply impairment of the validity of the ritual commandments to which view Jesus conformed both in word and deed. There is, as will be seen in the following, no etiological connection between the censures of Jesus and the doctrinal innovations of Paul, which latter were founded in the mysterium of Jesus' immolation.

Jesus, then, like his contemporaries, for all his and their emphasis on the ethical, was faithful to the accepted concept of the Torah and all that it implied. Insistence on righteous conduct did not weaken belief in the sanctity of the ritual laws, and Jesus' beliefs and opinions — including again his preoccupation with morality — conformed to the religious-national consciousness of his generation. There is no basis for the view that Jesus by his deepened faith and his emphasis on the ethical was removed, without his being aware of it, from the precincts of Jewry. The illusion that the ritual laws imply a degree of chauvinistic separation makes it impossible to understand Jewish history — and also the history of Christian origins. The individual Jew was required to obey the Law of Israel — this was an essentially religious obligation, whereby he shared in the blessing of the covenant. The religious regimen was, in fact, a barrier setting Israel apart from the nations; and the barrier held irrespective of the content of the Law, whether customs and rituals, or beliefs, or moral precepts. The Torah was a national barrier; Israel was separated by religious beliefs no less than by the ceremonies and rites. Thus even if it were assumed, contrary to fact, that Jesus renounced the ceremonial commandments, he certainly did not deny the unique sanctity of Israel's faith and Law. His concern was not "man" as such, but with those men for whom Torah was the word of God. The "deepening" of Jesus' faith, insofar as it refers to psychological and biographical facts and not' to some abstract intellectual concept, implies no diminution of Jesus' "nationalistic" attachment; even as the universalistic apho-, risms of Hillel and Akiba do not imply any dilution of Jewish identity.

Indeed, the statements of Jesus concerning non-Jews show that his outlook was wholly "nationalistic." Not only are the gentiles "dogs," as it were; they did not exist. Israel and only Israel — even if only the righteous and the pious of Israel — was summoned to the "kingdom of heaven." The thought that the transgressors of Israel will not be saved on the day of judgment implies no universilistic tendency nor any renunciation of the concept of "Israel," as Christian scholars are wont to think. The idea that a "remnant of Israel" will be saved was deeply rooted in Israel; it originated neither with Jesus nor with John the Baptist (see below).

Jesus and the Pharisees

There was, then, no contradiction between the views of Jesus and of contemporary Jewish orthodoxy with respect to the written Torah and the ceremonial law as a whole. Jesus accepted the oral law as taught by the Pharisees. The "scribes and Pharisees have taken Moses' seat" and whatever they prescribed must be observed (Matt. 23:1–2). Jesus' beliefs were wholly Pharisaic, and he argued against views of the Sadducees (Matt. 22:23–32, and the parallels). Nonetheless, the gospels record many disputations wherein Jesus differed with the Pharisees concerning numerous particulars of the Law, and also Jesus' harsh denunciations of the scribes and Pharisees. These reports give the impression that Jesus disagreed with the Pharisaic position as a whole and was opposed to the Pharisaic party. The prevailing opinion of Christian scholars that Jesus was in essential opposition to the Pharisaic Judaism of his day is based on these passages.

In Jesus' lifetime, the priestly faction which rejected the oral law *in toto* was dominant. It is naive to imagine the differences of opinion with respect to details of the ceremonial law could have brought the Pharisees at that time to seek Jesus' death and to hand him over to a Sadducean court. Certainly the Pharisees were not agreed concerning every detail of the Halakic law and of religious beliefs; the accounts of the gospels are in this respect misleading. But Jewish scholars also err when — in their tendency to apologetics — they seek to discredit those passages which tell that Jesus reviled the Pharisees, and conclude that the whole evangelical tradition is in this respect confused or a subsequent distortion.[15]

That Jesus denounced the Pharisees is beyond doubt, even though the reports of the encounters give a distorted view. After Jesus' death, the Sadducees persecuted his followers. But between the Pharisees and the Nazarenes, there was no dissension; the Pharisees tended to justify them, and many even joined the new sect. Subsequently, the Christian church became antagonistic to Jewry as a whole ("the synagogue of Satan") but not particularly to the Pharisees. Thus, it is most unlikely that the authors of the gospels invented the tradition of Jesus' opposition specifically to the Pharisees. There certainly was dispute. But the dispute centered in the

---

15 D. Chwolsohn, *Das letzte Passamahl Chisti und der Tag seines Todes,* 1892, 1908, 113f., suggests that later copyists wrote "Pharisees" or appended the words "and Pharisees", in place of the word "scribes" (which originally referred to scribes of the Sadducees — there were Sadducean "scribes" who knew the Law); this because there were then — in the later period — only Pharisaic scribes. A. Büchler, *Die Priester und der Cultus im letzten Zeitalter des Jerusalemischen Tempels,* 1895, 81f., thinks that Jesus argued with the priests, not with Pharisees, and that originally the (Aramaic) word "the priests" (and not "the scribes") was used in the gospels. Again, D. Chwolsohn, 117, expresses the opinion that Jesus denounced only the most unfaithful Pharisees ("the plague of the Pharisees" of Sotah 3:4), and that subsequently the qualification was removed. M. Friedländer, *Die religiösen Bewegungen innerhalb des Judentums im Zeitalter Jesu,* 1905, 227–30, 316–20, thinks that denunciations against some Pharisees were generalized. J. Klausner, 345, et al., thinks that Jesus rebuked the Pharisees as though he were one of their party.

question: Was Jesus the messiah? Concerning matter of ethics, the Law, and ritual commandments, there was no basic or essential difference.

It is unnecessary at this point to examine the accounts of Jesus' disputations with the Pharisees in matters of ritual in order to prove that they are inexact. We have observed above that the evangelists attribute opinions to the Pharisees which they never held; or again, to Jesus, as though in opposition to all the Pharisees, views which various sages express in the Talmud.[16] Examination of the gospels shows that Jesus did not argue against "the Pharisees" as such. Rather, he engaged in disputations concerning points in the Law about which there were divergent opinions. Jesus stated his views and expounded Scripture along with other disputants, which fact appears clearly in the gospel reports of discussions respecting vows and oaths, to which we now turn.

In Matthew 23:16f., Jesus censures the Pharisees because they say: "If anyone swears by the sanctuary, it does not matter, but if anyone swears by the gold of the sanctuary, it is binding... If anyone swears by the altar, it does not matter, but if anyone swears

16 Cf. Matt. 5:31–33; 19:3. Jesus' opinion of divorce is the same as that of the Shammaites (see above). The view attributed to the Pharisees in Matt. 15:5 is not Pharisaic (see below). The bizarre story (Matt. 12:9–14; Mark 3:2–6; Luke 6:6–11) that Pharisees left the synagogue to plot Jesus' death because he healed on the Sabbath refers to medicaments (ground herbs), whereas Jesus healed by verbal incantations and blessings. Cf. Sanhedrin 101a: It is permitted to charm snakes and serpents on the Sabbath. With respect to the plucking of wheat (Matt. 12:1f., and the parallels), it is uncertain whether there was at that time a fixed Halakhic rule. We observe in Matt. 12:11 that in Jesus' time it was permitted to lift an animal from a pit on the Sabbath; but in the Talmud, the matter is otherwise (see Shabbat 128b). Re washing of hands (Matt. 15:1f.; Mark 7:1f.), see D. Chwolsohn, 94; Büchler, 82–83. Jesus' statement concerning prohibitions, that no one sews a patch of unshrunken cloth on an old garment (Mark 2:21) is on the whole not in disagreement with Pharisaic rulings; and certainly there is in this no significant deviation from Pharisaic views, as Klausner (289) opines. These prohibitions were, in fact, voluntary customs observed by the very pious but not required.

by the offering that is on it, it is binding." Jesus concludes on the basis of inference from minor to major: "Anyone who swears by the altar is swearing by it and by everything that is on it, and anyone who swears by the sanctuary is swearing by it and by him who dwells in it; and anyone who swears by heaven is swearing by the throne of God and by him who sits upon it." Nedarim (Vows) :3 reads: "If one says... as the Altar, or, as the Sanctuary, or as Jerusalem, or if one vowed by any one of the utensils of the Altar... this is a vow as if he had uttered the word offering." It has been observed that the Mishnah here seems to say the opposite of what Jesus attributes to the Pharisees. Nonetheless, on closer examination, it becomes evident that is not so. The distinction, which at first glance seems unlikely, between the sanctuary and the gold of the sanctuary, which Jesus attributes to the Pharisees, is not without substance.

In the first place, the account in Matthew should be emended, on the basis of the Mishnah, to apply to vows only, and not also to oaths. The authors of the gospels were laymen, and did not distinguish between oaths and vows, and thus reported Jesus' reasoning incorrectly. A similar confusion is to be found in Matt. 5:33, where vows are called "oaths." [17] The disputations in which Jesus joined had to do, it seems, with the Halakic rules of vows and oaths, and the evangelist mixed them together. In Matt. 23:16–22, "If anyone swears" should be: "If anyone vows." The logic of the discussion can be understood only if this correction is made, because it is based on the Halakic principle that a vow is valid only if the object vowed (that is, the thing which is to be devoted) can be offered. If the object vowed is sacred (or forbidden for votive offering), the vow is invalid.[18] It follows that a vow by

---

17 Matt. 5:33: "You shall not swear falsely, but you must fulfil your oaths to the Lord" refers to Lev. 19:12 — oaths, and to Deut. 23:22 — vows. The (Septuagint) citation is not exact.

18 Nedarim 2:1: "As the flesh of the swine, or as an idol... As the dough-offering and the priest's-due of Aaron," it is allowable; the reason for which is stated in the Gemara to this mishnah, p. 14: "And

the sanctuary, the altar, or Jerusalem is invalid because these could not be offered, to which opinion there is reference in the relevant mishnah.[19] Moreover, the basis of the accepted opinion — that such vows are binding — was the assumption or interpretation that the vower, "though he did not mention the word *qorbān* (offering, sacrifice)," intended only the sacrifice on the altar, in the sanctuary, (Nedarim 1:3). Thus we observe (if the disputation story is authentic) that Jesus disagreed with the Pharisaic ruling and considered vows by the "altar," the "sanctuary" valid. Jesus's rejection of the Halakic distinction between the altar and the gold of the altar is exegesis in the Pharisaic manner and in no sense contrary to the Pharisaic system of exegesis.[20]

The logic of the disputation concerning the laws of vowing in Matt. 15:3f. is similar. Jesus here reprimands the Pharisees because they say that whosoever tells his father or mother, "Anything of mine that might have been of use to you is given to God" [as a sacrifice] is not required to honor his parents. Thus, says Jesus, the Pharisees nullify God's command. From earliest times, Christian

---

it was taught even so: If one vows by the Torah, his words are of no effect." Cf. responsum of R. Nahman (ibid.), and Maimonides, *Mishneh Torah*, Hilkhot Shevuot par. 8, halakhot 3–5; Hilkhot Nedarim par. 1, halakah 27.

19 Nedarim 1: 3 (variant version). R. Judah says: If one says "as Jerusalem" he has not said anything.

20 On the other hand, Jesus' statements in Matt. 23:22 and 5:34–36 with respect to oaths are intended to stress reverence. They imply no disagreement with accepted Halakha. According to the Mishnah (Shevuot 4:13), an oath is valid only if by a specific name or designation. But if one adjures "by heaven and earth, he is exempt" (see Gemara Shevuot, 35). This means that one who violates such an oath is not liable to the penalty of flogging; but there are restrictions (see the objections of Abraham ibn Daud to Maimonides, *Mishneh Torah*, Hilkhot Shevuot 12, halakhot 3–4). Jesus considers the expressions, "heaven," "earth," "Jerusalem," terms for God (cf. question of Rabbah, Shevuot 35b) and warns against such oaths. Whether he considered those who violated such oaths liable to flogging is uncertain. In any case, there is nothing contrary to Pharisaic ideology in Jesus' statements concerning oaths.

scholars have taken pride in this rebuke; it is witness to the superiority of the ethics of Jesus over Pharisaic doctrine, which
schooled men in the ways of hypocrisy. Early Christian writers
interpret the term "sacrifice" as (something) dedicated and understood Jesus' reprimand to mean that the Pharisees permitted a
man to exempt himself from his filial duty by means of a sub-
terfuge — that is, by a fictitious dedication.[21] Those writers, also,
who recognize the error of the usual interpretation still find reason
to denigrate the Pharisaic as opposed to Jesus' superior ethic.[22]
They agree that the reference is to a vow (which is essentially a
"sacrifice") and not to a spurious dedication. But they still do
not realize that Jesus in this passage is reasoning in the manner
of the Pharisees about a legal point, and not judging a hypo-
thetical moral issue.

That the view attributed by Matthew to the Pharisees is not
to be found in the Talmud has been pointed out.[23] The Pharisaic
Halakah, as is assumed in the usual exegesis of Christian scholars,
is impossible,[24] and it is unnecessary to waste words to prove that

21 Thus Origenes to Matt. 15:5: Sons dedicate their property to a poor
fund in order to avoid support of parents. Luther also points with
pride, and exclaims that the "rabbinites" taught people to evade the
"fourth commandment" (*Von den Juden und ihren Lügen*), ed. 1919,
Weimar, 490). This interpretation, despite its refutation, is still current, thus: *Dah Evangelium des Matthäus*, expounded by T. Zahn,
1922, (to Matt. 15:5), and similarly, in all innocence, E. Meyer, II, 427,
note 3, to Mark 7:8. Büchler, 83, is at pains to explain — contrary
to the usage in Halakic writings — "sacrifice" in the sense of (something) dedicated, thus to conclude that Matt. 15:5 is directed against the
priests.
22 See H. Strack-P. Billerbeck, *Kommentar zum N.T. aus Talmud Mid-
rasch*, I, to Matt. 15:5: "sacrifice," *qorbān* is not something "dedicated."
But parents can be deprived of their "sustenance," according to Pharisaic doctrine, even more easily: by a vow, etc. (ibid., 716).
23 August Wünsche, *Neue Beiträge*, 181ff., cited by Büchler, who agrees
with Wünsche that the Pharisees taught the opposite. Also Chwolsohn,
95; the Pharisees taught "the very reverse" of what Matthew (15:5)
attributes to them. Also Klausner, see footnote 28 below.
24 That is, that a man who vows (away) his property is no longer re-

the Pharisees did not permit a man by means of a vow to avoid the duty of honoring parents.

Mark's version of the controversy is clearer: "You let him off from doing anything more for his father or mother" (7:12). That is, if a man vows to devote his property his vow is binding, and he cannot use the offering to support his parents, so long, that is, as he is not realeased from his vow. This interpretation is, in fact, in accord with Pharisaic Halakah,[25] and the problem becomes: Wherein did Jesus disagree? Jesus and the Pharisees agreed that a vow which left parents without support was sinful and contumacious, decidedly a "vow of the wicked." But was such a vow valid and did it require release; or was it invalid from the start? The evangelists say that Jesus here berated the Pharisees because they nullify what God had commanded, "in order to observe what has been handed down"; the evangelists, however are confused. Aside from the fact that this would have been a Sadducean argument (and not Pharisaic), the laws of vows and oaths are Pentateuchal, that is, not rabbinic (of the oral law which the Sadducees rejected). Moreover, Jesus warned insistently that oaths and vows are binding, and in this was more strict than the Pharisees.

Here, again, it must be understood that the matter at issue is

quired to "honor" his father and mother (by supporting them). Delitsch, for example, translates Matt. 15:5 in this sense.
25 Thus Nedarim 9:1: "But the Sages concede to R. Eliezer that, in a matter between one and his father and mother, they may find a way out for him by reason of the honour due to his father and mother." That is, if by his vow he deprived his parents of the benefit of his property, his vow was binding; but a way is nonetheless to be found by which he could honor — that is, assist, support — his parents. This is exactly the position of Jesus according to the version of Mark; not (as Klausner,306) opines, its "contrary." Votive property, that is, cannot be used for the parents' support until the vow is annulled. The intent of the Pharisaic halakah is evident from the further specification (Nedarim 9:4) that they "find a way" for one who has vowed in violation of the Law. Klausner, 305, cites Nedarim 3:2, which is not relevant. That mishnah deals with vows made under misapprehension.

Halakic detail. The Pharisaic rule, as stated in the Mishnah, dif-
ferentiates between vows and oaths, and determines that vows
which involve transgression of a commandment are valid; but oaths
are not.[26] That is, if a man swears in violation of a commandment,
he must abide by the commandment (and be punished by flogging
for his vain oath); but if he vowed contrary to the Law he may
not observe the commandment until he is released from his vow.
This Halakic distinction is based on the differentiation of oaths and
vows.[27] Whether the distinction was recognized in Jesus' time is
uncertain; but it is clear that Jesus' dispute with the Pharisees concerned the validity of a vow (and not of an oath) which would
violate a commandment. Even as reported in the gospel stories,
Jesus' argument is based on the Law. He indicates no disregard
for — indeed he insisted on the sanctity of — vows, and it was
not because he regarded the rules respecting vows as merely human
regulations. Jesus believed that a vow which implied violation of a
commandment was invalid; in this respect, Jesus made no distinction between oaths and vows, and applied to vows also the rule
which others (and the later Halakah) applied only to oaths. At
the time, the question was still open, and Jesus argued for his
view.

The emotional fervor of the disputation as described in the
gospels — and thereafter by Christian theologians — is unauthentic;
and insistence on the ethical superiority of Jesus' position over
that of the Pharisees reflects failure to understand. The difference
of opinions concerned Halakic niceties; and Jesus' reasoning is
definitely Pharisaic. Here, and throughout, Jesus joined in discussions of the Pharisees concerning the Halakah and presented his
views as one of them. The evangelists were unable to grasp the
arguments in context, and reported them inaccurately, as though
Jesus was opposed to the Pharisaic position as a whole. This evolve-

26 Nedarim 2:2, and exegeses.
27 Cf. Maimonides, *Mishneh Torah*, Hilkhot Nedarim 3:1, and especially
    3:6f.

ment of the Christian tradition was influenced by Jesus' relations with the Pharisees toward the end of his life.

We have observed above that Jesus' hatred of the Pharisees is an historic datum, but that it was a development of his last years. According to the gospels, Jesus associated with Pharisees and broke bread with them in their homes (Luke 7:36), and was warned by "some Pharisees" that Herod intended to slay him (ibid., 13:31). Though never a member of the sect, his views and leanings were definitely Pharisaic, and his relation to the party was in some degree that of the masses — the "am-ha-arez." The people adhered to the Pharisees, and the Pharisees were the wardens of their faith. But the Pharisees were at that time also a sect, marked off from the rest of the nation by customs and special fasts and their meticulous observance of various commandments. The populace, though devoted to their doctrine, were not enamored of — they even hated — the sectarians who held themselves aloof. "The Pharisees," as a party which upheld and fought for the Law encompassed, it can be said, the great majority of the nation; but as a sect they were a restricted fellowship. Jesus was in this respect of the majority, a Pharisee of the people; his religious commitment, like that of the mass of the nation, Pharisaic. But he was not a member of the sect and, in despite of his adherence to their doctrines, he might come even to the point of hating them. On the other hand Jesus was, it appears, well versed in the Law and adept in the Pharisaic manner of exegesis, and his dislike of the Pharisees was not that of the untutored "am-ha-arez" for the learned.

The source of his exasperation was specifically personal. Jesus considered himself the "messiah," the "son of God," and demanded that the nation recognize him as its king. He believed that he was sent of God to redeem Israel and establish the "kingdom of heaven." The sages of the day, however, were skeptical and refused to acknowledge his mission, which to Jesus was egregious sin and rebellion against God. (Re Jesus' gravamina, see below.) Jesus reacted bitterly against the Pharisees, whom he considered the spiritual guides of the nation — they who sat in the seat of Moses. In that the scribes and the Pharisees did not recognize him as the messiah sent into the world, they failed of their duty to give guidance to the people. In his last years, Jesus, while still adhering to their teaching, came to hate them specifically because they occupied "the seat of Moses."

Jesus associated with Pharisees from the beginning and argued with them about matters of the Law. Certainly, even then, ho scolded the hypocrites among them bitterly. But he did not condemn the Pharisees as a whole, and he continued to associate with them. Nonetheless, *pari passu* with increasing consciousness of his messianic vocation, and his demand that the nation and its leaders acknowledge his "kingship," he became incensed against the sect which rejected his claim.

The evangelists failed to distinguish — they combined and confused — earlier disputations concerning details of the Law with the virulent condemnation of the later, messianic period, and reported the events of both periods in the same vein. It was personal acrimony which opened Jesus' eyes and stirred him to diatribes against the party as a whole, charging hypocrisy, fawning, oppres‹ sion, and deceit. It is significant that Jesus testified that the Phari- sees observed the commandments meticulously. But he took them to task in that they would "not lift a finger" to move the "heavy loads" which they had "put on men's shoulders" (Matt. 23:3–5; Luke 11:46); as if, that is, they therewith violated the Law. Thus, Jesus did not refrain from condemnation for deeds which, according to his own testimony, they did not do. He distorts their exegesis of the Law and attaches the faults of some to the whole sect; he vilifies them all and threatens them with Gehenna. Christianity, recognizing the divinity of Jesus and dedicating churches in his name, naturally accepted his judgment. The historian, however, will not expect that one who considers himself the "Son of God" and demands that his nation consecrate him, will evaluate the actions of his contemporaries objectively.

Jesus, in sum, was, with respect to beliefs and opinions, a "Pharisee" to the end. The source of his hostility to the Pharisees as sect and party was his conviction of his messianic mission. Herewith we reach the core of the problem: that modern liberal Christianity which discards the historic bases of Christian belief, discovers a new historic basis for its "refined" faith in the moral teachings of Jesus. It seeks to "emend" Jesus to accord with its requirements, to "liberalize" him to the extent possible, and to purge his faith of "superstitions." It is at pains to be rid of Jesus the "messiah," the "redeemer of Israel," and to stress the religious and ethical aspects of his instruction and preaching. In particular, the fate of Jesus in Israel and the development of the early Christian church are to be explained as due to the clash between his ethical-religious views and those of contemporary Jewry. In this, it misses the essential, the personal moment in Jesus' confrontation, his demand that he be recognized as the messiah. Therewith, however, and therewith alone, his fate was determined, and the seed of the separation of the new Christian church from Jewry was sown.

Jesus did not intend to found a new religion. His faith was that of the Jew of his day, and there are parallels to almost everything he taught in the rabbinic literature, both before and after him.[28] The novelty of his teaching and preaching was the acerbity of his censure; and the source of that acerbity was his personal religious conviction and experience. The ancient concept of the primacy of the ethical — or, in Jesus' thought, the primacy of the ethical and of the *amor Dei* — became imprecation and condemnation of the society of his day. He sensed the danger latent in ritualism and warned his contemporaries against it; but that was a Jewish view, a concept in fact which was possible only within Jewry and to which no non-biblical faith gave birth.

28 See the apt summary, J. Klausner, 396–401 and, in particular, 415–23. Nonetheless, Klausner thinks that Jesus' teaching implied negation of Judaism. But the negative indications which Klausner discovers in Jesus' words are rarefied indeed, far too thin to support Klausner's thesis.

Jesus' tragic fate, however, and certainly the subsequent religious movement which was bound to his life and death are not to be explained by his moral preachments and his censure of the Pharisees. These did not bring him to the cross, and they were not foundation stones of the Pauline church. Neither did Jewry reject Jesus because of his moral strictures; these were of the essence of Judaism. But Judaism could not accept the doctrine of Jesus instead of the Torah of Moses, or equate it to the latter. The Torah had become the symbol and record of God's revelation, the divine and unchangeable word and law. Moreover, Jesus himself, in his beliefs and teaching, did not demand or assert that the law be supplanted or amended. The words of Jesus, his sermons, his moral exegeses, and his denunciations of "the hypocrites," might well have found their way into the nation's sacred anthology alongside other writings of the same genre. In them there was no principal rejection, no revolutionary doctrine. Jesus' fate, therefore, must find its explanation elsewhere, in the very special factor, the specific personal claim with which he challenged his contemporaries.

THE APOCALYPTIC MESSIAH

Jesus — Jewish Messiah

Between the belief, on the one hand, of the gentile Christians in a divine redeemer and, against this, the popular Jewish anticipation of a human redeemer, the fact of an unique mystic-occult trend in Jewish-mystic eschatology, which nurtured Christian origins, has been largely overlooked.

Jesus could become a divine being to the gentiles only because in his life history there was a motif which was consonant with such amazing development. This was the belief of his disciples from the beginning that there was, beyond the human, a divine element in Jesus' nature. The boundary between Jewish and gentile Christianity can be drawn between the Nazarene belief that

71

Jesus was heavenly, the son of God, more than merely human, but not divine, and the gentile belief that he was the Son of God, divine. Nonetheless the "Son of God" aura was at least latent in the Jewish Jesus-saga; his figure, as it emerges in the gospel narratives, is unlike that of any earlier man of God in Israel. He is the son, not a man of God. To Paul, Pharisee and Jew, Jesus, though not "God," was a heavenly being, superior to all creatures, the sublime *imago Dei*. This concept did not evolve of any Jewish-pagan syncretism. Judaism itself could give rise to an idea of this kind, and certainly there was the germ of the concept in Jesus' own consciousness. Jesus did not think of himself as "God," as formally divine, and would certainly have considered Christianity's attribution of divinity an abomination. He was always conscious of his nullity in the presence of God; he prayed to God, and rebuked those who addressed him as "good master"; no one, he said, "is good but God himself" (Mark 10:18; cf. Matt. 19:17). Satan tempted him after the manner of men; he withstood the worldly temptations and did not transgress the commandments (Matt. 4:1–10, and the parallels).

But, withal, Jesus believed in his uniquely ordained divine pre-eminence, to which belief two facts, which cannot be gainsaid, bear surprising and even bizarre witness. One, Jesus forgave sinners; and, two, he banished evil spirits on his own authority, and his disciples did the same in his name. Against which facts, all the efforts to make Jesus a preacher and teacher only falter and fail. To Jesus himself and to contemporary Jewry a man who pardoned sinners committed blasphemy. Yet, Jesus believed that he was endowed with authority to pardon. He was no ordinary "rabbi"; and the "authority" given him had been given to no man. In Jesus' time mystics, such as the Essenes, were accustomed to banish evil spirits by spells. But the banishments were accomplished by means of "names," specifically names of holy angels. Jesus, however, reviled and cast out on his own. The evangelists state explicity that the foul spirits knew who Jesus was (Mark 1:24, 27–28, 34 et al.). Jesus did, indeed, exorcise in his own name and in the name of angels (ibid., 9:38 et al.); but he also banished by means of the Holy Spirit and by prayer and fasting (ibid., 9:29). This implies that Jesus, in his and in his followers' opinion, was the "Son of God" in a special sense, unlike any man endowed, he forgave sins and cast out demons on his own is evidence that Jesus thought himself unique among men. We will observe in the following that his unprecedented belief in his heavenly provenance was expressed in a number of ways; and that his relationship to his contemporaries and theirs to him was determined by this belief.

It is not without significance that Jesus' kinfolk thought "he was out of his mind," and tried to stop him (Mark 3:21). A "rabbi" who performed miracles was no rare phenomenon in those days, and it was not because Jesus performed miracles that his family thought him out of his mind. It was his conduct as one possessed of authority, as a prince of the world of spirits, able to command angels and demons, which astounded people. The phenomenon of a heavenly being treading the earth was without precedent in Israel; gods and sons of gods might walk together in the highways and byways of the gentiles with none to question. But in Israel such a phenomenon was — though not impossible according to religious belief — yet in fact fraught with extreme peril. Jesus' fate cannot be understood if it is supposed to have been determined by his disputations with "the Pharisees" regarding individual Halakic rules concerning vows, fasts, and similar matters. The mythological climate of opinion which pervaded the eastern Mediterranean culture of the age must not be overlooked.

The kinfolk of Jesus might try to hush up the matter of his remarkable deeds by going out in public to "seize him," and the men of Nazareth might drive him out of town with derision and scorn. But Jewry as a whole could not take this kind of "family" point of view. Jesus was not "out of his mind," as those who were close to him might imagine. Rather, he was the conscious embodiment of a definitely mythical-eschatological afflatus, and he did

not merely forgive sinners and banish demons. He presented himself as the "Messiah," the "Son of Man," and roused a public
movement; his teachings and his unearthly origin and heavenly
mission were matters of public concern. His preaching and re-
proofs and also his "mighty deeds " were of eschatological import; and he stated openly that he was the expected paladin-deli-
verer, the bearer of the nation's hopes "in the end of days," of the
coming of the kingdom of heaven. Therewith be brought on messianic upheaval.

Nonetheless, Jesus, in that he considered himself the "Son of
God," was thereby not of the same category as the other Jewish
"messiahs" who appeared both before and especially after him.
He was not of the type of Bar-Kokba and also not of the Shabbetai-
Zevi mold. His was a complex personality, which helps to account
for the confusion and conflicting views with respect to his ministry
and calling. He did not merely preach and reprove, tell parables
and pronounce moral injunctions, pardon transgressions and drive
out demons. His Jewish disciples applied the current term "Messiah" to him, thinking it proper to do so, since he was the long-
awaited "son of David"; and Jesus himself believed that he was
the heir to David's throne and kingdom. He aspired, however, to be
more than the "Messiah" of popular tradition; his would be the
"kingdom of heaven." Even in the Jewish-Nazarene period of Christian beginnings, the political moment — the aspect which dominated all the messianic upheavals — was not primary; and Jesus
never intended a political rebellion. His followers might hope that
"he was to be the deliverer of Israel" (Luke 24:21), that he would
"reestablish the kingdom for Israel" (Acts 1:6); and, at the end,
Jesus went up with his disciples to Jerusalem and proclaimed
himself "king of Israel." He wanted to establish there, in the
earthly Jerusalem, the "kingdom of heaven," and demanded, as will
be seen below, that sovereignty be accorded him and his disciples.
Nonetheless, Jesus was no ordinary messiah; his was the vision
and figure of the apocalyptic redeemer-messiah.

A profound change occurred in Jewish eschatology at the end

of the period of the second Temple, the addition of an apocalyptic element absent from the earlier messianic visions of the prophets. This was the novel doctrine of the resurrection. The prophets had pictured the "end of days" in marvelous light and colors; the new theophany would alter the order of nature, the arrogance of empires would be shattered, and the kingdom of God established on Israel's soil. And yet — for all the marvels, the old order remained; it did not come to its end in the visions of the prophets. A new age would eventuate, but it would be of this world; the nature of the world and of man and his society would be as they were.

The apocalyptic seers, on the other hand, envisioned the advent of a new world, completely unlike the old; the "end of days" would be the end of this world. The earliest literary expression of the apocalyptic mood is to be found in the book of Daniel. In the end of days there will be a "time of trouble," the like of which had never been. "At that time shall Michael stand up, the great prince," the patron of Israel, to deliver Israel. Only those who "shall be found written in the book" will be delivered in the day of wrath. And then, not only will the kingdom of arrogance fall and the everlasting kingdom of the saintly nation be established but — the dead shall rise from their graves! Many shall awake, "some to everlasting life, and some to reproaches and everlasting abhorrence." The particulars of the new world of the arisen dead are not elaborated in Daniel; but it is a completely new world of men risen from Sheol, men unlike any who had hitherto trod the earth. These are they "that are wise," men who have been saved, that "shine as the brightness of the firmament," and that "turn the many to righteousness as the stars for ever and ever." They are a new breed, awakened "to everlasting life" and shining as stars forever (Dan., ch. 12). In this strain the apocalyptic literature, of which only a part has been preserved in the apocryphal writings, created a world of colorful visions and figures, concepts altogether at variance with the visions of the prophets. Of these hopes and visions, the phantasms of the book of Enoch are typical.

75

In addition to the resurrection, another and completely different belief gained credence at this time: that the soul lived on after death to be punished in Gehenna or rewarded in paradise. This idea, however, was distinctly subordinate; the dominant and characteristic eschatological belief was that the dead would rise from their graves when the time had come. Nonetheless — and for all these novel imaginings — the messianic dreams of the earlier prophecy did not pass into limbo. The literature of the end of the second Temple is replete with a strange confusion of prophetic and apocalyptic views and gradually, out of the confusion, two foci of belief tended to coalesce: one, the coming of the messiah, inclusive of the prophetic visions of the end of days; and, two, the new belief in the world to come. In the later rabbinic expository literature the two ideas are distinct, even though vestiges of the earlier confusion remain.

In the period of the emerging Christian faith, however, the two ideas were completely intermingled; and Jesus' beliefs and acts can be understood only if this essential fact is recognized. Jesus and his contemporaries did not distinguish between the world to come and the days of the messiah. The eschatology of this period is characterized by use of the term "kingdom of heaven" to signify the "end of days." Of this usage there is only a trace in Jewish writings;[29] it is confined almost entirely to the New Testament and the early Christian literature.

---

29 In the concluding prayer ("Aleinu") of the traditional service, *The Authorized Daily Prayer Book*, rev. ed., Joseph H. Hertz, New York, 1954, 210–11, "...when the world will be perfected under the kingdom of the Almighty..."; and in the doxology (Kaddish), "...May He establish His kingdom..." (ibid., 212, 213); with respect to content, cf. the prayer: "Now, therefore... impose thine awe..." in the additional service of the New Year (ibid, 896). In the rabbinic literature, the phrase "kingdom of heaven" occurs without eschatological connotation. On the other hand, it is used with eschatological connotation in the literature of the period of the second Temple; see Psalms of Solomon 5:18f.; 17:3; Sibyllines 3:46f.; Ascent of Moses 10:1; also in the Targumim. Cf. Strack-Billerbeck, I, 178f., to Matt. 4:17. In Jewish

In Jesus' day, the anticipated human redeemer, the future "anointed king," had become the dominant figure of the doctrine of the end of days. This concept of the "messiah" must have evolved in the Hasmonean period; it is not to be found in Daniel. In the book of Daniel, Michael brings redemption to Israel. The "messiah" of the time of Jesus, however, is the king of the house of David who will arise to defeat the nations, gather the dispersed of Israel, and restore the kingdom of David. (See below.) The belief in an human messiah-king was exoteric, nurtured by temporal events, the hope of breaking the yoke of foreign rule, of Israel's deliverance from "captivity." The nation yearned for political liberation and national sovereignty, and the yearning expressed itself from time to time in political agitation and in outright rebellion and bloodshed.

The doctrine of the resurrection was widely accepted, even though its relation to the messianic anticipation was not clearly drawn. Moreover, alongside these popular ideas, there were also apocalyptic beliefs wherein the "redemption" was imaged in completely different colors. In these, the "end" was not the end of

writings which are later than the gospels, the term "kingdom" refers to the days of the messiah. The phrase "the world to come," occurring in ancient prayers, does not have the significance it acquired subsequently in the apocalyptic visions of the end of days. The "Amidah" ("Eighteen Benedictions") includes petition for the days of the messiah, and (added later) also for the resurrection of the dead, which latter was the beginning of the belief in the "world to come." Here the two elements, the messianic and the apocalyptic, appear together, which reflects popular belief and is not wholly compatible with the subsequent distinction between the days of the messiah and the world to come. There is nothing in Jewish literature (except in apocalyptic writings) which corresponds precisely to the "kingdom of heaven" of the gospels. Thus, the effort of Strack-Billerbeck, I, 180f., (to Matt. 4:17), to equate the evangelical and the Talmudic eschatology by reason of the occurrence of the expression, "the kingdom of heaven," is without support. In the Talmud, the significance of the "kingdom" changed; in the gospels, its meaning was definitive and did not change. The concepts of later Jewish and Christian sources are essentially incommensurable.

dispersion and servitude and the restoration of the kingdom of David. It was the end of this world, the advent of a new heaven and a new earth. The popular messianism was essentially political and temporal, its basis the national and political conflict, Israel versus the nations. But the conflict was also religious, ideological; and Israel's victory would be the victory of the God of Israel. Although the apocalyptic hope was nourished to some extent by the secular conflict, its horizon was of a completely different order: the ideal a new humanity on earth, celestial, without death. Here was the longing to be released of earthly bonds, from the yoke of the body, from the maw of death. Redemption was not only from the "captivity," but also from bondage of another kind, from the earthly man and his portion. The "end" would be the demise of terrestrial rule and the initiation of the "kingdom of heaven." Men would be released from the dust, and become as the angels; the barriers would fall, and those on earth would dwell with those on high. This world was accursed, the domain of sin; the rule of idolatry is merely the most conspicuous of the many forms of the dominance of sin and evil, but the end of days will be the end of pagan empire and the pagan world. Sin and evil will be no more; the kingdom of the saintly and the righteous will come, to be brought about by the "Son of Man," the "messiah," and not by the sword and military might. The messiah-redeemer will appear at the head of troops of angels. He will do final battle with the "princes" of the nations and with Satan and his angels who rule in this world. He will vanquish them and the idolatrous kingdom. The dead will quicken, the world will be renewed; the righteous will sit at table with the patriarchs and the saintly of all the generations in the new "kingdom of heaven."

The Essenes and sectaries close to them were especially given to these fantasies. The masses of the nation attended to their ideas, but without abandoning their more "mundane" hopes. That is, they were concerned more with the scion of David than with the heavenly "Son of Man." On the other hand, even the most enthusiastic of the apocalyptic believers continued to anticipate the earthly sovereignty of the messiah. In the extracanonical scriptures the two ideas dwelt comfortably together. The doctrine of resurrection, with its merging of heaven and earth, was in the nature of a bridge between the nation as a whole, with its exoteric, basically political faith, and the sectarians.

The popular messianism was essentially solace and hope. The prophetic descriptions of the terrors of the "day of the Lord" were certainly realistic. But for all that, the "end" was the end of the captivity, of Israel's subjugation to the gentiles; and Israel's religious struggle with the idolatrous nations was the central motif. Postexilic Israel felt itself the "servant of the Lord" which suffered and was afflicted because it was faithful to the one God. This faith was the heritage of the whole of the nation, and thus the hope of redemption was the "expectation of the comforting of Israel" (Luke 2:25). The purging of idolatry from within Israel brought about another profound change in Israel's hopes. The earlier prophets had threatened Israel with great punishments which would leave only a "remnant." Now this was changed: Judgment would be of the wicked only. The nation as a whole, "Israel," would be saved on the day of judgment. Israel after the destruction of the first Temple, this Israel which kept faith with its God, which did not serve the gods of the gentiles, was the "remnant of this people" (Zech. 8:6, 11, 12; Hag. 1:12, 14; 2:2; Ezra 9:8, 13, 15; Neh. 1:3). Between the righteous and the wicked of Israel there was still opposition; the humble and the pious anticipated the divine judgment which would befall the wicked and those who violated the covenant. But those were the dregs of the nation, rejects. In the popular view Israel, all Israel, would be consoled in the end. In this way the messianic expectation would become the basis of recurrent political agitations, which engulfed the nation. Anticipation of consolation and redemption was the religious facet of the political struggle against the pagan imperium. Israel's warfare with the nations, God's people against the heathens, was primary; the judgment of the wicked was secondary.

John the Baptist

Sectarianism within Israel was, however, of a kind to foster a different view: emphasis of the element of rebuke and retribution in the messianic faith. Conflict between the righteous and the wicked within Israel here tended to overshadow that between Israel and the gentiles. Moreover, a new piety developed among the sectarians, compared to which the usual reverence and observance were looked upon as inferior. The *signum* of sectarian fragmentation was the hostility of the untutored masses (the "am-ha-arez") to the Pharisees. With respect to the Essenes the gap was even wider. For the Essenes, righteousness was a special way of life, withdrawal from the world and its society; and among the withdrawn the birth of a new sectarian eschatology, different from the popular views. Here, the longing for a new world, to be rid of this world, was overpowering, the mood of repentance overwhelming. This was an asceticism which gave rise to the mood of censure: "Israel" was not enough, only the way of piety and asceticism could justify. To this mood, the earlier prophetic concept of the "day of the Lord" as a day of retribution was more conformable than the current popular notion that the end would be redemption and solace. The sectarians did, indeed, also anticipate the coming of the "son of David," redemption and the end of idolatry and the restoration of the monarchy. But their messianic faith was also sectarian, with apocalyptic overtones and the dominant vein of denunciation.

John the Baptist, whose influence on Jesus was great, was of these pietistic-ascetic circles. John lived in the "wilderness," wore "clothing made of hair cloth," "a leather belt around his waist," and subsisted on "dried locusts and wild honey" (Matt. 3:1-4; Mark 1:4,6). Though not formally an Essene, John was close to them but even more ascetic and much more solitary. He called for "return" and preached the "kingdom of heaven." It is incorrect, however, to equate his summons to repent with the Talmudic doctrine of repentance and deliverance, as is often done. In the

Talmud repentance brings on, accelerates the coming of redemption, which depends on repentance; and Israel, if it will repent, will effect its redemption.[30] This was rooted in the popular faith wherein the "end" was essentially consolation to Israel. John, on the other hand, did not foretell solace to Israel and did not call for repentance in order to effect the "kingdom of heaven." He said: "Repent! for the Kingdom of Heaven is coming!"[31] It is characteristic of all the Christian good news which is related to John that the kingdom of heaven is not to be gained by repentance. The kingdom will come shortly: It will come of itself at the appointed time. Its beginning will be the day of judgment, and only those who repent in time will be saved on that terrible day. The kingdom of heaven is above all the judgment day, "the wrath that is coming" (Matt. 3:7; Luke 3:7). Moreover, repentance will save individuals only; it will not bring redemption to the congregation of Israel. It will not be the sequence: repentance-redemption; but more in the nature of Nineveh's repentance which averted the decree in the book of Jonah, repentance-deliverance. To the "crowds"[32] that came out to be baptized, John says: "You brood of snakes! Who warned you to escape from the wrath that is coming?" All have sinned, all require baptism to be forgiven of their sins; and whoever does not repent will be cast into the flames. John challenged: "produce fruit that will be consistent with your professed repentance" (Matt. 3:8; cf. Luke 3:8). In Luke (3:10-14), John com-

30 This view is basic to the doctrine of redemption as expounded in the Talmudic and midrashic literature. The exile was due to Israel's sin, and redemption will come when Israel is purged of sin by repentance, prayer, and chastisement. Thus, Sanhedrin 97b, R. Eliezer, R. Joshua, Rab Samuel, concerning repentance and redemption; ibid., 98a, response of the messiah to R. Joshua b. Levi; Yoma 86b, "Great is repentance because it brings about redemption." Many similar statements in the Talmud and in early and later expository literature. This is the popular view even to the present.

31 Matt. 3:2; Mark 1:2-3; Luke 3:3 (succinctly): "repentance ... in order to obtain the forgiveness of sins."

32 Luke 3:7; in Matt. 3:7, "... many of the Pharisees and the Sadducees ..."

mands the people concerning charity and righteousness. But it is from John's ascetic way of life that we learn the manner of the man.

The dominant motif of John's "gospel" was, then, castigation, not consolation. John's intention was not to comfort Israel in its afflictions and servitude, nor to arouse the people to repentance in order to hasten the release from pagan dominion. He came, rather, to warn that the day of judgment was nigh and to rouse men to repent so that they might escape the terrors of that day. It is true that a prophetic note sounds through John's denunciations, but it is different from the ancient prophetic censure. The prophets rebuked the people for their sins, and the repentance they required was principally abjuration of the sins. In the postexilic period, the idea of repentance was given a more positive content: purging in the sight of the Lord, baring of the soul, and turning to God to seek Him in complete spiritual commitment. The anchorite-preachers of the type of John did not want merely to stir men to consciousness of their guilt. They demanded a better way, the life of piety and asceticism. Their point of departure was the absence of piety rather than the fact of sin, and their goal was life after the manner of the Essenes or flight from the world and the way of the hermit in the wilderness. Repentance was "turning" from this world, redirection of the soul to the new order which was coming; more, that is, than righteousness and justice, and more even than piety and compassion, asceticism also, and the seclusion of the anchorite.

The individualistic note in John's preachment corresponds to this kind of repentance. John does not address "Israel," and there is no "national" reference in his preaching. It is a mistake to equate the messages of John and Jesus to those of Amos and Jeremiah, the prophets of doom (Wellhausen). In Jesus and John, and also in the Book of Enoch, it is not "Israel" which is the addressee. "Israel" as such is not the recipient of the good that is to come, rather the "elect" and the "righteous"; "Israel" is not even the subject of the visions of retribution. The prophets spoke to the nation Israel, a people then dwelling in its homeland and free of alien rule. They threatened destruction of the state and exile. The fate of the individual would be determined by the fate of the nation. In the period of the Second Temple, on the other hand, the people felt themselves as in "exile." God had taken what He once gave and had not restored it. The remnant of Israel, and the holy city, and whatever else, were no longer the right of the nation, gifts of God's grace to Israel. They were now a higher possession, symbol of Israel's faithfulness.

Thus, the warnings of this period did not apply to these treasures of the nation. Retribution and solace were individual, the destiny respectively of the "wicked" and the "righteous." And yet, it was only the punishment of the wicked which was wholly personal. "Israel" was already in exile and afflicted, distraught and pined away; only individuals — not the nation — could suffer added pain. With respect to consolation, the opposite was true; in that the righteous would attain reward, "Israel" would inherit glory. In the righteous, the nation was magnified and exalted. To the devout (the Hasidim) of the days of the second Temple, it was not enough to be of Israel, but "Israel" was essential to their piety, and the devout could not imagine a piety which was not of Israel and of the faith of Israel. Nonetheless, Israel was symbolized now by the righteous and saintly who were alert to any infraction of the Law and dedicated to purity and abstinence. In earlier times, the fate of the individual was determined in the fate of the nation. Now, that relationship was reversed. Israel, however, remained even as it had been.

Accordingly, there is no reason to think that John, and after him Jesus, predicted the destruction of Jerusalem and the Temple. Prophecies in the gospels which allude to such destruction are certainly of later composition. The terrors foretold by the evangelists were reserved for individuals. Those who did not "return" would be consumed in the fires of judgment day. This censure was more severe than that of the prophets; and its specific hallmark, the call to be baptized, was completely novel, marking off the new preaching from that of the prophets. The earlier prophecy. called for cessation of sin and for good deeds and compassion. But repentance, the turning from evil, was not distinguished by any specific ritual. Now a new ascetic pietism, maturing in the recesses of the nation, aspired to reform the nation according to its special life pattern. It retained the religious-ethical core of the earlier prophetic rebuke, but added its extreme asceticism, which in the final analysis was more than the nation could accept. The Pharisees spoke of "a demon" in John (Matt. 11:18; Luke 7:33); but John spoke to the people, and the very strangeness of his appearance and ways stirred them. Disciples gathered to him, and he taught them how to fast and to pray (Matt. 6:5f. et al.; Luke 11:1). Then they went among the people and baptized after his manner (cf. Acts 18:24–25).

Son of Man, Son of God

The gospel of Jesus is characterized by the same basic strain, denunciation and warning, threat and not consolation. Jesus came to the Jordan to be baptized by John (Matt. 3:13, and the parallels). He followed John and began to evangelize, it seems, not immediately when he was baptized but only after John was imprisoned or beheaded (Matt. 4:12, 17; Mark 1:14). The interval was a period of "trials" wherewith Satan tempted Jesus in the desert (Matt. 4:1–11; Mark 1:12–13). In this period Jesus, it appears, sat at the feet of John, now withdrawn into the wilderness. It was only after John's imprisonment that Jesus returned to Galilee to become a "prophet" in his own right. But it was as no ordinary prophet that he returned to Galilee; while still in the wilderness — when he was tempted by "the Satan" — he came to the belief, which was to determine the course of his life and death, that he was "the Son of Man."

This designation which Jesus applies to himself in the gospels is symbolic of his messianic and apocalyptic quality; and there can be no doubt that Jesus used the term. It is remarkable that this general term was not replaced by "Son of God," which is less ambiguous and more in keeping with Christian thought; in this, there is preserved evidence of the most intimate character of this amazing personality. Among all the epithets applied to Jesus both before and after his death — the Son of Man, prophet, messiah, the son of David, the Son of God, the Logos — it is "the Son of Man" which is specifically his, the name he gave himself. Jesus used the term "Son of God" in its usual Jewish sense or to express his own unique relation to God; but never to indicate his special substantive nature and role in this world. He was not a "prophet" and did not speak in the prophetic style or use the characteristic introduction: "thus saith the Lord"; nor did he relate "visions of God." God's will is revealed, he believes, in his speech; he explains what "Moses and the prophets" intended; he is "sent" of God. His is of the nature of a "prophet," and he knows hidden things; but "prophecy" is not his essence. He was not sent to make known the word as revealed to him of God; but to realize the word, to accomplish a specific task within the world, that is, the redemption. He accepts the titles "messiah" and "son of David" with their traditional implications, which was the only way his contemporaries could understand them; and he also could think of his mission as redeemer only in the context and with the connotations of the age.

Nonetheless, Jesus considered himself more than merely the "son of David"; he was greater than David, and David called him "my lord" (Matt. 22:41–45, and parallels). Jesus did not consider himself a divine being; he was a Jew, and thoroughly given to the concept of God's unity and uniqueness. The thought that God would descend to earth and become incarnate was completely alien to his thinking. But the idea of a bond between men here below and those who dwell on high, far from being alien, was characteristically Jewish. This involved no apotheosis, rather ascent of favored individuals to angelic status, the status of heavenly creatures. Jewish imagery knew beings of dual aspect, human and angelic, such as Enoch and Elijah, who were in a way proto-

types of Jesus. Jesus thought of himself as a creature of two na-
tures, human and angelic, of the family of the divine, commis-
sioned to this world, and endowed with authority here below.

The Jewish "Son of God" of the age was an angel, and the
"Son of Man" a man-angel. The concept of a revelation in human
form, whether old or new, concealed from the angels and those
who dwelt on high, was current at the time. People speculated
concerning the nature of Jesus; some said he was John the Baptist,
others that he was Elijah, still others that he was Jeremiah or
another of the prophets (Matt. 16:13–14, and parallels). Thus, it
was possible that some holy man of earlier times was reincarnate
in Jesus; he might be Elijah come down from heaven in human
form. Herod thought that Jesus was John the Baptist risen from
the dead (Matt. 14:1–2; Mark 6:14; Luke 9:7), and Jesus believed that John the Baptist was Elijah (Matt. 17:10–13; Mark
9:11–13; cf. Matt. 11:2–15; Luke 7:18–35). These ideas are of
prime importance for understanding how Jesus thought of himself;
they were of the "secrets" of the kingdom of heaven. Jesus in-
formed the disciples in "figures" — "Let him who has ears listen"
(see cited passages). John was not "John," that was the appearance; within was the covert reality, "Elijah." Of John-Elijah,
there were three likenesses: the man Elijah and the angel Elijah,
both now reappeared in the likeness of the man John; and now,
also himslf, Jesus, the redeemer whose coming John-Elijah had
announced. He was the man-form of the heavenly being, the apocalyptic "Son of Man," the foreordained redeemer who had descended from on high.

Jesus was, without question, thoroughly familiar with the contemporary apocalyptic prophecies. The influence of the book of
Enoch is evident in much that he said.[33] In Enoch, however, the

---

33 Jesus used the term "woe" in the manner of the Ethiopic Book of
Enoch, 94:6–99:16. This is the denunciatory "woe to ...," rather than
the prophetic "woe ... (is me)," expressive of the prophet's grief and
despair. The use of "woe" in direct (second person) speech with
"... for ..." ("since") is characteristic: Thus, "Woe to you, ye rich,

term "Son of Man" denotes a preexisting heavenly messiah. Enoch presents a developed imagery which was current in particular in circles given to mystic speculations in the time of Jesus, and a messiah-concept which was on the whole of recent vintage unknown to the prophets. In the prophetic literature, it is God who will appear in the end of days and establish His kingdom. The great and understanding king who will arise in Israel and rule justly and with wisdom is mentioned (thus Isa. 11:1f.), but the redeemer and savior will be God himself, not the king. It was only toward the close of the period of the second Temple that this new king of the house of David became a messiah and redeemer.

Another trend in Jewish apocalyptic literature, however, tended to ascribe the role of the divinely appointed redeemer to an angel. There is a trace of this thought in Daniel, thus: "And at that time [of the end] shall Michael stand up, the great prince" (12:1), and execute justice against the nations and their princes. The idea that Elijah, the man-angel, will be sent "Before the coming of the ... day of the Lord" (Mal. 3:23) is of this stream of thought. In the Ethiopic Book of Enoch, the man-angel, Enoch, will be the messiah (71:14–17). Enoch here appears suddenly as "the son of man," who will bring peace to the righteous in the time to come. This succession, Elijah, Michael, Enoch, is not incidental. In mystic circles, it was thought that the expected redeemer would be an angel or a man-angel, which thought may be the origin of the term "Son of Man" as applied to the messiah. A celestial man, born of a woman, who has consorted with angels, will accomplish heavenly redemtption on earth. Whatever its origin, however, the term "Son of Man" lost its original sense and acquired the meaning of heavenly redeemer. Elsewhere in Enoch, the referent of the term

for ye have trusted in your riches." The attitudes to wealth of the world of Jesus and the Book of Enoch are the same, as will be seen. Whether Jesus was acquainted with the Book of Enoch in its present form is uncertain, but he certainly knew writings of that kind.

is not the man Enoch.[34] It may be that the figures of the Book of Enoch are related to the "son of man" of the vision of Daniel (7:13–14), although the "son of man" in Daniel is Israel. But the mystic visionary who created the composite symbol may have been acquainted with the apocalyptic ideas connected with the "son of man"-redeemer, and have created a hybrid symbol. Authors of apocalypses characteristically removed symbols from their original context and reassembled them in colorful raiment and confusion. But it is possible also that the "son of man" in Daniel was the original source and prototype of the later concept. In any case, both the term and the concept appear in the Book of Enoch. The "Son of Man" is a preexisting celestial being: "Yea, before the sun and the signs were created, before the stars of heaven were made, His name was named before the Lord of spirits.... And for this reason hath he been chosen and hidden before Him, Before the creation of the world and forevermore" (Enoch 48:2–6). The "Son of Man" was the elect of God, chosen from before to judge the world, to subdue the rebellious angels who caused man to sin, and to cut off the wicked and save the righteous (45f).

After baptism by John and while alone in the wilderness, not far from John, Jesus came to the belief that he was, indeed, the "Son of Man." Whether his thought was in the exact pattern of the Book of Enoch cannot be known. But it was this conviction that set him apart from all other "men of God" in Israel, and made possible his subsequent apotheosis among the gentiles, even though the concept itself was grounded in Jewish-mystical fantasies. Therewith, Jesus was neither "prophet" nor "man of God"; he was an heavenly man, man-angel, descended from on high. It is significant that even in the beginning of his Parousia there is no report of a theophany similar to the prophetic consecrations. The "holy spirit" alighted upon him after his baptism, and the "voice from heaven" was heard; but there was no "word of the Lord" to him. Apparently, the decisive psychological experience occurred while

34 (Ethiopic) Enoch, 46:1–6; 48:2; 52:1–16; 59:24–29; 71:14–17.

he was in the wilderness, which is the essence of the story of the "temptations" of Satan (Matt. 4:1-14, and parallels).

After John was imprisoned, Jesus returned to the Galilee. There he assembled a group of followers and announced the good news of the "kingdom of heaven." He probably already believed in his celestial nature and his mission to realize the kingdom of heaven. But he did not voice his private belief openly; he only hinted at it by calling himself the "Son of Man." To the crowds and to his disciples, he was for the time being a herald of good tidings or "prophet." And yet he was, for all that, more than herald and prophet; he worked "wonders." He went about the land performing miracles, healing, expelling demons, and granting pardon to sinners; his battle against Satan and Satan's demons had begun. The crowds were amazed by his deeds and his words (Matt. 9:33); they conjectured and tried to figure out: Who was this man? Was he John risen from the dead? Elijah, Jeremiah, or another of the earlier prophets? (Matt. 14:1f.; 16:3-14, and parallels). But Jesus spoke as one to whom authority was given, and his belief in his mission became that of his disciples and passed over to the people. Men began to believe that Jesus was the "messiah," the "son of David"; they were predisposed to see him as the "son of David." But Jesus was not really the "son of David." He was the apocalyptic messiah, the "Son of Man"; and he had come not to found a new kingdom of this world but the "kingdom of heaven."

Kingdom of Heaven

Jesus' kingdom "of heaven" or "of God" is not a religious-moral-psychological concept. It is not the "inward" conversion of the individual, as Christian moralists since Renan and Tolstoy have tried to explicate it and make it plausible. It is an apocalyptic kingdom, which was destined to come at the time appointed, at the time of the "end" which had been fixed from the beginning. Jesus believed that it would eventuate while he was yet living (Matt. 10:23; 16:28), and held to that belief to the last despairing cry on

the cross. In all this, Jesus' beliefs were those of the Jewish masses
of his time. The foundation stone of his (and Paul's) concept of
the "kingdom of heaven" was the resurrection. Jesus believed also
that the soul lived on after death, and in the popular phantasma-
goria of paradise and Gehenna. The essential, however, to Jesus
was the resurrection of the dead; Jesus and his contemporaries
held to both concepts — resurrection and the immortality of the
soul — in all innocence; and Jesus cited Scripture to prove the
resurrection: "I am the God of Abraham, the God of Isaac, and
the God of Jacob." He is not the God of dead men but of living
(Matt. 22:31–32, and parallels). The soul, that is, cannot live on
without the body; and the essential is the resurrection of the body,
not the immortality of the soul. Thus, Jesus in that context speaks
of Abraham sitting at the gate of paradise and receiving the souls
of the righteous to himself, and of Moses and Elijah "talking with
him" (Matt. 17:1f., and parallels). Jesus, then, even though he
believed also in paradise and Gehenna, held firmly to the popular
faith in the approaching resurrection which would be the core event
of the "kingdom of heaven" or of "the world to come." In the
synoptic gospels, there are no detailed descriptions of the "kingdom
of heaven" which can without exegesis be attributed to Jesus.
But, in general, what is said of the kingdom of heaven conforms
closely to Jesus' views; and conclusions with respect to their beliefs
may be drawn from the descriptions of the evangelists.

The evangelical "kindom of heaven," like the kingdom of the
time to come of the apocryphal literature, is a variegated and
bizarre configuration, the product of overwrought feverish imaginings. The outstanding characteristic of this eschatology is, as stated,
the absence of any boundary between the days of the messiah and
the world to come. The kingdom is described against the radiant-
ghastly backdrop of the resurrection; the quick and the dead, men
and angels, heaven and earth cast alike in one "kingdom." The
rising of the dead is the key symbol; reembodied man enters the
"kingdom." This kingdom is no realm of unsubstantial spirits; the
dead will have emerged from their graves, renewed in body, to enter

through the gates. These reincarnate men are, however, immortal, a
new creation. The "kingdom" is not wholly apart from this earth;
earthly and heavenly visions are inextricably intertwined.

In the kingdom of heaven, the righteous will "take their places
at the feast with Abraham, Isaac and Jacob" and all the prophets.[35]
Herewith, the boundary between the living and the dead is erased;
he kingdom of heaven is included in the promise of the "resurrection of the upright," [36] or of "life" or "eternal life." [37] It will
come with the "end of the world," [38] at the time of the "new
world" [39] into which men shall enter bodily, possibly even with
maimed bodies.[40] At the appointed time, the "Son of Man" will
appear "coming upon the clouds of the sky," [41] accompanied by
holy angels to take his seat on his glorious throne.[42] The apostles
will sit "upon twelve thrones, and judge the twelve tribes of Israel," [43] or even all the nations.[44] The "Son of Man" and his
apostles, together with the heavenly angels, will judge the world; they
will separate the righteous from the wicked, the former to life
eternal and the latter to everlasting punishment.[45] At the time of
the end, the Son of Man will dispatch his angels to assemble the
wicked, the seed of Satan, to cast them into the fire, and to bring
the righteous into the kingdom.[46] After the resurrection there will
be "no marrying or being married"; men will "live as angels do

---

35 Matt. 8:11f., "take their places at the feast with Abraham," etc. See
    Luke 13:28. In Matthew, allusion to the repentance of the gentiles
    and the rejection of "the heirs to the kingdom" (the Jews). Since
    Jesus did not send messengers to proclaim the good tidings to the
    gentiles, the whole passage may be considered a gloss. In Luke (13:
    28–29), there is no such allusion. It would appear that Jesus said that
    only the righteous will enter into life everlasting and that those who
    rejected him will inherit Gehenna. The allusion in Matthew was added
    later. Cf. the parable of the host who, when those who had been in-
    vited (those who were "called") did not come, brought in the poor,
    the maimed, the blind, and the lame in their stead (Luke 14:16f.).
    Jesus had invited the leaders and sages who rejected him, which is
    the thought of many passages.

36 Luke 14:14.

in heaven." ⁴⁷ The "upright will shine out like the sun, in their
Father's kingdom," ⁴⁸ and the apostles will be privileged "to eat
and drink" at Jesus' table in his kingdom.⁴⁹ In the musings of the
time sexual intercourse could be renounced, but not "the banquet."
In Jesus' kingdom of heaven there will be a table laden with food,
and benches whereon to recline while feasting. At the last Passover supper Jesus tells the apostles that he "will never eat" the
paschal meal again until "it reaches its fulfillment in the kingdom
of God," ⁵⁰ and that he "will never drink this product of the vine

37 Matt. 18:8–9; 19:29 and parallels, et al. Mark 9:43, 45.
38 Matt. 13:39f., explication of the weeds (24:3). See Mark 13:7; Luke
    21:9 concerning "the end." The detail in these visions is certainly of
    later date, but their phraseology is characteristic of the period of
    Christian beginnings harking back to the time of Jesus. Thus in the
    Nazarene prayer: "Let grace come and let this world pass away"
    (*Apostles' Manual*, The Didache, X, 7).
39 Matt. 19:28.
40 Mark 9:43–47: "You might better get into the Kingdom of God with
    only one eye..."; Matt. 18:8–9.
41 Matt. 26:64; Mark 14:62; cf. Matt. 24:30; Mark 13:26; Luke 21:27f.
    The "Son of Man" and "cloud(s) of heaven" are a conventional
    combination. Cf. Dan. 7:13.
42 Matt. 25:31.
43 Matt. 19:28, and parallels.
44 Matt. 25:32. The authenticity of this vision is questioned, but the idea
    that all the nations will be judged is early.
45 Matt. 25:46.
46 Matt. 13:36–49.
47 Matt. 22:30, and parallels.
48 Matt. 13:43, following Dan. 12:3. This figure also in the Book of
    Enoch.
49 Luke 22:30. Cf. 14:15: "the banquet in the Kingdom of God," pre-
    ceded by the reference to "the resurrection of the upright." Also the
    "Son of God" in his glory. Cf. the account of Jesus' resurrection (Luke
    24:30f.). Jesus took his place at the table, and blessed the bread and
    broke it in pieces, etc. prior to his ascent to sit at the right hand
    of the Almighty. Cf. Acts 10:41: "...by us, who ate and drank
    with him after he had risen from the dead." Cf. Enoch 62:13–14:
    "And the righteous and elect.... And with the Son of Man shall they
    eat and lie down and rise up forever and ever.."
50 Luke 22:16.

again till the day when I shall drink the new wine with you in my Father's kingdom." [51] The paschal lamb, that is, will be eaten and wine drunk in the kingdom. This conforms to the statement attributed by Papias to the elders of his time, that Jesus discoursed of the marvelous fruitfulness of the soil in the time to come, especially the abundance of grapes and wine.[52]

The "Son of Man" seated on his throne will be the first in "the kingdom." In the gospels this is Jesus, who has died and ascended to heaven and who, with angelic retinue, will reappear on earth. However, Jesus himself believed that he together with his disciples and all the righteous of his generation would enter into the kingdom of heaven while yet living. The kingdom would come "before the present age passes away" (Mark 13:30), at a time when the apostles "will not [yet] have gone through all the towns of Israel" (Matt. 10:23). Jesus assured his disciples that some of them would not taste of death, and that they would "live to see the reign of God come in its might" (Mark 9:1), and he did not believe that he, the Son of Man, the redeemer-king, would die. We cannot know how he imagined his enthronement. After his death, the faithful anticipated a theophany; but Christian scripture does not give a clear picture of Jesus' thoughts in this respect. However, he and the disciples believed that they, while yet living, would sit at the head of the kingdom of heaven — alongside Abraham, Isaac, and Jacob. Thus, Jesus imagined the "kingdom of heaven" as a realm of men-angels who live a celestial existence on earth. The center of the kingdom is Jerusalem; there Jesus would appear amidst clouds of glory and gather the children of Jerusalem around him, "as a hen gathers her brood" (Matt. 23:37; Luke 13:34), and a new temple, "made without hands," would be built (Mark 14:58). Jesus would sit upon his throne, and the twelve apostles

51 Matt. 26:29, and the parallels.
52 Irenaeus, *Adversus haereses*, V, 33. Re the nationalistic component in the eschatology of Jesus, see J. Klausner, 434f. However, this nationalistic element is generally legendary, popular, and not specifically "Jewish."

upon their thrones; and there, it appears, the judgment of the nations would take place. The descriptions of the new Jerusalem
descended from heaven in the Revelation of John are certainly
close to the thought of Jesus. The boundary between the "days
of the messiah" and "the world to come" is blurred. The day
of the "Son of Man" is the time of the ingathering of the exiles,
the downfall of the gentiles, the resurrection and the renewal of
the kingdom of David. The apocalyptic Jesus, therefore, could go
up with his disciples to establish the kingdom in Jerusalem; he
may have thought that his kingdom would be established even
before the end of days and the resurrection of the dead. Thus, he
promised the faithful homes and fields even "in this time" (Luke
18:28–30; Mark 10:28–31; Matt. 19:29. Jesus' statement, it seems,
is not in original form). Nonetheless, the marvelous kingdom is,
for all this, of "the world to come," a kingdom wherein celestial
men will live in the company of the righteous of ancient days, and
death and evil will have given way to everlasting joy and splendor.
For all its terrestrial and material bases, the kingdom was of heaven,
apocalyptic, not of this world.[53]

However, a terrible, universal Judgment Day will precede the
advent of the kingdom. The message of Jesus, as that of John the
Baptist, is of reproof and warning, not a gospel of consolation.
Jesus was a sectarian, not a "popular prophet," a pietiest and
ascetic even though not easily assigned to any of the various sec-

---

53 John 18:36. Although Jesus' reply to Pilate is not authentic, the
statement is indicative of the nature of the "kingdom" of the "Son of
Man" and his angels subsequent to the "resurrection of the righteous."
Klausner, 376, says that "Jesus the Jew" could not have uttered these
words. However, the nationalistic character of Jesus' beliefs, which
Klausner correctly stresses, is wholly compatible with this statement
if it is properly understood. The "kingdom of heaven" of "Jesus the
Jew" was the kingdom of contemporary popular Jewish rumination.
The "kingdom" wherein the righteous will dine with Abraham, Isaac,
and Jacob and the prophets and will mingle with the angels is not
"of this world." In the New Testament, there is no definite demarca-
tion between the "days of the Messiah" and "the world to come."

tarian movements of his day. Certainly his thought is close to that of the Essenes in many respects. He had been a follower of John the Baptist, and it was John who awakened him to the idea of his message. That he continued to be influenced by John's Nazaritic asceticism is evident in his animadversions on family life [54] and on the wealth and pleasures of this world.[55]

But Jesus does not merely denigrate wealth; he condemns concern with the affairs of this world and spurns labor. He is a mendicant and migrant, not a true Essene; and in his piety there is a negative component beyond that of the usual Essenism. The Essenes supported themselves by physical labor performed in common. Jesus, on the other hand, founded an itinerant fraternity based even in principle on nonemployment. The communism of the Essenes was of a society of workers; that of the early Christians founded by Jesus a communism of supplicants, paupers, eleemosynary. Jesus not only forbade the service of "mammon"; he charged his disciples not to concern themselves with the morrow,

54 Jesus' ideal is the eunuch "for the sake of the Kingdom of Heaven" (Matt. 19:12). Paul tells the Corinthians in Jesus' name that "it is an excellent thing for a man to remain unmarried" (I Cor. 7:1f.). Neither Jesus nor Paul married, and the Essenes generally avoided contact with women.

55 Poverty is a virtue and wealth a vice. The wealthy and "those who rejoice" take their portion in this world and have no share in the world to come (Luke 6:20f.; cf. Matt. 5:3, "those who feel their spiritual need" is a gloss.) Cf. the parable of the "beggar named Lazarus" (Luke 16:19f.). Jesus and the disciples do not afflict themselves by fasting, but this is only because they are "wedding guests" who rejoice with the "bridegroom" who is among them (Mark 2:15–19); see Matt. 11:19; Luke 7:34. In the Book of Enoch, also, "woe" is proclaimed for the rich (see 94:6f.), but there specifically for those who have achieved wealth by injustice. "An afflicted and poor people" (Zeph. 3:12) is a prominent theme in earlier prophecy. But in Enoch, there is the new note that this world is to be negated. The garden of Eden is prepared for those "who love God and loved neither gold nor silver nor any of the good things which are in the world, but gave over their bodies to torture. Who, since they came into being, longed not after earthly good, but regarded everything as a passing breath, and lived accordingly..." (Enoch 108:8–10).

"wondering what you will have to eat or drink ... what you will have to wear." They must be concerned only for their souls; concern about bodily needs is the way of the gentiles unbecoming to pious Jews who fear God (Matt. 6:24–33; Luke 12:16–21, the parable of the rich man who built larger granaries and died). Jesus and his disciples were wayfarers, eating at the tables of others and subsisting on alms. In this, there is some resemblance to the prophetic bands in ancient Israel. But the ideological basis was completely new: negation of this world and its demands, the ideal of asceticism and mendicant piety without labor, of which the archetype is to be found in India.

Jesus' ascetic approach to life was the basis of his ethical teaching. Love of the enemy, turning the other cheek, humility, and nonresistance were pietistic ways, without which the kingdom of heaven could not be attained. These ideas did not originate with Jesus, but he gave them extreme formulation; they were necessary conditions of the "kingdom of heaven." The logic of the "redemption" was reformulated in terms of ascetic pietism.

Thus Jesus, like John the Baptist before him, came before the people with a summons to repent, not to proclaim the good news of redemption. The kindom of heaven was nigh; but it would be preceded by the terrible judgment day, and there was hope only for those who would repent in time. Neither John nor Jesus — nor in their footsteps, subsequently, Christianity — called for repentance in order to bring about the kingdom of heaven. Jesus preached terror, not solace, for the nation; the kingdom of heaven would come of its own, and only the righteous would be justified. All the rest would be lost; therefore, let him who wishes to be saved on Judgment Day repent now. The kingdom of heaven is of the pious, the anchorites, this a sectarian and exclusive gospel. Jesus was not sent (as Jonah) to warn the gentiles — not even the Samaritans, whom the Pharisees considered very close to Jewry; all the gentiles will be rejected on Judgment Day. Moreover, even of Israel only a remnant would be saved which, again, is indicative of the sectarian character of the message.

In proclaiming that Jews would not be saved by the merit of the patriarchs (Matt. 3:9, and the parallels), John's intent was not to widen the compass of those saved by abolishing the limitation of physical descent but to restrict; not only would the gentiles be condemned, there was no assurance also for Israel. That the entrance to the kingdom is narrow and that "only a few are to be saved" are basic themes in Jesus' gospel (Luke 13:23f.). "Go in at the narrow gate. For the road that leads to destruction is broad and spacious, and there are many who go in by it. But the gate is narrow and the road is hard that leads to life, and there are few that find it" (Matt. 7:13–14). "For many are invited but few chosen" (Matt. 22:14). The kingdom of heaven is for the "little flock" of Jesus' disciples (Luke 12:32); and Jesus speaks in parables so that the many will not comprehend the secrets of the kingdom. He explains to the disciples, "To you has been intrusted the secret of the reign of God, but to those outsiders, everything is offered in figures, so that 'They may look and look and yet not see, And listen and listen and yet not understand, Lest possibly they should turn and be forgiven'" (Mark 4:11–12; Matt. 13:11–15; Luke 8:10). Jesus "said nothing to them [the crowds, the outsiders] except in figures, but in private he explained everything to his own disciples" (Mark 4:34; cf. Matt. 13.34). Only the very pious, those whose "uprightness is far superior to that of the scribes and Pharisees," who observe the Law meticulously and even go beyond its requirements, will enter the kingdom of heaven (Matt. 5:19f.). Hope is only for the poor, the mourners, the afflicted, the hungry, those who wail, the eunuchs, the Nazarites who have abandoned the world, their homes, their parents, brothers, wives, and children for the sake of the kingdom of God (Matt. 19:16–29; Mark 10:17–30; Luke 18:18–30).

Obviously, from this point of view, the world is condemned. The Galileans killed by Pilate and the eighteen Jerusalemites who died when the tower fell on them were not worse men than others. "No, I tell you; unless you repent, you will all perish as they did" (Luke 13:1–5). Jesus likened the day of the kingdom of heaven to the times of the flood and the destruction of Sodom. Just as in Noah's generation, men were occupied with the things of daily life "up to the very day that Noah got into the ark and the flood came and destroyed them all," and "as it was in Lot's time; they went on eating, drinking, buying, selling, planting and building," and suddenly came the brimstone. So it will be "on the day when the Son of Man appears" (Luke 17:27–30).[56] Eating, drinking, buying, selling, planting, and building — these are sins, it is a wicked and faithless age (Matt. 12:39, Mark 8:38). Jesus compared his contemporaries to the men of Nineveh and himself to Noah. He does not want to give them a "sign" which would cause them to believe in him. If they will not believe in him and repent, the fate which Jonah proclaimed for Nineveh will be theirs (Luke 11:29–30; cf. Matt. 12:38–40). This was no good news of "redemption"; it was proclamation of "the flood" and the "fire and brimstone" of Sodom, a doomsday when none but the saintly would be saved.

Faith in Jesus

In addition to the sectarian, there is also the specifically personal note in this gospel. Beyond and above repentance and good deeds, Jesus requires belief in himself. He was, he said, "gentle and humble-minded" (Matt. 11:29). And yet, if even a few of the statements attributed to him in the synoptic gospels are original, his was an inordinate and incomparable degree of self-esteem; never before had any man of Israel spoken of himself as Jesus did. This posture is explicable only against the background of Jesus' belief in his celestial origin, that he was the "Son of Man" sent of God to found "the kingdom" on earth. His contemporaries must accept, beyond his message, himself!

56 Cf. Matt. 24:37–39. The same figures with contrary significance appear in a later vision of the signs which will precede the end of days. Jesus the "Son of Man," clothed in glory and accompanied by angel hosts, would suddenly confront an unbelieving generation. The combination of diverse elements, as in the visions, is characteristic.

More than teacher, Jesus was savior and redeemer, greater than the Temple, greater than Jonah or Solomon (Matt. 12:6, 41–42; Luke 11:31–32). Prophets and upright men and kings had longed to hear his words and could not (Matt. 13:17; Luke 10:24); he was the "bridegroom," and so long as the bridegroom was present there was joy in the world (Matt. 9:15, and parallels). The harlot merited pardon because she wept and kissed his feet and put perfume on them. Jesus reproved the Pharisee who was his host because he did not wash his feet and kiss him and put oil on his head (Luke 7:36–48). To Jesus, preacher of humility, the pouring of perfume of myrrh on his feet was a *mitzvah*; [57] he was the "heir of the kingdom," the king's son, supreme among men. He granted pardon to transgressors, which fact alone is proof of the disingenuousness of those theologians who would deny Jesus' "messianic" self-awareness, or dispraise the significance of his belief that he was the messiah and explain his fate as due to the opposition of the Pharisees to his teachings. Jesus pardoned sinners which, according to contemporary opinion and also to the view of Jesus himself, only God could do, as we have said above. Jesus did not preach a new "personal religion"; he required faith in himself. This was the novelty of his phenomenon. Prophets who claimed to be messengers of God had arisen aforetime in Israel; but Jesus thought himself a celestial being, not "God" and not the "Son of God" in a Christian-pagan sense, but one of the divine retinue, the "Son of Man." It is difficult for Christians, even the nonorthodox, and also to a certain degree for Jews of the present day — after two millenia of the apotheosis and worship of the Galilean Jew Jesus throughout the Christian world — to appreciate the

---

57 Cf. the parallel accounts, Matt. 26:6–13; Mark 14:3–9, re the woman who pours a flask of precious perfume on Jesus' head while in the house of Simon the leper in Bethany. The disciples were indignant at the squandering of money which might have been given to the needy; but Jesus praised the woman's deed, which would be recounted to the latest generation. The allusion to the preparation "for burial" (Matt. 26:12; Mark 14:8) is added.

anomaly of Jesus' assertion of his special celestial quality to the Jews of his time. A Galilean carpenter, "gentle and humble-minded," crisscrossed the land at the head of a heterogeneous band of fishermen and tax collectors and votaries of both sexes. He pardoned sinners and threatened all who refused to "believe" in him with the torments of hell. The enthusiasm of the believers and the bitterness of the nonbelievers were alike intense. The faith in Jesus, that he was the "Son of Man" or the "Son of God," was Jewish-mystical, not pagan. Very few would have denied the possibility that a "Son of Man" could be sent of heaven. The Jews of the period believed that Elijah would return and mystics believed also in the coming of Michael, the "Son of Man," or of Enoch. But never before had a member of the heavenly family trod the earth in human form. Was, then, this Galilean in truth the Son of Man? The phenomenon was at the very least likely to cause public disorder, in particular as the movement gathered momentum; and when Jesus and his followers went up to Jerusalem "to restore the kingdom to Israel," it bordered on rebellion. The tragic finale had become inevitable: either the political-messianic excitation would end in the establishment of the terrestrial sovereignty of the "Son of Man," or "his angels" would appear to shield him, to be a sign to the whole world.

Therewith, the guilt of that generation was compounded by an additional, egregious sin: the people did not have faith in him. The gospel of the "kingdom of heaven" became the gospel of the "kingdom of Jesus"; it was obligatory to believe that Jesus would summon "his angels," that he would raise the dead to new life, judge the world, and occupy the throne of glory in the world to come. Jesus demanded humility, love, withdrawal, asceticism, abstention, complete trust and, above all, belief in him and his authority. He called on the Jew who observed the Law to do more: "Sell your property and give the money to the poor, and you will have riches in heaven. Then come back and be a follower of mine" (Matt. 19:16, 21, and parallels). The "apostles" would sit upon twelve thrones to "judge the twelve tribes of Israel" because they had given up everything and followed Jesus (ibid., 27–29, and parallels); this the only meritorious deed attributed to the apostles in the gospels. They were "uneducated men with no advantages" (Acts 4:13) who did not understand Jesus' discourses; they strove with one another as to who would be "the first" among them, and were eager to sit at his right and left in "his kingdom." Everyone who abandoned property and family for Jesus' sake was assured a share in life eternal (Matt. 19:29, and parallels). Anyone "who loves father or mother" or "son or daughter" more than Jesus was not "worthy" of him, but "whoever loses his life for my sake will gain it" (Matt. 10:36f.). The expressions, "I," "my name," "for my sake," "after me," mark the speech of this Galilean "rabbi"; "the Son of Man" takes the place of the Law of Moses.

People began to follow Jesus. He healed them; they were hallowed by the touch of his garment. They addressed him "Lord, Lord," and anticipated salvation at his hand. Jesus took note of this and admonished: "Why do you call me 'Lord! Lord!' and not do what I tell you?" [58] He seemed to anticipate the beginning evolution of the Christian church which would make the apotheosis of Jesus the essential, and disregard his teachings.

That development, however, was implicit in Jesus' message. Jesus was never merely a "teacher." He was the heavenly redeemer, endued with authority, who healed the sick, drove out demons, and pardoned sinners; these were the signs of the "new teaching" (Mark 1:27). The Law retreated before the manifestations of heavenly "power" which Jesus wrought himself and imparted to his apostles. An unnatural power communicated by contact with Jesus' body and clothing healed (Matt. 9:21f.); nor did Jesus perform his miracles for their own sake, as other miracle workers. To him, they were an attribute of his destiny as the redeemer, of

---

58 Luke 6:46; cf. Matt. 7:21f., where the question is put in the context of the (later) contention of "prophets" and "apostles" within the Christian communities.

the arsenal of his war with foul spirits and Satan their master. The infirm and the sinners were involved with Satan and his demons — whereas healing and forgiving of Jesus were of a single authority and power (cf. the story of the paralytic, Matt. 9:2f., and parallels). Refusing to cure the daughter of the Canaanite woman, Jesus explained, "I am sent only to the lost sheep of Israel's house" (Matt. 15:24); that is, the healing was a function of his "messianic" mission, one phase in his battle with Satan. Against the Pharisees who charged that he could not drive out demons except by the aid of Beelzebub, he explained, "Any kingdom that is disunited is on the way to destruction... If Satan is driving Satan out, he is disunited, and so how can his kingdom last?... But if I am driving the demons out by the aid of God's Spirit, then the Kingdom of God has overtaken you" (Matt. 12: 24–29, and parallels). Exorcism of the evil spirits is the beginning of the fall of the dominion of Satan and, therefore, also the beginning of the kingdom of God. Jesus endows the apostles with "power over the foul spirits" and charged them to heal the sick, drive out demons, and preach the kingdom of heaven (Mark 6:7–13; Luke 9:1–6; Matt. 10:1f.). The disciples — the seventy-two (Luke 10:17)[59] — were "delighted" to report back that the very demons had submitted to them; and Jesus responds: "I saw Satan fall from heaven like a flash of lightning!" (ibid., 18).

To Jesus, therefore, the lack of faith in him and his mission to destroy the kingdom of Satan and the demons who cause men to sin and afflict them in body and soul was a mortal sin which beset

---

59 Concerning the "seventy [seventy-two]" see Luke 10:1f. There are many additions to Jesus' speeches, particularly in Matthew. But there is no reason to doubt the gospel accounts which tell that Jesus sent messengers to the cities of Israel with orders to heal, to evict demons, and to preach the kingdom. Witness the prophecy which was not fulfilled: "...for I tell you, you will not have gone through all the towns of Israel before the Son of Man arrives" (Matt. 10:23). It is probable, however, that the messengers were sent only to the towns and villages of the Galilee region and not of all Israel.

the whole generation. He did not distinguish between belief in God and belief in his own "power." Most of his complaints of absence of "faith" refer to faith in himself and his power; thus, he says "faith" will help. The spirit whereby he works wonders is the "holy Spirit," and "whoever speaks against the holy Spirit cannot be forgiven for it, either in this world or in the world to come" (Matt. 12:31–32, and parallels). His generation has witnessed mighty deeds but has not "returned"; therefore, he pours out his wrath upon it and prophesies the terrors of the flood and Sodom, and pronounces the message of Jonah against it. For, even though the crowds followed him and believed in him, Jesus knew that the nation did not. The people were drawn to him, but the leaders waited for a "sign." He said, "I thank you, Father, Lord of heaven and earth, for hiding all this from the learned and intelligent and revealing it to children" (Matt. 11:25; Luke 10:21). He called his apostles "children"; the uneducated, the tax collectors, and harlots were drawn to him; the world was upside down. Jesus had descended from heaven to save Israel, and now the heads of the nation, those who knew the Law, rejected him! His exasperation with the Pharisees is to be understood, as stated, against this background.

At first, Pharisees had come to hear Jesus; they were able to bear with pietistic sectarians such as the Essenes and with John and his disciples. But shortly their attitude toward Jesus changed; Jesus required belief in himself; those who had faith must abandon all to follow him. He threatened nonbelievers with Gehenna, and when his conviction that he was the "Son of Man" intensified, the disbelief of the sages became a sin too grievous to be borne. "The tax-collectors and prostitutes are going into the Kingdom of God ahead" of the leaders of the people (Matt. 21:31–32; Luke 7:29–30). Whereas the masses believed in John, the Pharisees and the sages did not. Jesus was concerned, of course, less with unbelief in John-Elijah, the herald of the messiah, than with unbelief in the redeemer himself, the "Son of Man." The experts of the Law were stumbling blocks to the whole generation; they had "taken the key to the door of knowledge," and the people trusted them. But they did not follow the "Son of Man"; they would neither themselves enter the kindom of heaven "nor let those enter who are trying to do so" (Matt. 23:14; Luke 11:52).

The sages of the Law considered the possibility that Jesus might be the messiah but, in the light of their responsibility, they were unwilling to acknowledge him as the messiah until he gave a "sign." The miracles which he and his disciples performed might stir "the tax collectors and prostitutes," but the leaders were not satisfied. They asked an unmistakable omen from heaven; how difficult to satisfy this nation for whom the Red Sea had been split, and which had stood at Mount Sinai. Jesus replied, not without acrimony, to such "a wicked and faithless age... no sign will be given it but the sign of the prophet Jonah" (Matt. 12:39, and parallels). The kingdom of heaven, he explained to the Pharisees, would not come "visibly." Its beginning would not be with signs and omens in the heavens and on earth: "for the Kingdom of God is within you" (Luke 17:21). The kingdom of God had already begun in the revelation which was Jesus. Even now, the "Son of Man" was among them, and whoever would be saved must leave all and follow him; then he would merit the goodly heritage of those who had faith. But the Pharisees did not "believe," and Jesus gradually came to terms with this upside down world. Tax collectors and harlots, the simple folk believed; they would enter the kingdom. The apostles, the "children," would occupy the twelve thrones, while the sages, those who were expert in the Law, would be banished to Gehenna. Jesus cast the leaders of the nation into Gehenna and set the apostles over the twelve tribes of Israel; "those who are last now will be first then, and those who are first will be last" (Matt. 20:16, 19:30; Mark 10:31; Luke 13:30). God had chosen to give "the kingdom" to the "little flock" of the saintly (Luke 12:32). The cause of Jesus' indignation with the Pharisees was his conviction that he was "the Son of Man," the ruler of the heavenly kingdom, whose sovereignty the sages of the Law — the offspring of those who had slain the prophets (Matt. 23:29–31; Luke 11:46–48) — would not acknowledge.

Jesus and Jewish Nationalism

The expression, "the Son of Man," is symbolic of the apocalyptic gospel of Jesus and his sectarian denunciations, wherein the nationalistic aspects of prophetic messianism tend to disappear. Jesus' message was based almost altogether on the earlier messianic prophecies of consolation, and yet there is scarcely a trace of this in the gospels. This is the result, in some degree, of a kind of "natural selection" which is grounded in the severance of Christianity from its Jewish roots. In fact, however, the gospel of Jesus was in general not messianic-nationalistic, and the prophecies of national consolation were no "stumbling block" to the development of Christianity. The crown of "Israel" was given to the church, and there was no need to forget or tendentiously to conceal the nationalistic prophecies.

Nonetheless, it is a serious mistake to find an inclination toward "universalism," disavowal of the "nation" in favor of "humanity," and negation of "nationalism" in Jesus' teachings. Like John the Baptist, Jesus rejects Israel as such in favor of "the righteous," the ascetic pietists, the believers. But this is not repudiation of Israel in favor of "mankind." The nationalistic-messianic element is overshadowed by the apocalyptic and sectarian, but it remains and cannot be distilled away. Jesus is devoted, heart and soul, to "Israel"; his existence is wholly within the world of Jewry. His heaven is the heaven of Israel, of Israel's God, angels, patriarchs, prophets, and saints; and the Satan also and the demons whom he battles are "Jewish" demons. He is come to this earth from the Jewish heaven, from among the Jewish entourage of God. The "kingdom of heaven" which he proclaimed was the kingdom of Abraham, Isaac, and Jacob; and the gentiles had no share in it.

The nations are as nothing to him; they are as beasts, "dogs"; at most, they may eat the crumbs which fall from the table of "the children," "their masters" (Matt. 15:21–27; Mark 7:27–28). Jesus instructed the apostles that they should "not go among the heathen, or to any Samaritan town" (Matt. 10:5–6). The kingdom of heaven was of no more concern to the heathen than to the beasts. The apostles were destined to judge "the twelve tribes of Israel"; there would be no gentile nations. The epithets, "gentile" and "tax collector," are interchangeable (Matt. 18:17), but the terms, "son of Israel," "descendant of Abraham," and "daughter of Abraham," connote the most distinguished pedigree (John 1:47; Luke 19:9, cf. 13:16). Jesus was "sent" to the house of Israel only; wherefore it was incumbent upon him to resolve not only the problem of this world and the next, but in addition that of Israel's captivity and redemption, and Israel's contention with the nations.

In Jesus' thought, the "days of the messiah" tend to be absorbed into "the world to come," wherewith the nationalistic tone of his message is obscured. Jesus is "the Son of Man," and Israel's "Son of Man" could not escape the messianic task. As "Son of Man," Jesus was also the "son of David," the "messiah." Jesus was hesitant; the "Son of Man" was not really the "son of David," but a heavenly being whom David addressed as "my Lord." Nonetheless, to the people, including the disciples, Jesus was the messianic heir to David's throne. In the popular mind the messianic and apocalyptic visions cohabited comfortably, and the messianic hope was sustained and intensified by the very realistic conflict between Israel and the pagan nations. To the Jewish masses, the apocalyptic visions had become a kind of prophecy growing out of the longing for liberation. It was in the nature of things that Jesus, the "Son of Man," was looked upon as the expected "son of David," and his peremptory call to repent was heard and understood in accord with the popular point of view. The populace wanted to meet his demand to "return"; they were attentive to the doctrine of their new "prophet," deeply stirred by his censure, his asceticism, and also by his threats and cries of "woe," which were attributes marking the "saint." What Jesus demanded, however, was exceedingly difficult; it was impossible for a whole people to abandon family and property, to love their enemies. The nation could not emasculate itself for the sake of the kingdom of heaven, become a nation of mendicants in order to follow Jesus. Yet, the people anticipated the coming of the "messiah" and, interpreting Jesus' teachings according to their own ways of thinking, they saw in him the realization of their hopes. He was the messiah, the son of David, who would defeat Rome and redeem Israel. The anticipation was of dual aspect, at once celestial-apocalyptic and terrestrial-messianic. Thus, the two elements could merge in the figure of "the messiah." Little wonder that the masses of the nation discovered the long-awaited messianic "son of David" in the "Son of Man."

Moreover, Jesus himself, in despite of his apocalyptic predisposition, was not unmindful of the political implication of his role as messiah. His eschatological view derived from the "scriptures," including, of course, their nationalistic-messianic elements. The messiah would be of the stock of Jesse, he would renew the kingdom of David on this earth and gather in the dispersed of Israel. His throne would be in Jerusalem and he would subdue the gentiles, even if by angelic legions rather than with the sword and an army. The "Son of Man," in short, would fulfill the task of the "son of David." The apocalyptic "kingdom" of Abraham, Isaac, and Jacob and all the dead who would rise from their graves would merge with the terrestrial kingdom of the house of David. Jesus was and was not the "son of David"; he was "the son of David— the Son of Man." The ambiguity of the concept is sign and symbol of the fusion and confusion of the messianic and apocalyptic beliefs of Jesus and contemporary Jewry. Thus it was that when Jesus returned from the wasteland where he prayed in solitude to speak to the crowds, he became the "king of Israel." This title, preserved in the gospels, testifies to the messianic-political aspect of the figure of Jesus. Jesus did not intend to liberate Israel by

107

armed rebellion; it was not in his nature to assemble troops and lead the nation in battle. He would found his "kingdom of heaven," subdue Satan, and put an end to sin and death on earth; and the fall of Satan and his demons would be the end of idolatry, of pagan empire on earth. The societal aspect of the "kingdom of heaven" was political, and that implied revolt against Rome; the "kingdom of heaven" was inextricably involved in the immediate political situation. Jerusalem was, indeed, symbolic of the celestial kingdom; and the "Son of Man" would appear "in heavenly clouds" with his angelic hosts. But for all that, the locus of his appearance was the earthly Jerusalem, the holy city, the city of the line of David. The "Son of Man" must enter "his kingdom" through the gates of Jerusalem.

Political Implications of Jesus' Thought

In the final period of his life Jesus resolved to go up to Jerusalem at the time of the Passover, there to enter into "his kingdom." In what manner he anticipated his enthronement is unclear. But it is certain that he went to Jerusalem for the specific purpose of establishing the monarchy of David.

Christian scholarship generally accepts the view of the gospels that Jesus went to Jerusalem in order to die there. When he saw that the nation did not repent, he despaired of his message and determined to die in order to atone by his blood for the transgression of the people and thereby to effect their redemption. But this opinion and also the view that he went to Jerusalem in order to endure suffering [60] are contradicted by the fact that Jesus hid from

---

60 This is the opinion of J. Klausner, 320 f., 325 (concerning "the cup of affliction"), 337f. But Jesus' conduct prior to the arrest, and the actions of his disciples, who fled immediately after he was seized, prove that not only the crucifixion, but even the arrest, was wholly unexpected. It had not occurred to the disciples that the "Messiah" might be arrested. If Jesus had foretold the "tortures," the disciples would have viewed his arrest as confirmation of his prophecy (since they did

the authorities when he suspected that the leaders of the people were plotting against him, that he stayed in a remote part of town, and that he moved from place to place. That is, he attempted to avoid suffering and death (it will be seen in the following that to the last he did not believe that these would be his fate). In addition, in Jesus' eschatological beliefs, as they are reflected in his preaching and parables, there is no place for the death of "the Son of Man."

The hypothesis that Jesus went up to Jerusalem in order to die and to effect atonement and redemption by his passion or death is rooted in the prevailing confusion with respect to the character. of the summons to repent of John and Jesus, which we have considered above. In fact, for John and Jesus the "kingdom of heaven" was at hand, and its coming did not depend on "return." There was no need to hasten its advent by repentance and certainly not by the suffering and immolation of the redeemer. Repentance was the way of salvation for individuals in Israel. Jesus preached the flood and the brimstone of Sodom; only "the little flock," his followers, were destined to the "kingdom," and he preferred not to reveal the secret of the kingdom to those who were doomed. For whom, then, would he have gone up to Jerusalem to be afflicted and to die? In the parables of the "harlots" and the "tares," and elsewhere, Jesus explains that the masses will not enter the kingdom. His angels will separate the faithful from the rest of mankind, the former for the kingdom and the others for Gehenna. There was but one way to believe in him.

In all this, there is nothing of an atonement of death. The "Son of Man" was come to rule, not to die; for which reason the disciples were so bewildered when the catastrophe occurred. The very thought of the messiah's death was remote; nothing of this

not know at that moment that he would be sentenced to die). It will be observed in the following that Jesus went to Jerusalem, not in order to preach repentance and to suffer (Klausner, 337) but specifically to demand that the leaders of the nation recognize him as king of Israel, the heir of David.

sort had even been heard. In the "scriptures" there was nothing of it ("testimonies" were discovered only after the event) and Jesus, when he dispatched the apostles to proclaim the good news, had assured them that his kingdom would come soon (Matt. 10:23; Mark 9:1; Luke 9:27).

Both Jesus and his disciples believed that they would rule in Jerusalem and judge Israel. It was only natural, however, that, after the tragic events, none of the disciples were able to recall events of the days immediately preceding the crucifixion as they had appeared to them at the time. What had happened now appeared in a new light. Jesus had not thought that he would be put to death or have to endure torture, and never hinted at any such event in his discourses with his followers. If he had done so his disciples, as (H. S.) Reimarus points out, would not have been so appalled when he was arrested, and they would not have fled. In the synoptic gospels it is stated that Jesus told the apostles that he was destined to suffer affliction and be killed and to rise again on the third day, and that the disciples "did not understand what he meant" (Mark 9:31–32; 10:33–34; Luke 18:32–34). The agony and death appear in this context in all the accounts whereby the actual course of events and the purposes of the actions are obscured. That the disciples did not "understand" the very clear words spoken to them can have only one explanation: They were wholly unaware of the discourse. Jesus could not have imagined that he must die or be afflicted. What happened to John and to other prophets was no precedent: He was not a prophet, he had been sent to accomplish, not to pronounce. He was a "power." The "Son of Man" and his angels stood ready to support him in his battle with Satan and his other opponents; that was the end to which he was sent. The predictions of torture and death of the evangelists are a somewhat naive embellishment, obviously and awkwardly inserted, and easily detached. They center attention on the sequence of affliction and death; and in this light the earlier events are seen, as it were, in distorted reflection.

The details of the journey indicate clearly that Jesus went to

Jerusalem to become ruler of Israel. This was his belief and that of his followers and of the crowds which gathered to him. Jesus believed that sovereignty would now be restored to Israel. In addition, in despite of his apocalyptic point of view, he now confronted the people and the leaders with a specific political challenge: They must recognize him as the messiah-king, enthrone him as the heir of David. He did not go up to Jerusalem merely to preach "repentance" and to await there the advent of the kingdom of heaven. He came to demand his rightful sovereignty, even though he conceived that sovereignty in his own very special way.

On the way to Jerusalem, near Capernaum, a discussion broke out among the disciples as to "which of them was the greatest." [61] Jesus, as Mark tells the story, overheard them. When they had gathered in a house in Capernaum, he asked them what they had been discussing on the way. Not wanting to renew the dispute in his presence, they were silent. The significance of the disciples' contention is indicated by the incident which occurred shortly after, as they approached Jericho. James and John, the sons of Zebedee, came to Jesus and asked that they be allowed to sit respectively at his right and left hand in his "triumph" (Mark 10:35f.). Their mother joined her sons to ask the same "favor" of Jesus (Matt. 20:20f.). It is clear that this was sequel to the contention on the way to Capernaum. The other apostles were "very indignant at the two brothers" (ibid., v. 24). Here again, as elsewhere, the authors of the gospels anticipate the difficulty and relate the incident as occurring after Jesus had told "the Twelve" that he was going up to Jerusalem to die (ibid., vv. 17–19, and parallels). But if they had known or even suspected that they were shortly to witness the torture and death of their lord, they could not possibly have continued to argue about who was "greatest," even to the point of bringing at least one mother into the affair. Actually, the problem was urgent: Who would be the greatest in the "kingdom" which was close at hand? This is adumbrated in Jesus' reply.

61 Mark 9:33–37; Luke 9:46–48; Matt. 18:1f.

The gospels here include reference to the "cup" which Jesus is to drink and the baptism which he will undergo (Mark 10:38f.; cf. Matt. 20:22f.). The double entendre of Jesus' answer shows clearly that the passage is a later gloss. A statement referring to afflictions is no answer to the request of the sons of Zebedee and their mother; and Jesus' question, whether they could drink his cup and undergo his baptism, is gratuitous. Jesus' reply, it is clear, was only that the assignment of thrones was not his but God's to give. At another time (apparently another dispute) Jesus told the Twelve that they should not be like "the rulers of the heathen" and "their great men" who "lord it over them." They must be servants, "everybody's slave," "to wait on other people," (Matt. 20:25–28; Mark 10:42–45). This comparison to "the rulers of the heathen" is evidence that Jesus himself, as well as his disciples, believed that in Jerusalem the "kingdom" would be theirs.

We comprehend the content of this quarrel when we consider Luke 19:11: When Jesus and the Twelve were near Jerusalem, the faithful "supposed that the Kingdom of God was immediately going to appear." To them and to Jesus, the going up to Jerusalem was ascent to the kingdom. That this was the belief of Jesus is evident from the parable which he told in Jericho — shortly after the argument about who would be greatest — to the crowds who welcomed him as the heir who was about to receive his kingdom. In Luke this parable is joined with another related in Matt. 25: 14–30, whereby it is in some degree garbled and its meaning obscured. The parable appears in Luke 19:12–16 and also in verses 17 and 19, which concern authority over the ten and five towns. A nobleman, it is stated, went to a distant country to secure "his appointment to a kingdom," but "his countrymen hated him." Following a digression (vv. 20–26) the nobleman, having returned to his own country, after he had entered into his kingdom, commanded that those enemies who hated him be slaughtered (v. 27). The digression passage tells of his faithful servants and their compensation and the governorships awarded them. The combination of the two parables is confusing, but the sense is clear: Jesus is going up to Jerusalem to assume sovereignty.[62] Many — in particular "his countrymen," the Galileans — rejected him. After he will have obtained "the kingdom," he will apportion the governorships among his faithful "servants" and cast his enemies into Gehenna, as he had threatened many times. Jesus' deeds and words in Jerusalem and his fate, as they are reported in the synoptic gospels, can be understood only against the background of these anticipations and the excitation of the time.

Jesus entered Jerusalem at the head of a "messianic" procession in the bright light of popular acclaim. He sat astride a donkey, in conformity to Zech. 9:9. Some of his followers cast their garments on the donkey, "and Jesus seated himself upon them." Onlookers spread their coats in his way or cut branches and strewed them before him. Multitudes went before and after him, shouting: "Hosanna! Blessed be he who comes in the Lord's name." "Blessed be the reign of our father David which is coming!" "God bless him from on high!" or: "God bless the Son of David!" (Matt. 21:1–9; Mark 11:1–10). According to Luke 19:38, the people cried: "Blessed is the king who comes in the Lord's name." [63] This "messianic" procession cannot be explained on the assump-

---

62 According to Luke 19:12, the "nobleman once went to a distant country to secure his appointment to a kingdom and then return." The accepted interpretation of the parable is based on this "return," whereby Jesus supposedly intimated that he would ascend to heaven and then return to punish those (that is, Israel) who had rejected him. But both the "distant country" and the "return" of the parable are borrowed from the parable of the slaves (in Matt. 25) to whom their master entrusted money when he went on a journey; they are not of the parable in Luke concerning the king. Cf. Y. Kaufmann, *The Final Ascent of Jesus to Jerusalem* (Hebrew), HaGoren, X, 34–35.

63 H. Graetz's opinion that the accounts of Jesus' entry to Jerusalem are fictitious is erroneous. Christians tended subsequently to stress the guilt of the Jewish people in that they did not acknowledge the "Messiah" and caused his death, which is the dominant theme of the evangelical accounts. What, then, could have been the purpose of inventing stories of a messianic procession which is so contrary to the principal motif?

tion that Jesus came to call for "repentance," and to suffer and die. It was the "son of David," the nation's king, not the "Son of Man," who rode on the ass. The "son of David" astride the donkey was the terrestrial counterpart of the "Son of Man" who was destined to appear in heavenly clouds; but the goal of the messianic cavalcade was openly political. This was no entry to the end of an "inner" spiritual religious revival intended to establish the "kingdom of heaven" in men's hearts. Jesus came as the king entering his regal residence. He would not rebuke the disciples when they cried, "Blessed is the king who comes in the Lord's name," or the young men in the Temple who shouted, "God bless the Son of David!" (Luke 19:38–40; Matt. 21:15–16). He was the king, the son of David, now come to the royal city of David.

Jesus' idea of the relationship of his "kingdom" to Rome is indicated in his response to those who asked him if it was right to pay the poll tax to the emperor: "Pay the emperor what belongs to the emperor, and pay God what belongs to God" (Matt. 22:21, and parallels). The "liberal" exegesis that the "kingdom" of Jesus was "within," wholly a matter of faith, and that the continued rule of the pagan empire did not conflict with Jesus' kingdom, is unfounded. In the kingdom of Abraham, Isaac, and Jacob, there was no room for an "emperor"; in the kingdom of heaven, after the terrible judgment of all mankind, the "heathen kingdom" could no longer exist. Moreover, Jesus could not have been so innocent, so unacquainted with the ways of the world, as to think that deeds such as his messianic entry and the cries of "Blessed is the king" would go unnoticed in the "kingdom of idolatry." The view that in his response to the question of paying the poll tax Jesus renounced the messianic kingdom and the hope of restoring the Davidic monarchy is mistaken.

In fact, Jesus' response is the key to understanding the practical content of his messianic claim at that moment. He did not enter Jerusalem as a rebel, as leader of an insurrection (although there is indication that he was prepared for fighting; see Luke 22:36–38); and the advent of his kingdom did not depend on the fall of Rome. Nonetheless, he came before the leaders of the nation with a specific political — even if political-religious — demand: That they acknowledge his "messianic" right to the throne of David and recognize him as king of Israel, of which fact the very question (concerning the poll tax) is evidence. After the messianic procession, the people looked upon Jesus as the rival of Caesar, the claimant to the throne, which is also the context of Jesus' answer. The disciples, through whom the account has come down, were unable later on to understand what Jesus had said, and gave it the erroneous interpretation which has misled ever since.

The sense of Jesus' response was his claim of sovereignty, but with emphasis wholly on the religious aspect. Jesus' political demand did not apply to taxation; it was of the essence of his belief that the religious obligation must be fulfilled. His right of sovereignty, the kingdom of the "Son of God," was heavenly and he was, therefore, unconcerned with denarii and taxes. Both Jesus and the emperor were "kings," and the people must, for the time being, give to each what was his, to the emperor what belonged to him, and to Jesus that which belonged to God. Jesus did not contest Caesar's right to the tax; let the people pay what is due to the emperor for the present. But at the same time, the nation must acknowledge Jesus' sovereignty, that is, their religious obligation, a duty owing "God." This was fulfillment of his political-religious requirement; the people must recognize him as "king-messiah," and seat him on David's throne until he shall come with his angels to establish the "kingdom of Israel," that is, the "kingdom of heaven." Then will come the end of emperor and empire together with the fall of Satan and his demons; with Satan, the emperor falls. In the world cataclysm, the "flood," the day of Sodom, the kingdom of idolatry will collapse of itself.

Jesus demanded, therefore, that he be given "what belongs to God," the diadem of the kingdom of God, this the sense of his astute response to the provisional problem of "Caesar." Jesus knew that he was entering the terrestrial Jerusalem as "king," and as king of Jerusalem here below he stated his case before the leaders of the nation. He was incensed when they doubted and asked him by what authority he acted. He related a parable which clearly shows that he demanded that they acknowledge his sovereignty: A land owner planted a vineyard and leased it to tenants, and left the neighborhood. At the proper time, he sent a slave to the tenants to obtain a share of the vintage. The tenants beat the slave and sent him back empty-handed. He sent more slaves, of whom the tenants beat some and killed others. There was yet one more to send, a dearly beloved son. But the tenants seized the son, the "heir," slew him (according to the gospel stories), and cast his body outside the vineyard. "What will the owner of the vineyard do? He will come back and put the tenants to death and give the vineyard to others" (Mark 12:1-9, and parallels). The meaning of the parable is obvious: The "tenants" are the leaders of the nation to whom Jesus "began to speak in figures"; the "others" are those who believed in Jesus, his faithful followers and disciples to whom he promised "cities" and "thrones." They were destined to be princes in Israel in place of the present leaders who rejected the "son" and "heir." The vineyard is Israel or Jerusalem. The murder of the son in the parable is a subsequent addition; Jesus had told that the tenants conspired to drive the "heir" away, and were punished for their crime. Jesus now came in person before the "tenants"; he demanded the "vineyard" and threatened that he would execute judgment against them. He said: "That stone which the builders [that is, the nation's leaders] rejected has become the cornerstone" (Mark 12:10-11, and parallels). The heads of the nation might reject him, but unto him the "vineyard" had been given.

The prophecy of the ingathering of the exiles, which was preserved in the gospels as by a miracle, brings this out clearly. Matt. 23:37-39 and Luke 13:34-35 read: "O Jerusalem, Jerusalem! murdering the prophets, and stoning those who are sent to her, how often I have longed to gather your children around me, as a hen gathers her brood under her wings, but you refused! Now your house is left unto you desolate.* For I tell you, you will never see me again until you say, 'Blessed be he who comes in the Lord's name!' " This splendid apostrophe is Jesus' only prophecy in which the messianic-national point of view is in sharp focus, and since there is no indication of the arrest and crucifixion in it, it must be authentic. Its exact time is evident: Jesus was despairing of the people, he was prepared to flee for dear life. The men of Israel did not "consent" to be redeemed; the messiah would depart and leave their house "desolate." Jesus believed that he would return shortly, but Jerusalem would not see him again until he returned in glory. That is, he did not then know that the men of Jerusalem not only would see him again but, in addition, would seize and crucify him. This prophecy was spoken, therefore, before his arrest.

The purpose of Jesus' going up to Jerusalem is stated explicitly in this prophecy. He is here, essentially, the Jewish "messiah" come to gather the children of Jerusalem to himself. Jesus states what he requires of the men of Jerusalem: that they greet him with the cry, "Blessed be he who comes in the Lord's name." They must acknowledge his mission to gather in the exiled; they must recognize him as the messiah-king. But the people did not believe, and Jesus was forced to flee. Nonetheless, he was certain that the people of Jerusalem would behold him soon in his glory as the messiah who will assemble the dispersed of Israel.

In all four gospels it is stated that the words, *Rex Judaeorum*, were inscribed on the cross,[64] which is evidence that the people understood that Jesus claimed to be the sovereign, and that the issue was: Is Jesus king of Israel? There is no reason to question the

---

* Matt. 23:38, Luke 13:35. Goodspeed, American translation: "Now I leave you to yourselves." King James: "Behold, your house is left unto you desolate." [Translator's note.]

64 Matt. 27:37; Mark 15:26–27; Luke 23:38; John 19:21. According to John the Jews asked Pilate to inscribe: "He said, I am [i.e. pretended to be] the king of the Jews"; and not: "The king of the Jews."

fact of the inscription; certainly there was no reason to invent
this detail at a later time. Further evidence that the problem was
the messianic sovereignty of Jesus is the fact that in the days
immediately following the crucifixion when it was rumored that
Jesus had risen, his followers remained in Jerusalem. They anticipated his return within a few days, "to re-establish the kingdom
for Israel" (Acts 1:6). That expectation was the natural sequence
of the disciples' earlier contention with respect to the leadership
in Israel, the messianic procession and Jesus' arraignment of the
leaders of the nation. Therewith, the logic and purpose of the ascent
to Jerusalem is clear: to restore the monarchy to Israel and to
gather the dispersed children of Jerusalem from the ends of the
earth.

Jesus' own faith that his kingdom was nigh was steadfast even
to the Last Supper. The tradition of the Last Supper of Jesus and
the Twelve is early, and was known in its present form to Paul.
But in the Acts of the Apostles 2:42, the sacramental meal (with
drinking of wine), which in the earliest period was observed by
the Nazarene congregation on the eve of the Sabbath, is not mentioned. This indicates that the tradition of the Last Supper does
not go back to the time of the events. It is natural that the events
of that last evening would be viewed subsequently by the disciples
in the light of the tragic finale. But at the time of the supper, their
thoughts were on the approaching kingdom. It is possible that
Jesus broke bread and shared wine with the Twelve and entered
into a "new testament" with them. But the thought that the bread
and wine symbolized his body and blood came later. Jesus said
that he would not "eat this Passover supper" again "until it reaches
its fulfillment in the Kingdom of God," nor drink the fruit of the
vine again "until the Kingdom of God comes" (Luke 22:15–18;
Matt. 26:29; Mark 14:25). That is, the "end" would come before
the next Passover. It is not impossible — following the version of
Luke (22:14–30) — that Jesus confirmed the covenant with the
apostles and solemnly promised them once more that he would
appoint them judges over Israel.

Similarly, in the last prayer which he prayed in the night of his arrest there is an authentic kernel. But why was Jesus depressed, and for exactly what did he pray?

Trial of Jesus

Certainly he did not pray for early death; and it is understandable that, even though his belief in his mission was unimpaired, he was not jubilant. The need to flee Jerusalem was a severe blow; his flight would try the faith of his followers, and even the disciples were beginning to waver (Luke 22:31–32). It is no wonder that he was distressed to the point that his heart was "almost breaking" (Matt. 26:38; Mark 14:34). The "cup" which he sought to escape by prayer was that of the shame of flight; it was not the cup of tortures and death. Jesus, then, even when he appeared before the Sanhedrin did not believe that he would soon die. To the question whether he was the messiah, he replied, according to Mark 14:62 and Matt. 26:64, "I am! and you [or: and now you] will see the Son of Man seated at the right hand of the Almighty and coming in the clouds of the sky." (In Luke 22:70, only: "I am, as you say!") That the conclusion of the response (in Mark and Matthew) is a later gloss is indicated by its duality. Jesus was seated "at the right hand of the Almighty" only after the Nazarenes came to believe that he had risen again. Jesus told the Sanhedrin he was indeed the Messiah; and in a little while they would witness his ascent to heaven and his return in heavenly clouds. This belief is not more strange than others of his beliefs, his war with Satan and Satan's demons; or his promises of thrones to his disciples and salvation to his followers in the day of judgment, To his last despairing cry, "My God! My God! Why have you forsaken me?" Jesus believed that his angels would appear. The crowds and the Galilean women went to Golgotha to watch and to observe; some expected, even to the last, that Elijah would appear to save Jesus.

The frenzied excitement which broke out in Jerusalem when

Jesus entered the city astride an ass and accompanied by disciples and followers who proclaimed the kingdom and roused the multitude inevitably brought catastrophe. There is no telling what might have happened if the scribes and leaders of the people had invested Jesus with the crown of David; or if Jesus had been installed as "king" in Jerusalem by his disciples, and the populace had risen to his defense in defiance of the city fathers. In fact, the Jewish leaders themselves were prepared to believe if only he would give a "sign." But Jesus did not give a "sign"; he continued to threaten them, his opponents, with Gehenna and to speak in "figures" and allusions, which everyone now understood — even the children who welcomed him in the Temple with cries of: "Hosanna, the Son of David!" For all the apocalyptic tendencies of the fervor, it certainly would have ended in rebellion against the Roman authority. Jesus himself was in no way suited to lead an armed insurrection and guide a political coup; but political leaders would have arisen among the adherents of the messianic upheaval.

Obviously, it was necessary to bring matters to a decision. The heads of the nation assembled to question Jesus, "What authority have you for doing as you do, and who gave you this authority?" (Matt. 21:23, and parallels.) Again, instead of a direct answer, Jesus responded with a very obvious hint: He asked whether John's baptism was "from heaven, or from men." From their point of view, Jesus' conviction that John was "Elijah" was the foundation of his belief in his mission: John was Elijah and he, Jesus, the messiah, the king of Israel of the dynasty of David. The leaders of the nation had not recognized John when still living, and now they did not know who Jesus was and whence his "authority." The Pharisees and Sadducees alike were forced either to take stand against him or seat him on "the throne of David." The opinion that the leaders seized Jesus and tried him because they were convinced beforehand that he was a false messiah, or because they wanted to punish him for his attacks on the Pharisees, is erroneous. The gospel accounts tell that the Pharisees and chief priests seized and questioned Jesus with intent to destroy him. Of course Jesus had enemies, and there were those who hated him; but to the nation as a whole he was a problem which demanded immediate solution; [65] to which fact the final question put to Jesus by the high priest is witness.

According to Luke 22:63–65, the men who took Jesus into custody began to maltreat him even before his trial. Luke, however, has confused matters. Jesus was abused and mishandled only after the judgment had been made, as reported in Mark 14:65 and Matt. 26:67–68, and certainly not by the court. The decision to arrest Jesus and interrogate him is not proof that he had been condemned in advance. The Jewish leaders were anxious to determine if he really was "the messiah." In this, they were probably spurred by the political danger, but a religious problem was also involved. Jesus was politicaly "dangerous" only if he was a false messiah; this question, therefore, had to be clarified. This was essentially a religious problem of the first order, for Jesus was a messiah-prophet, not a messiah-warrior. Unlike Bar Kokba, the protagonist of the nation's messianic dream of independence, Jesus was not a man to arouse the masses to rebellion. He proclaimed himself the "son of David" and "king" without performing any political act whatsoever. His claim, that is, was religious and prophetic; he came before the nation as one acqainted with God's will, as "prophet" and apostle of the Lord. Now that he appeared publicly as "king" to whom Israel must give not that which was "the emperor's," but that which was "God's," it was requisite that the hidden will of God be revealed.

The gospel accounts of the trial are inexact; they were reported by disciples who were not present. The three synoptic gospels, however, tell that at the close of the trial the high priest asked Jesus to state before the court whether he was the messiah. What, then, was the purpose of that solemn question? The gospel reports,

---

65 The pervading attitude at the time is accurately reflected in the statement attributed to R. Gamaliel in Acts 5:34–39.

according to which the high priest immediately tore his clothing (Matt. 26:65; Mark 14:63) when Jesus answered in the affirmative, are certainly defective. But the intermediating posture of the high priest, his solemn question, and the oath "by the living God" (Matt. 26:63) by which he adjured Jesus, show that his purpose was not simply to extract words from Jesus in order to condemn him, and that Jesus' affirmative reply was not of itself "blasphemy" in the opinion of the high priest. The high priest wanted Jesus to state in open court whether he was the messiah; that is, he asked a sign of Jesus at the trial, even as had been asked earlier (cf. the words of the high priests and the elders at the crucifixion, Matt. 27:41–43; Mark 15:31–32). At the trial, however, the sign was asked in court and with oath. The form of the question must have been: Give us a sign that you are the messiah, the Son of God. And if not, you are a false prophet, which would conform to the explicit statute of Deut. 18:20–22.[66] Jesus replied that he was, indeed, the messiah, and the sign was coming "upon the clouds of the sky."

Jesus was sentenced to death as a false messiah-prophet and for blasphemy; with which event Christian and Jewish scholars have been occupied without end. Jewish scholars have tried to prove that it was the Romans, not the Jews, who passed sentence. According to Jewish law, Jesus was not subject to the death penalty,

---

66 The progress of the court trial is not reported exactly in the gospels; in particular, the essential fact of the demand for a sign is omitted. Thus, the impression is given that the whole procedure was merely the formalizing of a verdict which had been determined in advance. It cannot, however, be assumed that the judges — given the prevailing beliefs of that age — were convinced in advance of the trial that Jesus was a false messiah. J. Wellhausen. *Das Evangelium Marci, übersetzt und erklärt*, Berlin, 1903, 124, argues correctly that Jesus committed a transgression (acknowledgment of his messiahship) only when the high priest questioned him directly, and that he was condemned for saying what he had not wanted to say. Wellhausen, however, following the gospel accounts, completely misunderstands the essential nature of the trial. A true messiah would not have been condemned to death if he acknowledged that he was the messiah. The purpose of the

and the procedure of the trial as described in the gospels is con-trary to Jewish practice. It was a Sadducean, not a Pharisaic court, which judged Jesus; or, again, what is reported in the gospels was a preliminary investigation, not a trial at all.[67] In fact, this is not the case. Crucifixion was Roman and, in this respect, it is not correct to say that the Jews "crucified Jesus." However, according to Jewish law, Jesus was liable to the death sentence. It is true that an unique instance such as this — Jesus' assertion that he

court was not to determine whether Jesus claimed to be the messiah, but whether he claimed rightfully. The court did not ask him if he considered himself the messiah, and was not trying to get him to say that he was. From the time of the messianic procession, they knew that Jesus had proclaimed himself the Messiah, and that the crowds who followed him considered him the "son of David." Thus, it was incumbent upon them to find out if he was able to verify what was being said of him. The question put to him was whether he was in truth the blessed messiah; that is, give us a sign that you are the messiah. This was what the Pharisees had been asking of Jesus earlier and what the Jewish Nazarenes asked later (cf. Paul's complaint, I Cor. 1:22); cf. H. Strack-P. Billerbeck, I, 1017, to Matt. 26:65 (B 5): The blasphemy consisted in Jesus' saying that he would be seated at the right hand of the Almighty, "seemingly by reason of his own authority and without divine sanction." Jesus's reply could not, however, have been understood in this sense.

67 D. Chwolsohn argues that Jesus was not liable to the death penalty according to Pharisaic law; and that he was tried by a Sadducean court. According to mishnaic statutes, Jesus would not be considered a false prophet (Chwolsohn, 88, n. 1), not guilty of blasphemy (ibid., 119). Concerning blasphemy, see Sanhedrin 7:5. W. Bousset, *Kyrios Christos*, 1913, 53, also argues that, according to mishnaic statutes, Jesus was not guilty of blasphemy. R.W. Husband, *The Prosecution of Jesus*, 1916, tries to prove that the court proceedings were only an inquest. J. Klausner, 362f., seemingly agrees with Husband. Klausner thinks that the Pharisees would not have sentenced Jesus to death, even if they had held him to be a sorcerer because, "after all, he was one of themselves" (ibid., 364). As if the Pharisees would not have con-demned "one of themselves" to die as a sorcerer if he was deserving of the death sentence according to the Law! Klausner also argues that, according to the statutes of the Mishnah, the death sentence would not have applied to Jesus as blasphemer or as a false prophet (ibid., 373–74); all of which is in error (see below).

123

was the messiah, the Son of God, the messiah called prophetically to be the redeemer of Israel — is not explicitly spelled out in the statutes of the Torah, and no such case is mentioned in the Mishnah. But the Pentateuchal statutes concerning false prophets and blasphemy applied in the case of Jesus.

Jesus came before the people as prophet and apostle of God. He, the Galilean rabbi, neither king nor military leader nor conqueror of the nations, could know that he was "the messiah" (as understood by the Jews of his time) only by prophetic revelation, by the Holy Spirit. He said that he was the "Son of God" (even if as understood by the Jews of his time), a heavenly king, one of the celestial family. The mishnaic statute (Sanhedrin 7:5) concerning blasphemy is unrelated to the procedure in the trial of Jesus; and it is in vain that Jewish scholars try to prove by reference to it that Jesus was not judged according to Pharisaic law; that, according to the Mishnah, the blasphemer is guilty only when he expressly pronounces the Name ("such as 'may Jose smite Jose' "), which is certainly a late version of the statute. Earlier, blasphemy had been understood in the general sense of any statement which was disparaging of the deity.[68] Thus, to claim to be

---

68 An instance of the obligation to tear one's clothing when one hears blasphemy, II Kings 18:37 (Eliakim, Shebna, and Joah rent their clothes when they heard the blasphemy of Rab-shakeh); see Sanhedrin 60a. Rab-shakeh did not curse but said that the Lord could not deliver Israel. The custom of rending garments for blasphemy is mentioned also in the gospel accounts of Jesus' trial. In the gospels, the term "blasphemy" is used in broad sense; Jesus' pardoning of sinners was considered blasphemy (Matt. 9:3, and parallels). Jesus considered a statement of the Pharisees that he banished foul spirits by aid of Beelzebub "abusive speech" which "cannot be forgiven" (Matt. 12: 31-32, and parallels). E. Meyer, II, 452, note, correctly calls attention — against those who question the gospel accounts on the basis of Sanhedrin 7:5 — to the stoning of Stephen as a blaphemer (Acts 6:8-7:60), and says that Stephen also was not guilty according to the mishnaic statute. However, Meyer also is in error in saying that the Sanhedrin trial was "merely a formality," the seeking of a pretext to hand Jesus over to Pilate as a rebel. In fact, the primary purpose of the Sanhedrin was to determine the question at issue in accord

the "Son of God" was irreverent, "blasphemy." [69] In any event, according to mishnaic law, the sentence would be death. In Sanhedrin 11:5, it is stated that "the false prophet is he that prophesies what he has not heard or what has not been told to him." His death (by strangulation) is "by the hands of man" (cf. Sanhedrin, see 11:1). This mishnah is merely a restatement of the statute of Deut. 18:20–22 and was, therefore, not a matter of dispute between the Pharisees and Sadducees. According to Deut. 18:20–22 (cf. Deut. 13:2–3), a prophet is to be examined or tested by means of a sign; and there is no doubt that this was the procedure in Jesus' trial. The high priest charged him on oath to state before the court whether he was the messiah, that is, to reveal his mystery, and give proof that he was the messiah; but Jesus would not give a "sign." To the Sanhedrin, his refusal after the solemn charge of the high priest was a sign that he was a false prophet, which meant that Jesus was guilty of blasphemy;[70] the verdict followed.

with the Pentateuchal statute. That the crowds which followed Jesus proclaimed him "the son of David" was sufficient for Pilate.

69 In Acts 7:56–57, it is stated that the members of the Sanhedrin "stopped their ears" when they heard Stephen say that he could see "the Son of Man standing at God's right hand," and that Stephen was stoned because he made that statement. In Justin Martyr, *Dialogue with Trypho the Jew*, ch. 38, the Jews says that the doctrine of the previous existence of the messiah is blasphemous; and how much the more the belief in "another God besides the Maker of all things" (chs. 55f., 68, 74, et al.). Certain "contrived expositions" of scriptural passages are also blasphemous (ch. 79), etc.

70 D. Chwolsohn, 88, n. 1, thinks that Jesus was not condemned as a false prophet because a false prophet is not liable to the death penalty unless he had enticed to idolatry. In this, however, Chwolsohn is in error; he has confused the false prophet — who is liable to death by strangulation — with those who entice or mislead (to idolatry) — who are to be stoned to death. J. Klausner expresses the same (mistaken) opinion in a number of places in his *Jesus of Nazareth*. On page 380, he says that Jesus was not a false prophet and had not beguiled men into worshiping other gods in the biblical, or even the mishnaic, meaning of these terms. On pages 374f. (first edition), he includes the false prophet with the blasphemer and the enticer in the

The hearing was not a preliminary inquest. It was completely outside the context of Roman law, and it could not serve as basis for secular (Roman) prosecution. The Sanhedrin had to investigate the matter first of all from the religious point of view, which was irrelevant to the Romans, in order to determine whether it should demand the sentence of death in this case. The judges of the Sanhedrin appeared before Pilate as prosecutors, not as examiners. The political implications of the charges, which to many may have been the essential, had already been decided by the religious determination. If Jesus was not a true messiah, it followed that he was politically dangerous and likely to cause great harm to the nation. The nation's leaders faithfully performed their duty as prescribed by the nation's law codes; and any authority in their situation would have had to act as they did. Inasmuch as Jesus could

category of those liable to death by stoning. See also pages 363f. and 372f. (first edition). Chwolsohn refers to Deut. 18:20f., apparently confusing that passage with Deut. 13:2. In any event, the error is obvious. According to the explicit terms of the mishnaic statute, Jesus was a false prophet and, as stated above, he was liable for death also according to the statute of Deuteronomy. It is possible, however, to interpret Deut. 18:20 as placing the execution of the sentence in God's hands. Nonetheless, if the false prophet is equated with him "that shall speak in the name of other gods," (Deut. 18:20), the execution of the sentence would be in the competence of a terrestrial — not the heavenly — court. There is, in any case, no basis to assume that the passage was ever understood as giving over the execution of the sentence to "the hands of heaven." Re the blasphemy, see above. It is possible that Jesus was also condemned as a sorcerer, and that his claim to effect miracles by means of the Holy Spirit was considered blasphemous. (Jesus himself considered the charges of sorcery "abusive speech" (Matt. 12:31-32, and parallels). Statements in the Talmud, according to which Jesus was condemned as a sorcerer, may be reminiscent of this. At first glance, it seems surprising that the Talmud does not state that Jesus was sentenced as a false prophet. But Jesus was a false prophet only in that he claimed to be the messiah, and the Talmud makes no reference whatsoever to that claim. In *The Life of Jesus* (*Toledoth Yeshu*, Hebrew), on the other hand, Jesus is repeatedly called a false prophet. See the versions in S. Krauss, *Das Leben Jesu nach jüdischen Quellen*, Berlin, 1902, 41, 47, 73, 81, 119, 120, 129; re death by strangulation, ibid., 79, 80 81.

not produce a "sign," he was, according to the Pentateuchal statute, liable to the death penalty. He constituted a grave threat in that he proclaimed himself "king," and that in Jerusalem during the Passover season — a place and time well suited to rebellion. The police did not dare to arrest him during the day because they feared the populace. Such was the pass to which the situation had evolved, and if Judas Iscariot had not betrayed him, he probably would have escaped.

The invalidity of the opinion that Jesus was put to death because he vilified the Pharisees is indicated by the attitude of the people toward Jesus. They defended him, and the authorities were forced to arrest him at night when no one was there to help him. To the people, Jesus was not just another messiah who would rouse the nation and gather troops. This was a messiah who was also a prophet, and who would succeed by the "might" of the divine. The populace also awaited a "sign"; if he was the "messiah," he could not be put to death. They hoped for the immediate advent of "the end." Among those who cried "Crucify him," there must have been many who thought that would be the moment of doom for Pilate. Jesus was caught in a web of tragic circumstances. The crowds who were inclined to follow him — aside, that is, from the ardent faithful — naturally would opt for a "testing," to force Jesus to reveal his "might" against the power of Rome. So far as the masses were concerned, the Sanhedrin's verdict of "blasphemy" was conditional; there was still the possibility of a very different issue. When they rejected Pilate's offer of a Passover amnesty to Jesus, it was not to take vengeance against him because of his preaching and his teachings. To these they were given to the last moment; they had not suddenly turned against Jesus. Rather, their view of the problem was specifically "messianic"; they sought confrontation between Rome and Israel's "messiah"; they wanted to force the battle of the end. Thus, Jesus was crucified by those also who believed in him. His death had become tragic necessity, that of a false messiah-prophet.

Jesus summoned to repentance and taught a sublime ethic. But he also demanded that he be consecrated and revered as the "Son of Man"; that the people have faith in his mission. They must believe that he was come to subdue Satan and the demons, to overcome the gentile nations and to gather in the dispersed of Israel, to renew the kingdom of David and establish the heavenly temple in Jerusalem, to raise the dead and to sit on the glorious throne in the heavenly kingdom and at the table with Abraham, Isaac, and Jacob. All these ideas were in accord with Jewish tradition; they were in no way contrary to Jewish doctrine. The sole problem was whether he, Jesus the Galilean, had been sent to do all this. He was not condemned because of his ethical teachings, but because he said that he was sent to do these things — and now he had not done them and he would not give a "sign." The problem was within Jewry, like that of Bar Kokba and Shabbetai Zevi. In the life and teaching of Jesus there was no denial of Jewish doctrine or "nationality." Jesus — the Jewish messiah to whom the gentiles were as dogs — could then become the Savior of the gentiles only in the wake of a fundamental metamorphosis, of which the seed in Jesus' life and teaching was the apocalyptio element.

THE CHRISTIAN GOSPEL

Nationalist Elements of Early Christianity

The politically oriented messianism of Jewry was fostered by the antagonism of the pagan world to Israel and Israel's religious values. Only Jews and those who were drawn to the religion of Israel and who, like the Jews, came to abhor idolatry, could comprehend and experience the pathos of Jewish messianism. The ideal was, in fact, nonpolitical and nonnationalistic. For all its this-worldly aspect, the goal of prophetic messianism was realization of the kingdom of God; that all nations should come to know the Lord, a concept at once religious-national and humanistic-national. With the passage of time, the purely religious element became ever more dominant. Israel's zealotry was zeal for the Lord, and the condemnations of paganism were ever more pronounced. Monotheism came to be required also of the gentiles, and idolatry wherever practiced was a sin for which there was no expiation. The wellspring, however, of this "messianic" urgency, the desire to realize the kingdom here and now, was Jewish-religious, Jewry's negation of idolatry.

In contrast, the apocalyptic doctrine of the "end of days" was unequivocally universalistic, embracing all mankind. The apocalyptic confrontation was not of Israel and the nations, but of good and evil, life and death, flesh and the spirit, salvation and damnation — of heaven and earth. It was not just the defect which was Israel's exile and subjugation to the gentiles which would be corrected in the apocalyptic kingdom of God; it was the cosmic evil. In the end of days, there would be no death, no illness, afflictions, pestilence, wars; man's life on earth would be without end.

In sum, the goal of Jewry's political messianism was the end of exilic defeat and subjugation; that of its apocalyptic messianism, the end of corruption and evil on earth. At this point, Jewish eschatology made contact with the mystery faiths of paganism.

Alongside that messianism which was religious and nationalistic — the ideal of redemption from the exile — there was in Jewry also the transcendent vision of a world without death and the ills of the flesh, and beyond the self-appraisal of the nation the moral accounting of the individual. This welding of diverse elements, nationalistic and universally human, social and individual, is given classic expression in the fourth Ezra (II Esdras), which is the most profound of the apocryphal writings. The author seeks an eschatological answer to the burning question: eradication of cosmic evil which weighs so heavily on mankind. His visions of the ingathering of the exiles and the downfall of pagan dominion are religious-nationalistic, the quickening of the dead and life without evil universally human, all woven together in Jewish eschatology.

Nonetheless, the specifically apocalyptic element can be precipitated out of the amalgam. The apocalyptic ideal as such did not grow out of the opposition between Israel and the nations or

of the Jewish church and its adversaries. The source of apocalyptic
aspirations in general was not religious or ethnic or political conflict; rather the cosmic opposition of good and evil, of life and
death. The apocalyptic vision promised redemption from the ills
of earthly existence and therewith, in the apocalyptic ideology,
to some degree release from dependence on the fate of the nation
and messianic political redemption. In the apocalyptic visions, the
fate of Israel in this world was of no significance; in the end of
days, there would be no more wars of the nations, and the outcome
of Israel's struggle with the gentiles would be determined in the
battle of the angels with Satan.

The roadblock in the way of the acceptance of the religion of
Israel among the nations was the fact of Israel's exile and subjugation. In the apocalyptic visions, this obstacle was removed; the
struggle against Satan, the power of evil in the world, was without
political and nationalistic bounds.

Jesus was an apocalyptic Messiah; he believed that he would
redeem Israel, subdue the nations, assemble the dispersed of Israel, and establish his throne in Jerusalem. But he also fought Satan,
anticipated the resurrection of the dead, and promised angelic
life, the "kingdom of heaven"; all of which conformed to the
prevailing Jewish ideology of the day. Nonetheless, his purpose
was not military; he did not intend insurrection. The political
aspects were no more than incidental to his messianic gospel. His
purpose was to put an end to the world as it was, to effect the
resurrection of the dead and to realize man's celestial life. He was
the "Son of Man" not merely the "son of David"; wherefore he
could become the "Redeemer" also of those to whom the quarrel
of Israel with the nations was meaningless. In him, the apocalyptic
ideal could be detached from Israel's nationalistic hope. This possibility would be realized very quickly in the thought and preaching of Paul.

Paul grew up as a follower of Pharisaic Judaism and patriotic
Jew, wholly devoted to the "hope of Israel," yet, in fact, utterly
untouched by Jewish political aspirations. His hope of redemption

was not the removal of the yoke of the "kingdom of arrogance"; Israel's quarrel with the nations was consigned to oblivion. Paul was zealous for the promise which was Israel's by reason of the merit of the fathers. But the "redemption" would not come until Israel returned in full repentance. His ideal was wholly apocalyptic. His "messiah" did battle with Satan, with death, with Sheol, but not with the nations; in Satan's fall, the "nations" would be the vanquished. The ancient conflict between Israel and the nations continued; in the Day of Judgment, the nations would be destroyed, and only "Israel" — the "true" Israel, the "remnant of Israel" — would be saved. The dominant theme, however, was changed; the world, not just Israel, would be renewed, death and Sheol overcome. The national messiah, who had longed to gather Jerusalem's children "as a hen gathers her brood" and to restore the kingdom to Israel, disappeared in the apocalyptic messiah of Paul. Therewith, the historical Israel became the symbolic Israel. The latent potential of the Jewish apocalyptic was beginning to unfold in the Christianity of Paul.

The detachment of the faith of Israel from the nation Israel was not, however, due wholly to this Pauline element; Christianity evolved through a number of transformations before the separation was definitive. The first stage was the increasing emphasis of the mythological significance of the person of Jesus. Jesus believed in his celestial origin and the essentiality of "belief" in him and in his power and ministry. For Jesus, however, that belief had not reached the status of an abstract article of faith; it was still a personal matter. He had been sent to found the "kingdom of heaven"; he was first in the kingdom and fought Satan; wherefore the kingdom was given to those who acknowledged him and labored with him for its realization. His personal faith, however, and his doctrine and teaching were of Israel, the oral and written Torah. The added duty which he imposed on his followers — to forsake the world and follow him — was of the moment, the time of the approaching end, of the advent of the "kingdom" of which he was the "bridegroom" and the "king." Therewith, he required extreme piety — that his followers separate themselves from the world and its pleasures, that they abstain and pray and repent before the "end."

In Christianity, however, Jesus' person, his life and death became the permanent basis of faith. The magic-mythological ritual of the church factually supplanted Jesus' call for repentance and his ethical demands. His teachings were abandoned and himself retained; Christianity evolved as a magic *ritus* drawing from the Christian myth of the sacrifice of the Son of God. Its origin was not, as commonly argued, the substitution of faith and ethics for the Jewish ceremonial law and commandments. Jesus himself had become the instrument of consecration, his acceptance of unique and supreme importance. The dispensation of the new testament revealed in Jesus displaced the Law given at Sinai. The temporal messianic movement, the fulfillment of the promise given Israel, now became a permanent religious covenant, a new theophany: The "king of Israel" became the bearer of "grace," the redeemer and savior.

The question at this point was whether this new revelation and testament would be bound in with the fate of the people Israel, or separated from Israel to become a "covenant" to the gentiles. The attitude of Jewry to the new testament would be decisive.

Golgotha was the watershed of the messianic movement which Jesus roused. The people beheld no "sign" and despaired. The disciples who had accompanied their master to Jerusalem in order to be present at the founding of the kingdom of heaven fled for their lives; their trust in his promises faltered. Jesus himself was surely the last to lose faith. To the end he believed that help would come from heaven, and it was only with his last breath that he cried: "My God! my God! Why have you forsaken me?" It was at that moment that he felt himself abandoned of God, misled by a dream which had failed; thus, his awesome personal tragedy.

For three days the messianic ferment subsided; the sudden catastrophe which negated all the hopes and assurances of Jesus seemingly had put an end to the movement. But on the third day after the crucifixion, there occurred the event which would determine the course of development of Christianity: The body of Jesus vanished from the grave. Just how that happened is unknown, but the disappearance of the corpse was certainly the occasion of the renewal of the messianic movement. There are scholars who opine that the belief in Jesus' resurrection derived wholly from his appearance before the disciples (that is, in a vision unconnected with bodily resurrection), which opinion is, however, in error. Jesus' appearance was considered a miracle; it brought renewal of faith after the disappointment of Golgotha — and reunited the scattered disciples. The appearance, on the other hand, of the "spirit" or ghost of a departed in a vision would not have been a miracle.

The disappearance of the body was, therefore, the beginning. It is not impossible that the miracle is to be explained like thousands of instances of "rebirth" of the dead which have occurred from ancient times to the present; that Jesus did not die on the cross, but lost consciousness, and then revived and rose from his grave and fell in some other place. Whatever the facts, the legend of the resurrection instilled the faithful with new hope. Many of them "beheld" Jesus; they reassembled and renewed their broken fellowship. The masses of the people, however, were not now drawn into the movement. So long as Jesus lived, they were able to see him as the "messiah," the "son of David." But a dead messiah was unsuited to the popular mood. Only the faithful who stood apart, the sectarians, were able to believe in a messiah who had died. The new Christian congregation which came together after the death of Jesus was a sect, and within Israel it could be nothing more. The political element, which was the basis of its earlier popular appeal, was gone.

Nonetheless, the new faith won followers in the days immediately following the reports of the resurrection. At the season of Pentecost, seven weeks after the Passover of Jesus' crucifixion, a mass movement began in Jerusalem (Acts, ch. 2). Many believers sold their belongings and gave the proceeds to the new congregation which was organized on the principles of the earlier mendicant communism of Jesus (ibid., vv. 44f.). Peter and his associates wrought miracles and healed in the name of Jesus; the excitement spread to neighboring villages, and crowds came to Jerusalem bringing the sick to the apostles to be healed (ibid., 3:1–11; 5:12–16). The Sadducean Sanhedrin tried to suppress the excitement and began to persecute the apostles. According to Acts 5:34–39, Rabban Gamaliel opposed these persecutions. Later, in Paul's time, thousands of Pharisees, "zealous upholders of the Law," were drawn to the movement (ibid., 21:20).

Popular Religion and Jewish Law

The new religion was at this stage essentially an eschatological faith. At first the resurrection had been, to the believers, the continuation of Jesus' earthly existence. The disciples thought that Jesus was risen from the grave "to restore the kingdom to Israel" now. But after some weeks of waiting, and after Jesus had ceased to "show himself" (Acts 1:3), the faithful concluded that Jesus had ascended to heaven for the time being and would shortly return to redeem Israel (ibid., 1:3, 6f.). The tenet that Jesus died in order to atone for men's sins came later. In the earlier period, the essential was the resurrection rather than the death. Jesus had not died to obtain forgiveness for sinners — an idea foreign to the thought of contemporary Jewry — but to fulfill Scripture (in which the believers now began to search diligently) and to give a sign to men so that they would repent. The purpose of the death and the resurrection was to reveal to all mankind the "powers" of Jesus; and to bear witness to the truth of his divine ministry. In the synoptic gospels, and also in the Acts of the Apostles, there are references to the concept of atonement by death;[71] but it is

71 Cf. the "interpretations" of the Acts of the Apostles, in particular 2:36, 3:15, 18, 21; 4:10–12; 5:30–31 (God "raised Jesus to life...

not a major theme. The essential article of faith is that it is now known to all that Jesus is endowed with the power of the divine, that he is "both Lord and Christ" (Acts 2:36), that he will return to judge the quick and the dead, and that "everyone that believes in him will have his sins forgiven in his name" (ibid., 10:43). Jesus was sent not to atone by his death, but by his might and power to do battle on earth with Satan and to overcome him. Even now, after Jesus' death, it was not imagined that redemption would come as a result of his sacrificial death; rather, Jesus would triumph over Satan by his return, by his reappearance on earth. The apostles required repentance and faith; these, in the name of Jesus, were the only way of pardon for transgressions. The hope of the followers had been the anticipation of the redeemer; now, the coming of the crucified redeemer who had risen from the dead and would soon return.

This faith, however, even in the early stages, included a specific article by which Christianity would be disjoined from the messianism of Jewry. This was the obligation to believe in Jesus, to be saved in Jesus' name; not just repentance and good deeds, observing the *mitzvoth*, piety, poverty, asceticism, but the faith that Jesus, and none other, is the redeemer. Israel had believed that God would send a redeemer; and over the generations the people had attached their messianic hope to various figures. But neither before nor after Jesus was belief in the messiah, when he appeared, a religious obligation. Rather, Israel and all the nations would recognize the messiah by his deeds of redemption.

Christianity's determination of the redeemer in the person of a messiah who had not yet effected "the redemption," and its re-

in order to give repentance and forgiveness of sins..."); 7:52. In 8:32–35, which refer to Isa. 53, the verses which include allusions to atoning death are not quoted. In Paul's sermon in Athens, Jesus' death and resurrection are mentioned only as a sign which God has given to mankind so that they would believe and repent. See Acts 17:31: "a man... whom he has guaranteed to all men by raising him from the dead." The essential is the resurrection, not the death.

quirement of belief in him, were concepts wholly foreign to Judaism. And there was more: belief in Jesus was the condition of forgiveness of sins (Acts 10:43; et al.). In this tenet, which became an essential article of faith, Christianity followed Jesus. Even during his lifetime, Jesus had insisted on belief in himself and had assured the "kingdom of heaven" to those who followed him. Now, however, as belief in the redeemer who had died, it became the essential, the first article of the creed. It was the kernel from which Paul would subsequently develop the negation of the Law; although at first no opposition was felt between this doctrine and the "yoke" of the Law. Belief in Jesus, although of major, even decisive importance, was still only one more duty added in the end of days to the older commandments. The extreme conclusion that the Law was abolished would be drawn by Paul only in the next period.

The rejection of the Law was the consequence of the heightened mythological-magic appreciation of the person of Jesus and his life history. It was not due to opposition to Jewish "ritualism," denial of the worth of the Temple and its sacrificial system, or the idea of the primacy of the ethical which Jesus had stressed. The Nazarene congregation in Jerusalem was not opposed to the keeping of the Law and the commandments, nor to the Temple and the Temple sacrifices; and the intermittent persecutions which it suffered were not because it transgressed in these respects. The doctrine of the primacy of the ethical had already been relegated to second place, and Paul also would speak of it only incidentally. The congregation of Jerusalem was much concerned with the Law and the commandments. New pietistic precepts were introduced, additional fasts and prayers; and the Temple service meticulously scrutinized. Jesus had been zealous for the sanctity of the Temple, and his disciples followed him in this. Paul prayed in the Temple and, while in a trance, beheld Jesus in the Temple (Acts 22:17–18). The very many who joined the Nazarene movement did not cease to be "zealous upholders of the Law." Because of them and the founding elders of the congregation, Paul was forced to sacrifice in the Temple as though he, too, was faithful to the Law (Acts 21:17ff., 26). The Nazarene congregation of Jerusalem was persecuted by the Sadducees, but defended at times by the Pharisees.[72]

The idea that the Law was abrogated developed and took hold only gradually, and without any connection with the teachings of Jesus and his moral strictures. The root of the doctrine as Paul developed it was not the will to "refine" the faith or denial of the worth of works and rituals as such. Elsewhere in this work* we have considered the fact that the character of the Christian religion which enabled it to win pagan peoples — who were certainly unprepared to accept a "refined religion" purged of rituals — was

---

72 The Sadducees persecuted the Nazarenes because they taught "that in the case of Jesus there had been a resurrection from the dead" (Acts 4:1-2). We have mentioned above that Rabban Gamaliel spoke in their defense. Also, "some scribes of the Pharisees' party" argued in defense of Paul (ibid., 23:9); this because Paul misled them by saying that he was "a Pharisee, and the son of Pharisees" and by implying that he was on trial only because of his "hope for the resurrection of the dead" (ibid., v. 6). Again, however, Pharisees joined in the persecutions, which we learn from the fact of Paul's participation in the murder of Stephen when he was still Saul, the Pharisee. But the opinion that Stephen was killed because he denied the Law or the Temple is baseless. Stephen spoke only of what Jesus would do when he returned in glory (ibid., 6:14), which prediction the Jews considered blasphemous (ibid., v. 11). But Stephen did not advocate the abrogation of the Law. The peroration of Stephen's answer in the court (ibid., 7:47f.) is confused and incomplete, and its specific intent difficult to determine. Vv. 48-49 are not disparagement of the Temple. Vv. 49-50 are a direct quotation from Isa. 66:1-2 and could not be a ground for the sentencing of Stephen. In verse 7:53, Stephen castigates Israel in that it was given the Law by angels, "and did not obey it." In Stephen's language, there is indication of the influence of Luke (author of The Acts of the Apostles), Paul's disciple. It is not impossible that Stephen said that Jesus would "tear down" the Temple and build a new Temple (cf. Acts 6:14), as Jesus himself had said. But he was condemned because of his statement that he could see "the Son of Man standing at God's right hand" (7:56f.).

* *Golah ve-Nekhar*, I, ch. 6 (The Israelite Religion and Heathenism), p. 284f.

not that it had been purified and refined by abrogation of the commandments. Moreover, the abrogation of the Law and the commandments was, even from the point of view of church dogma, unconnected with any "liberal" tendency to purge religion of ceremonialism. In the apocryphal Christian literature of the period following the Acts of the Apostles, there is indeed an effort to base the denial of the ceremonial laws on their lesser significance as compared to refined beliefs and morality. The commandments of Judaism and the Temple and its sacrifices are negated and considered the product of failure to understand the esoteric content of Scripture.[73] These and similar ideas represent, however, only subordinate trends in Christian writings which are close to the pagan-gnostic ideologies of the period. Orthodox Christianity which followed Paul limited the scope and validity of the Law but did not deny its sanctity and its commandments, nor that of the Temple and its sacrificial system. Jewish Law was divinely given, but with the coming of Jesus no longer incumbent, wherein there is no rejection as such of the commandments generally and the sacrifices in particular. Paul did not base his dogma on the doctrine of the primacy of the ethical and never referred to the statements of Jesus concerning the validity of the Law and the commandments. The commandments were divinely ordained; the Law was altogether sacred, without blemish. But now, the old was replaced by new rites based on the mystique of the life and death of Jesus. This was diversion to myth and magic, not ascent to "purified" religion.

It is, indeed, an egregious error to find the origin of Christianity in the so-called "liberal" movements within Jewry; thus in particular, in Hellenistic Jewry with its tendency to "refine" the faith, to interpret the Pentateuch allegorically, to deny the absolute value of the ceremonial law, to emphasize ethics and monotheism, to

---

73 This point of view is expressed in particular in the apocryphal "Epistle of Barnabas." However, the author adheres to all the mystic ritualism of the church, and thus unintentionally denies the "refined" religion, which fact easily escapes notice.

remove the "barriers" and "universalize" the religion of Jewry. This error is tied in with another of more general character: the tendentious discovery of the roots of Christianity in Greek philosophy and its late outgrowths. In fact, there was a certain "philosophic" current in Christianity. But, on the whole, Christianity was, as we have observed, a popular faith begotten of the most ingenuous beliefs of the masses. "Higher faiths" evolve, for the most part, through scholarly efforts to purge popular beliefs of their cruder aspects and to discover tendencies in them which are acceptable intellectually and philosophically. Normally, these two procedures follow one another. In Christianity, however, they were contemporaneous. During the very years when the popular beliefs were evolving in characteristic fashion, there was an associated "intellectual" current, which strove to bring the popular beliefs into conformity with Hellenistic philosophy. Christianity was provided, as it were, with a kind of "philosophical" exegesis, even though the exegesis was of little significance in its conquest of the Roman world. In that period, Christianity was conscious of its popular character, and even prided itself on its obscurantism (I Cor. 1:23), that it was an *absurdum*, anti-intellectual and illogical. It is not without significance that Luther — nearly fifteen centuries later — would wish to banish reason, the "evil beast," from the classroom.

The evolution, therefore, of Christianity and, in particular, its negative evaluation of the commandments are not to be explained as a tendency to more refined or sublimated religious concepts; and also not to be related to philosophic thought in general, or more specifically to philosophic tendencies in Jewish thought. There was no connection whatsoever between the philosophic exegesis of Hellenistic Jewry and the humbler circles which were attracted to Jewish and Christian homiletics. The Hellenistic-Jewish reinterpretation of Jewish Scripture in conformity with Greek thought could appeal only to a very restricted intellectual elite, and even there its influence was minimal. The profound ignorance of things Jewish among Greek and Roman scholars and authors is surprising. At a time when Jewish customs were spreading and converts were numerous, Romans such as Seneca and Tacitus held very bizarre notions of Judaism. The so-called "philosophic" Hellenism certainly did not pave the way for penetration of Jewish ideas into the Greek-Roman world; no one came to Judaism because he had read Philo or Josephus. The attraction of Jewish ideas and practice was a popular phenomenon, with women the more susceptible.

Certainly Christianity in its beginning was not influenced by any Jewish intellectualism. For all its abolition of "the commandments" (that is, the "old" Law), it was anything but a "purified" religion. Its beginning — from Jesus onward — was banishment of foul spirits, warfare against Satan, the resurrection of the dead, the banquet of the righteous in the time to come and, in addition, the conception of Jesus by the Holy Ghost. Christianity proclaimed, that God had taken the form of a Galilean Jew, been put to death, and risen again; and had threatened all who did not believe in him with the fires of hell! The popular mythological outlook of the day was that of Jesus and his disciples — these, the "uneducated" who were given to all the current superstitions. The "resurrection of the dead" was the central theme of the new religion and a very special stumbling block to Greek intellectuals (Acts 17:31–32). The welding of the resurrection doctrine with the belief in Jesus' divinity is characteristic: Jesus was the "Son of God," the primeval divine substance by which the world had been created. He was not divested in death of the body formed in the female womb in order to ascend to heaven; the created body had risen from the grave: it had ascended to heaven to be seated "at the right hand of the Almighty." The gospels state that Jesus appeared before his disciples after the crucifixion not as a "spirit" but corporeally, "flesh and bones" with hands and feet; that the disciples touched him and saw the marks of the nails on his hands; that he ate "broiled fish," and that he remained with his disciples about forty days before his ascent to heaven. The "Son of God," therefore, ascended bodily, with staff and garments. The "logos" of the gospel, ac-

140

cording to John, is a tenuous construct, fine-spun out of the popular legend which is the origin of Christianity. Thereby, the legend
becomes wholly illogical; to magnify it seems the merit and reward
of those who believe *"quia absurdum."*

This is also the position of Paul. Paul was acquainted in a superficial way with the popular Hellenistic "enlightenment" of the
time, but he was consciously inhospitable to "enlightened" religious
ideas. He despised "what this world calls wisdom" and took pride
in the "folly of the gospel message," which to him was the wisdom
of God (I Cor., chs. 1–2, et al.). For all his perspicacious casuistry,
his views are anthropomorphic and exoteric; he does not understand the Greek concept of the soul and can imagine no entity,
even if it is spiritual, which is not also corporeal. There is for
Paul — as also for Jesus (Matt. 22:29–32) — no life of the soul
without a body. The resurrection is the essential of Paul's faith;
if there were no resurrection, if the Messiah did not rise from the
dead, all belief is vain: "If Christ was not raised, your faith is a
delusion ... those who have fallen asleep in trust in Christ have
perished" (I Cor. 15:17–18); there is no hope for man. "If the dead
do not rise at all, 'Let us eat and drink, for we will be dead to-
morrow" (ibid., v. 32; cf. I Thess. 4:15f., et al.).[74]

The efforts to find traces of Hellenistic Jewry's philosophizing

74 Christian theologians seem to sense no contradiction when they say
that "la voix des simples" — of the masses — speaks in the gospels,
and at the same time that "Christianity does not and cannot include
any doctrines and any morality other than those of Hellenic philosophy" (Ernest Havet, *Le christianisme et ses origines,* 1878, III, 485). But
the primary dogma of Christian faith was belief in Jesus and his
divinity, which belief is wholly foreign both to "Hellenic philosophy"
and to the concept of the "Logos," to which it was related even by the
earliest Christian "philosophers." The doctrine of the divinity of a
Galilean Jew cannot be derived in any sense from Greek philosophy
or from the idea of "the Logos" or from the abstract concept of
"the Trinity." The origin of Christianity, both the belief in Jesus
and the other specific tenets of Christianity, lay in popular beliefs and
not in "Greek philosophy." The philosophic exegeses were secondary
and subsidiary.

exegesis and to interpret the early Christian innovations with respect to the commandments as an innate "liberalizing" movement — a tendency to "purify" the older religion and to remove its "restrictions" — are without basis. The founders of Christianity were not followers of Philo and the other Hellenistic Jewish exegetes; they shared the superstitions of the Jewish masses of the time. Alexandrian Jewry might interpret the narratives of Scripture "allegorically" and seek rationalistic explanations for the commandments, but the early Christian accepted the biblical stories with all their anthropomorphisms literally. To Hellenistic Jewry, the Pentateuch was essentially law, *nomos*; but Christianity annulled "the Law," that is, the commandments, and retained the narrative. Rites were not, however, unimportant; the Christian rituals which replaced the older Jewish practices were invested with specific religious significance, which was unrelated to philosophic or intellectual refinements of belief. The role of sacrifice in Christian beliefs is a striking example of this. In the apocryphal literature of the church there are "rationalistic" arguments against the Temple and its sacrificial order, which arguments go back to the preexilic prophets. Nonetheless, the rationalistic arguments were not decisive. Not only did Christianity accept the sanctity (though limited in time) of the Temple and the sacrificial service, it received and incorporated the concept of sacrifice and, in fact, attached more importance to it than did Judaism. The basic premise of Christianity was the sacrifice of God's "Son," his immolation in order by his blood to make atonement for the transgressions of men. In this, the pagan-mythological motif within the sacrificial cult came to full and even exaggerated expression. It is not only the concept of sacrifice and of the atonement of the blood, it is the idea of human sacrifice, and the awesome, fearful idea of the sacrifice of the "Son of God." The mood which gave birth to this idea certainly was not of a nature to deny the Temple and its sacrifices because of "enlightened" considerations.

Christianity's sacrificial system was characteristic. In the Eucharist, the "body" and "blood" of the Christ was partaken of by the faithful. And if — even before Paul — the Nazarene community did not observe all the traditional sacrifices, this was because they had already fallen into disuse in Jewry due to their restriction to the precincts of the Temple in Jerusalem. Christianity was subject to the same circumstance which prevailed in Israel from the discovery of the book of Deuteronomy in the time of Josiah; it was impossible to sacrifice to "God the Father" outside Jerusalem, and for the Christian congregation, also, there was no temple other than that of Jerusalem. The destruction of the Temple, therefore, was the end also of the sacrificial shrine of Christianity — including Pauline Christianity. Christianity could not build shrines to Jesus outside Jerusalem and was driven to substitute the symbolic sacrifice of the Messiah.

Discernment of the ideological basis of the abolition of the traditional sacrificial system enables us to understand the rationale of the "abolition of the Law." Christianity accepted and maintained the legendary and narrative portions both of Scripture and the oral tradition, and required the faithful to believe. Indeed, Christianity went beyond Judaism in this respect. The biblical cosmogony was given "dogmatic" sanction, and heretics were condemned to die for every minor deviation. The Law, that is, was not "abrogated" insofar as it was narrative and legend; only that part which was commandment was negated.

To understand this negation, it must be borne in mind that all the ceremonial commandments, not just those for which there was no "reason," were annulled. Christianity also abolished the festivals and holy days without which no religion — indeed, no human society — can exist, and even the Sabbath, the supreme benefit with which Judaism endowed humanity. Christianity also did away with Jewish jurisprudence, which of itself disproves the view that the abolition of the Law was the consequence of a striving for a "higher" or "enlightened" faith, or corollary to the rejection of "ritualism." As the Christian congregation outgrew the sectarian exaltation of the Sermon on the Mount, it felt the need of institutional procedures. Even at the beginning, a fiscal organization was set up with rules and regulations. The precept, "judge not lest ye be judged," might suffice for the mendicant community subsisting totally on charity which Jesus had founded. But, since the church did not consist wholly of "saints" of Jerusalem, and the great majority of the communicants remained bound to worldly affairs, some juridical system was necessary. Paul sensed the need of a civil law and reproved the Corinthians for bringing "ordinary matters" before a heathen court (I Cor. 6:1f.). There was, however, at that time no Christian jurisprudence; canon law would be created later to fill the gaps of the secular law. Christianity took over the beliefs and concepts of Judaism and its world of song and legend but rejected its jurisprudence and attached the pagan law, the *"corpus juris"* of Rome, to the gospels.

Herein is the "great error" which has misled Christian scholarship to this day. Christianity, it is said, did away with the superficial trappings of Judaism which obscured its elevated morality. This, according to Wellhausen, is the merit of Christianity, the "remainder" which is half of all. However, Jesus, and certainly the early Christianity which followed him, did not remove the trappings. Jesus preached to a pauper congregation which had withdrawn from the world in order to prepare for the coming of the kingdom — the imminent event! But, insofar as thought was given at all to "this world," it did not occur to anyone to abandon the Law. Pauline Christianity would abrogate the Law and its jurisprudence and graft the gospel onto the tradition of Rome. This Christianity is not the gospel, as is customarily assumed, but the gospel with the Catholic sacrament and, in particular, with the Roman *corpus juris* and other secular, non-Jewish codes; the sacred element — the sectarian agape and the profane element — the secular statutes and justice. In Judaism there was no such dualism; Jewish jurisprudence was of the divine law. Christian jurisprudence, however, since it was "secular," could be disavowed as such, and religious law be cloaked in the mantle which was wholly "love." This interpretation, however, is the "great error." The "remainder" — the inevitable "remainder!" — of Christianity is the pagan code of the "Christian" state; and, until the development of the Christian state, the pagan code as such. Pagan legislation remained in force with all its cruelties: torture to extort confessions, barbaric executions, slavery, and extreme class inequalities. Christianity intended no political revolution or social amelioration; Paul warned his flock and taught that secular society would remain as it was. The abrogation of Jewish Law was not inevitable. The Nazarenes withdrew from their compatriots as a separate, proscribed community and were able to live in some measure by their private code. Christianity would shortly draw the logical conclusion: the annulment of the Law.

The abrogation of the Jewish jurisprudence is proof that the annulment of the Law implied no opposition to "ritualism" and religious forms. The annulment was, as we have stressed, the consequence of the increasingly mythological-magical appreciation of Jesus, and especially of his sacrificial death. The world was redeemed by Jesus' "blood," not by his ethic and doctrine.

We have observed in the foregoing that, for the Nazarene community in Jerusalem, the essential event was not the death of Jesus, but the resurrection and the expected immediate return which would bring about "the end." To Paul, on the other hand, the essential was the mystery of the death. Christianity could not content itself with the idea that the redeemer had died to "fulfill the scriptures"; the crucifixion was utterly earthshaking, awe-inspiring. Why had God allowed the "Son of Man" to suffer that cruel, repulsive death? Belief tried to understand the suffering of Jesus; it sensed a great mystery, an occult significance in Jesus' immolation, and found it in the concept of the atonement: God had given the redeemer as sacrifice to atone for the iniquity of man. In this light, the events of Jesus' life acquired new meaning; it was no longer the resurrection, but the death which was now the essential. Jesus' death was the mighty, awful deed of God, the culminating event in the history of man. The Christian "good news" was centered in the association of man in the divinely ordained sacrifice of the "Son of God." Repentance, good deeds, the good life, withdrawal, humility, asceticism, love, all these were preparation for association in the divine redemptive sacrifice, the reconciliation by the blood of the "Son of God." The ethical instruction of Jesus was absorbed into the mythical doctrine of this sacrificial redemption, and the Law of Judaism rendered obsolete. A new sacramental ritual with mythical-magic import evolved. Baptism implied sanctification and salvation, and in the Eucharist the participant partook of the body of Jesus and shared in the "grace" which had come to the world by the divine sacrifice. Herewith, the event of Golgotha became of importance immeasurably greater than the theophany of Sinai.

The evolved doctrine of the redemptive sacrifice is to be found in the epistles of Paul. We can do no more than surmise the course of its development. Certainly Paul had not thought at first that the new cult and its sacraments would supplant the Law. After his "repentance," he went to "Arabia" (Gal. 1:17–18) and pondered the new "truth" which had been revealed to him. On his return to Jerusalem, three years later, he prayed in the Temple (Acts 22:17) even as the earlier Nazarenes and received personal instruction from them (I Cor. 15:3). According to the account in the Acts of the Apostles, it would seem that the original formulation of Paul's new doctrine is that of his sermon at Antioch in Pisidia (Acts 13:16–41). In this, Paul reverts to the idea that in the death of Jesus the "utterances of the prophets" and "everything that had been said about him" had been fulfilled. But, in addition, he explicates the connection between the phenomenon which was Jesus and the "Law." It is not just that the "forgiveness of sins" is announced through Jesus; Paul insists that which "the Law of Moses" cannot do — remove the guilt of men — is effected through "union" with Jesus of "everyone who believes" (ibid., vv. 38–39). The obligation of the Law is not annulled, but the Law alone cannot "justify"; to attain to the salvation of life eternal the Jew must believe in Jesus. Belief in Jesus — not piety and moral conduct — is more important than the whole of the Law, even though the Law is not yet abrogated.

Nonetheless, in the understanding of Jesus' death as a divine sacrifice, the divine mythological soteriology, and the tenet that belief in the mystery is the *sine qua non* of salvation and life eternal, the negation of the Law is implicit. The implications of the doctrine were developed, it would seem, in connection with the problem of gentile proselytization which, though subsidiary and external to the evolution of doctrine, was of decisive importance in the development of Christianity. The origin, however, and determination of the abolition of the Law were the magic-mythological direction which, in Paul, became the essential basis of Christian dogma and not any inherent tendency within Christianity toward "universalism" and removal of the "barrier" of the Law.

Universalist Elements of Christianity and Judaism

The references in the New Testament to the problems connected with the preaching of the gospel to the gentiles are obscure and confused. The Jewish Christians, on whom it devolved to resolve the problems, dealt with them in general terms which do not really come to grips with the issues. Thus, the difficulties of research are magnified, and it is not surprising that contemporary Christian scholarship understands what transpired according to its preconceptions.

In reading the New Testament sources which relate to the question of gentile proselytes, one might think that the founders of Christianity faced a completely new problem which Jewry had not previously resolved, and that their solution — that of the Nazarene congregation — was essentially new. This, indeed, has always been and still is the view of Christian scholars! Judaism confined God's grace to the "seed of Abraham," and Christianity removed the "barrier" opening the gates of faith to all mankind. An eminent contemporary historian, Eduard Meyer, says that the essence of the question — to preach the good news to the gentiles — was whether the providence of the Creator extends to all His creatures; [75] as though Jewry had not faced and resolved that problem long since! However, when we turn to the references in the New Testament, we are amazed to find that two Jews, Peter and Paul — nearly two thousand years before Harnack, Meyer, and company — spoke in much the same vein. Jewry had been receiving proselytes of all nations, yet Peter says that he "now" really understands "that God shows no partiality, but welcomes the man of any nation who reveres him and does what is right" (Acts 10:34–35); [76] and Paul — as if the thought was new in Israel and the issue between him and his opponents — asks: "Does God belong to the Jews alone? Does he not belong to the heathen too?" (Rom. 3:29). The God of Israel, Paul says, is the God of all men and desires that all peoples turn to him in repentance. One might imagine that Paul's thought, to which he returns so often, that in the association of faith all differences between Jews and Greeks, barbarians and Scythians, are removed, [77] was original with him. But Jewry likewise gave the name "Israel" to every gentile who accepted the faith of Israel. Or again, the ideas that it is not the seed of Abraham in the flesh, but that all those who accept the faith of Abraham are in truth beloved of God and the true seed of Abraham (the "father of all proselytes"), [78] and that the branches of the wild olive can be grafted on the cultivated olive. [79] So, also, that the barrier between Israel and the nations is "broken down" by common faith and the "two" made "one," and that the gentiles, when they accept Israel's faith, share in the "commonwealth of Israel," in the promises assured to Israel [80] — that all these originated in Christianity.

In sum, Peter and Paul seem to be saying that Christianity first

---

75 Meyer, III, 99.
76 *Cf.* Paul (Rom. 2:11): "... for God shows no partiality," and all who sin will be punished without distinction, whether Jew or Greek.
77 Gal. 3:28; I Cor. 12:13; Col. 3:11; cf. Rom. 10:12.
78 Rom. ch. 4; 9:7f.; Gal. 3:14–29.
79 Rom. ch. 11.
80 Eph. 2:11f.; also 1:12 f., et al.

attained to the thought that it was not just the "seed of Abraham" for whom there was hope, but that gentiles also would be saved if they accepted the true faith; that is, that the institution of religious conversion was a Christian, not a Jewish, creation.[81]

The obscurity of this problem is due in no small measure to the ambiguous use of the word gentile, *goi*, to denote: (1) alien(s), that is, (peoples) non-Israelite by descent; and (2) idol worshipers, that is, (peoples) non-Israelite by religion. The same applies to the Judaeo-Greek equivalent, *etné*, and the translations of that word in various languages. If this ambiguity is borne in mind, it will be seen that Christianity's proclamation of the gospel to the gentiles conforms to the spirit of Pharisaic Judaism, and that the two faiths are equally firm in their evaluation of the significance — or insignificance — of racial origin. In both Christianity and Judaism, the heathen peoples were without hope or future. But the individual's ethnic-racial affiliation did not determine: The "alien" became "Israel" by religious conversion. This concept, which Christianity received from Judaism, was the basis of gentile proselytization. The gentile who remained heathen was lost, but for the *goi* who accepted the faith of Israel there was hope — this was the common doctrine of Judaism and Christianity. The problem

---

81 Christian scholarship has never understood the nature of Jewish proselytism in the post-biblical period and has not realized that Paul's proselytization of the gentiles was in accord with Jewish practice. This is due, on the one hand, to the way in which the discussion of gentile proselytization is reported in the New Testament, and certainly also to the fact that Christian scholars have, with rarest exceptions, known nothing of the source materials of later Judaism. Early Christian scholars, as well as those of the modern period, were unaware of the nature of the religious conversion of Jewry. Augustine, for example, argued that there were righteous men among the gentiles, which even the Jews did not make bold to deny, and cites as proof Job, ". . . neither a native, nor a proselyte, an alien (*advena*) to the people Israel, but of the Idumean nation, there born and buried" (*Civitas Dei*, Book 18, ch. 47; Jacque Paul Migne, *Patrologiae Latina*, XLI, 609). Thus, the "proselyte" is *advena*, the alien dwelling in the land of Israel among the people Israel.

with which the founders of Christianity struggled was, therefore, not that of racial or ethnic origin, whether the God of Israel "welcomes the man of any nation who reveres him and does what is right." Judaism had already resolved that problem.

In fact, the problem facing the Christian fathers concerned the essentials of the "faith of Israel" which the alien must accept in order to be saved. The clash within the Christian community of the new mythological cult and the older religion of the Torah developed from this problem. Baptism and circumcision were the symbols respectively of the new and the old, and the problem was basically inner-Jewish. The Jewish Christians held that the Law alone could not "justify"; by observance of the commandments the Jew could not merit the "kingdom of heaven." He must, in addition, believe in the salvation of Jesus and be baptized in Jesus' name. The problem came to the fore in connection with gentile proselytization: Did baptism alone suffice — that is, without circumcision and without observance of the commandments? Therewith, the change in the Nazarene creed, which had evolved of the Christian mythus, found explicit expression.

The mission to the gentiles, however, was not an innovation; it was not victory over ethnic narrowness, removal of ethnic-racial "barriers" — a novel tendency to "universalism." Neither Christianity nor Judaism proclaimed salvation and solace to all men irrespective of religion. Redemption was only for proselytes, those who were grafted onto the "cultivated olive" and become "Israel" of the spirit. Christianity's innovation was baptism as the specific rite of conversion. The perplexity of the Nazarene community resembles in some respect that of the time of Ezra and Nehemiah and the succeeding generation, when the concept of religious conversion was in process of formulation. The Christian solution to the question of conversion derives from the change in Judaism. It was both formally and in substance the Jewish principle that without the faith of Israel there is no salvation. To this concept the Christian church now attached new rites centered in the life and person of Jesus. Therewith, the obligations of the old Law and its commandments were abrogated; they were no longer a condition of entry into the "kingdom of heaven."

Nonetheless, the theoretical validity of the Torah, as such, was not denied. It was still incumbent on the gentile who became a Christian to acknowledge its unique sanctity; he must believe in the cosmogony and the narrative portions of the written and, to some extent, also of the oral law. But now — in this age of a new testament — he was not required to observe the commandments. He must accept the whole of the Jewish-Christian cosmogony from the beginning, that is Genesis to the resurrection of the dead, including the exorcism of demons, the war with the Satan, and the corporeal ascent of Jesus to heaven. The hypothesis that Christianity required of the gentile convert only that he "believe," that for the rest he could remain what he had been, is the product of the obliquities of liberal theologians. The new Christian accepted a world of new beliefs, ideas, and legends which he had not known before. This was the universe of belief and legendry which had grown out of the historical experience of the nation Israel; the religion which the new Christian accepted was "only" the whole of Jewish legendry.

Christian conversion was in a sense "haggadic" — historical-legendary — rather than "Halakhic," that is, regulatory. The gentile proselyte was not required to observe the Sabbath, but he had to believe in its cosmogenic aetiology, the six days of creation. He need not observe the Passover but must believe in the biblical account of the exodus from Egypt. He did not have to be circumcised, but he must believe that circumcision was required — in its time — of God. He did not have to observe the Jewish holy days but must believe in their sanctity, that is, of the time when the "old" Law was still valid. He was relieved of the yoke of the commandments; but he accepted the "Satan," the "resurrection of the dead," "Abraham, Isaac, and Jacob," and the primeval Adam, denial of these and similar beliefs would bring condemnation in the Catholic church. It was only in the sphere of the ritual commandments that Christianity, engaged in the creation of a

151

new cultic corpus based on the Christian mythology, made concessions.

The perplexity of the Nazarene congregation with respect to the mission to the gentiles was in essence a phase in the birth pangs of the evolving haggadic-mythological rites of conversion in the period of transition from Jewish to Christian ideology. That was the proximate but there was also, a second important factor: the event of gentile proselytes, which to the Nazarenes seemed something very new and wonderful, the workings of the "finger of God." Paul says that salvation has come to the heathen because of Israel's "stumbling," [82] and therewith explains Israel's disbelief in Jesus and his mission: This is God's great "secret." God hardened the heart of Israel not in order to destroy Israel but to open the way for the gentiles. The gentiles are reconciled in the rejection of the Jews, but when "all the heathen have come in" Israel will be saved.[83] The "gospel" and the "promise" are the inheritance of Israel "according to the flesh." Jesus "has become an agent of circumcision," and God in his mercy has caused the gentiles to share in the promises made to the patriarchs.[84] In Acts, Luke reports several times that Paul turned to the gentiles after the Jews rejected him. In Antioch of Pisidia, Paul and Barnabas tell the Jews: "God's message had to be told to you first, but since you thrust it off and judge yourselves unworthy of eternal life, we now turn to the heathen." [85] Thus, the first Christians believed

---

82 Rom. 11:11: "Through their false step salvation has gone to the heathen...."
83 Ibid., 11:25–26, and other verses of the chapter.
84 Ibid., 15:8f. Paul bases the claim of "the poor among God's people in Jerusalem" to contributions of the gentiles on this: "...for if the heathen have shared their spiritual blessings, they ought to do them a service in material ways" (ibid. 15:26–27).
85 Acts 13:46. Paul spoke in the same vein to the Jews of Corinth. After trying without success to convince them that Jesus was the messiah, he said: "Your blood be on your own heads! I am not to blame for it! After this I will go to the heathen" (ibid., 18:1–6). He spoke similarly in Rome (ibid., 28:25–28).

that the gospel was intended for Israel and that the gentiles were permitted to share only after the Jews rejected. This belief is to be viewed against the background of Jesus' instruction to the disciples when he sent them to preach the good news: "Do not go among the heathen, or to any Samaritan town, but proceed instead to the lost sheep of Israel's house" (Matt. 10:5–6). Jesus, unwilling to heal the daughter of a Canaanite woman, explained that he was "sent only to the lost sheep of Israel's house" (ibid., 15:24, 26; Mark 7:27). Indeed, we know that the disciples preached first to Jews and turned to the gentiles only later.

The Gentiles

This narrowly nationalistic tendency in the earliest stage of Christian development is, at first glance, passing strange. At the time when Jesus ordered his apostles not to preach to the gentiles and Paul, the "apostle to the gentiles," thought that salvation was awarded the gentiles only because Israel had "stumbled," Jewry had been preaching its Torah and winning converts everywhere for some hundreds of years. The early Christian restriction was to any proselytization of the gentiles, not just to the specific Pauline doctrine of conversion without fulfillment of the commandments. This is the only possible meaning of Jesus' above-mentioned instruction to the apostles. In contrast, Judaism at that time was trying to win the gentiles to a better way, to bring them salvation without reference to Israel's "trespass" or dependence on it. It remains to inquire into the cause of the greater parochialism of early Christianity as compared to Pharisaic Judaism.

We recall at this point the distinction made above [86] between the specifically religious element in Jewish thought and the messianic-historic factor. As religion, Judaism was altogether universalist, making no distinction between "Jew" and "Greek" except as they differed in religious belief and practice. But the religion of Israel

86 Y. Kaufmann, *Golah ve-Nekhar*, I, ch. 5.

was confined as a result of the circumstances of its development
to a single nation, and this historic restriction was reflected and
symbolized in particular in the messianic doctrine. Postexilic Jewry
did not believe that the nations would accept its Law and tended
to envisage the future redemption as liberation from the gentile
yoke, the end of the dominion of idolatry.[87]

Christianity, on the other hand, was messianic from the beginning and as such imbued with the messianic mood of the Jewish
nation rather than the inherent universalism of Jewish religious
thought. Christianity proclaimed the Day of Judgment, the coming
of the end, and did not, at first, feel itself a distinct religion.
Christianity preached the gospel of the end to Jews, "the lost sheep
of the house of Israel," and did not regard its mission as the conversion of the gentiles to the faith of Israel. Its message, moreover,
was sectarian, the way of pious ascetics, which threatened Israel
also, non-idolaters, with Gehenna. Indeed, only the few were
called and would be saved, not all Israel; and certainly there was
no good news to be preached to the gentiles. The gospel was for
the salvation of the righteous and the pious; it was not appointed
to the masses. The parochial sectarian bond was breached only
later, when Christianity had become for its adherents a new and
independent form of the religion of Israel.

Christianity, therefore, had to remove two roadblocks in its
way to proselytization of the gentiles: First, the nationalistic-
messianic restriction with its characteristic sectarian approach; and
second, the Jewish rites of conversion, for which Christianity would
substitute a new ritual conformable to the greater significance of
the mythical element as compared with the old Law. It was only
when it had surmounted the two barriers that it regained the universalism of Pharisaic Jewry and breached the nationalistic charge
of Jesus.

The "new" insight, therefore, of the founders of Christianity
that God welcomes all those who revere him "of any nation" and

87 Ibid., 220f.

"shows no partiality" was not new to Jewry. It marked, however, the internal crisis within the Christian community, and the struggle to overcome the parochialism of its origins. The view that the preaching of the gospel should no longer be restricted to Israel is expressed in the words of Peter and Paul: God desires that the souls of the gentiles also be redeemed before the "end." Secondly, the statements of Peter and Paul reflect the development of the new conversion whereby the detachment of Christianity from Judaism would be definitive. God accepts all who revere him, those also whose conversion is belief in the mythological-magic lore of Christianity and who do not observe the commandments. This, as stated, is a shift in religious values, but not a new or changed evaluation of the ethnic factor. On the basis of the foregoing, we are prepared to understand the beginnings of gentile Christianity.

Beginnings of Gentile Christianity

Pauline Christianity, which was to become the faith of the gentiles, was also constructed on bases which Judaism had laid. The circles in which gentile Christianity evolved were, as is generally agreed by Christian scholars, the judaizers, the half-proselytes, the "God-fearers" who were given to Jewish ways but not, or not yet, Jews by conversion.

The story of the baptism of the captain Cornelius and his household (Acts, chs. 10–11) reflects the nature of the beginnings of gentile Christianity. Cornelius, "a devout man, who feared God," who was "liberal in his charities to the people [the Jews] and always prayed to God," and who had "a good reputation with the whole Jewish nation" (Acts 10:2, 22), became acquainted with the Christian message and believed. Wanting to be baptized with the members of his household, he approached Peter, who fell into a trance and beheld "a thing like a great sheet ... with all kinds of quadrupeds, reptiles and wild birds in it." A voice ordered him, "Kill something [of those unclean things] and eat it!" Peter interpreted the vision as applying to Cornelius and his uncircumcised household. Then, when Peter and Cornelius and their associates were conversing, the "holy Spirit" descended suddenly upon Cornelius and his retinue; and the Jewish followers of Peter "heard them speaking in foreign languages and declaring the greatness of God." Peter and the Jewish believers with him "were amazed because the gift of the holy Spirit had been showered upon the heathen too." Then Peter said, "Can anyone refuse the use of water to baptize these people when they have received the holy Spirit just as we did?" and "directed that they should be baptized in the name of Jesus Christ" (ibid., 10:42–48).

This event, the alighting of the "holy Spirit" on gentiles, was the birth of gentile Christianity. Peter justified himself before the Jerusalem congregation by the argument: "So if God had given them the same gift that we received when we believed in the Lord Jesus Christ, who was I, to be able to interfere with God?" (ibid., 11:17). Peter's opponents "heard this... made no further objection..." and said, "Then God has given even the heathen... the hope of life" (ibid., v. 18). To the Christian congregation, the descent of the "holy Spirit" upon the gentiles was "the finger of God," a sure sign that God desired the return of the gentiles. Later, at the time of the dispute between Paul and his opponents concerning gentile proselytization, when Paul and Barnabas returned to Jerusalem to consider the matter in a meeting with the apostles and elders, the same decisive argument is attributed to Peter: "And God who knows men's hearts testified for them by giving them the holy Spirit just as he had done to us, making no difference between us and them..." (ibid., 15:8–9). Paul and Barnabas also "told of the signs and wonders which God had done among the heathen through them" (ibid., v. 12); the "holy Spirit" and the "wonders" were sure signs of God's will. Paul used the same argument against the Galatians who wanted to observe the Law: "This is all I want to ask you: Did you receive the Spirit through doing what the Law commands, or through believing the message you heard?... When he supplies you with the Spirit and works wonders among you, is it because you do what the Law commands, or because you believe the message you heard?" (Gal. 3:2, 5; cf. Eph. 1:13).

The phenomenon was, in fact, without precedent in Israel. To the Jews, an ecstatic religious movement among gentiles was in the nature of things unclean, an abomination even as all the manifestations of idolatry. However, in the period of the second Temple, in wake of the penetration of Jewish ideas, a special class of gentiles had gradually evolved around the Jewish communities of the Roman diaspora. These were the half-proselytes who had abandoned idolatry, gentile judaizers, disposed to follow Jewish religious practice and influenced by what went on in Jewry, but not become wholly Jews. Enthusiasm within Jewry was likely to communicate itself to them; and, in since they were attached to the religion of the Jews, fervid visionary manifestations among them were not considered the product of pagan impurities and foul spirits. This state of affairs was of decisive importance in the development of Christianity. Great numbers of Jews were roused to fervor by the events of Jesus' life and the saga of his passion, and their excitement naturally affected the "God-fearing" gentiles. Signs and miracles, healing and "wonders" of all kinds, ecstasies, speaking in tongues, prophecies, visions, all the phenomena which at that time were thought to be evidence of the "holy Spirit" occurred in the nature of things among the half-proselytes also. The Nazarene community observed the faith of the God-fearing gentiles in the Jesus saga and were deeply stirred. They were convinced that the signs and wonders were the working of the "holy Spirit" with which Jesus had endowed those who believed in him. This, in the context of their religious ideas, became "the baptism of the holy Spirit." The Jewish Christians felt themselves at one with these God-fearing gentiles in this new faith which, in their view, could gain the "kingdom of heaven" for them. The ecstatic "baptism" of the holy Spirit was the foundation of gentile Chistianity. Jewry, by fostering the community of the "God-fearing," had created the human material of the earliest gentile-Christian church.

It was the special situation of these judaizing communities which had evolved under the influence of Judaism that diverted Christianity from its original nationalistic pattern, and not any ideological universalism. The origin of gentile Christianity was a religious and historic event, not a new religious concept. Religious Judaism longed for the return of the gentiles but, because of its historic experience and the continued dominance of idolatry among the gentiles, did not think that the gentiles would repent. Christianity, as a messianic movement, held at first to this historic messianic judgment of the nation Israel and refrained altogether from preaching the gospel to gentiles. But the gentiles were, so to speak, "evangelized" of themselves. They were deeply moved by the Christian mystery and received the glad tidings which had not been announced for them. It was this messianic acceptance among the "gentiles," that is, the judaizing gentiles — those "God-fearers" who had not yet become fully Jews — which turned Christianity from its original course. To the early Nazarenes, this Christian movement was a sign that God had not destined all the uncircumcised to perdition; thus their exclamation: "Then God has given even the heathen repentance and the hope of life!" (Acts 11:18). The idea that God desired the turn of the non-Jews to the faith of Israel had long been established in Israel. But that God had addressed the gospel of the kingdom of heaven also to the gentiles, that he might baptize them with the "holy Spirit" and work "wonders" among them — these things were altogether new. And in them, something else was implied: God has baptized these "God-fearers" who do not observe the commandments, these uncircumcised gentiles, with "the holy Spirit"; in this, he has given a sign that the "kingdom of heaven," which was vouchsafed only to the righteous few of this generation, is given also to those gentiles who believe in Jesus even though they do not observe the commandments. Therewith, Christianity began to function as the revelation of a new covenant, a new, divinely revealed distinct testament whereby, without dependence on the old, the proselytes could be received of the God of Israel. The triumphant future of Christianity is foreshadowed in the baptism of Cornelius and his company.

Complementary, as it were, to this development among the God-fearing gentiles, and its obverse, was the non-belief of the Jews. The "stiff-neckedness" of the Jews was no less astonishing to the Nazarenes than the belief of the gentiles. Those to whom the promise had been given, among whom the "messiah" with ministry to them was born, rebelled and hardened their hearts; this while these gentiles, to whom the messiah had not been sent, and who were without the merit of the fathers, believed. Paul, as we have observed, turned to the gentiles only after the failure of his efforts to win the Jews. He discerned a connection between the two phenomena: God had hardened Israel's heart for the time being in order to give of his grace to the gentiles. The significance of the unwillingness of the Jews to receive the "good tidings" for the development of gentile Christianity lies in Paul's conviction that without the "rebellion" of the Jews there would have been no salvation for the gentiles. Christianity turned of necessity in the way it had not intended; it was this historical circumstance, not intrinsic universalism, which impelled Christianity gradually beyond the limits of Israel. Universalism was certainly a necessary condition to the spread of Christianity beyond the confines of Israel. The concept, however, of universality was an inheritance of Judaism, and it was Judaism which, by reason of its innate universalism, had created those communities of half-proselytes among whom gentile Christianity originated. Christianity's special course was due to the particular circumstances of its emergence and not to some new concept which denied religious significance to ethnic attachments.

Jews and half-Jews, the judaizers, approached the new religion from different points of view. Jewry as a whole was unable to accept the Christian gospel, whereas the judaizers tended naturally to find the message of "the redemption" in it. After the death of Jesus, the gospel was no longer a messianic message and had become a religious challenge: to believe in Jesus and the absolute significance of the mystery of his life and death. In that period, many pious Jews accepted the Christian gospel and were not conscious of any diminishing of the validity of the Torah. But the majority did sense such diminution: Christianity required belief in a new theophany which was not less, rather far more important than that of Sinai. The lessened stature of Sinai did not yet imply the annulment of the Law and the commandments; Peter and James, the brother of Jesus, meticulously observed the commandments as Jesus had expressly charged. Even the new "inner freedom" and the tendency to reduce the significance and sanctity of the Law did not change this. To the Nazarene Congregation, the absolute sanctity of the Torah and the unconditional duty to abide by it — without any "inner freedom" — were fundamentals of faith; and Paul also did not in principle question this belief.

Nonetheless, in that Christianity made belief in Jesus a religious duty no less important than the obligation of the Torah, the significance of the Law even when it remained in force was lessened. Paul said that the Law alone could not "justify"; unless he sought forgiveness of his sins by baptism in the name of Jesus, the Jew could not attain to everlasting life. Although the apostles based belief in Jesus on the words of Torah and the prophets, the essential of the new faith was the unique sanctification of the man-messiah who, to his worshipers, was the symbol of a new theophany of no less significance than the revelation of the Law. Jesus was invested with divine sanctity. He was of himself instrument and conduit of holiness; and his sanctity did not derive from that of the Law and the prophets, even though it was confirmed by them. At that time, Jewry believed in the coming of the redeemer; this was destiny and hope and sure promise. But the idea that belief in any one man was a duty and condition of the pardoning of transgression and of entry into "the kingdom of heaven" was without precedent. It is probable that some of those Jews who opposed Christianity were prone to believe that Jesus was the messiah and would yet be proven the promised redeemer. But they were unable to accept the doctrine that this belief was a religious obligation without which there was no escaping the judgment of Gehenna. Acceptance of Jesus as the promised redeemer — for which there is basis in the preaching of Jesus himself — and especially of the further proposition that "belief in him" was a religious duty, even the supreme duty and the way of personal salvation, was exceedingly difficult for Jews, and was met with bitter recrimination and invective. Christianity had become more than a "messianic" movement, and Jesus the personification of a new myth and the instrument of holiness. Belief in Jesus, as the apostles preached the new faith, was lessening of the Law even if the apostles themselves were not conscious of that. "The Law," even if not yet abrogated, had to make room for a second revelation. Jewry, however, was devoted to "the Law," its faith in the Law absolute; the nation as a whole could not accept the "good news." It could not believe that faith in Jesus, and not observance of the Law, was the way of salvation.

The Judaizers

The ideological situation of the judaizers was wholly different; they were spiritually in the mood, as it were, of the days of Sinai. Analysis of the attitudes of these "God-fearers," who constituted the early gentile church, will elucidate the formative factors of gentile Christianity. These were men and women who had come under the influence of Judaism, accepted its beliefs and followed many of its practices; and certainly very many of them refrained from the worship of the gods of Rome. They were of various categories: Some accepted only isolated Jewish beliefs and practices, while others, though closer to Judaism, were still not proselytes. For much the greater part, they were not of the intelligentsia; they knew little or nothing of the current "philosophy" and did not come to Judaism by way of logic and speculation. They were drawn to Judaism by its religious charisma, the lore of the hidden God, master of the universe, who rules with wisdom, loving kindness, and mercy, and is faithful to reward those who love him. The lure of Judaism was popular, not esoteric, not unlike that which had overwhelmed the nation at Sinai and changed its way of life for all time. Why, then, it may be asked, did the judaizers stop at midpoint? Why did they not accept Judaism altogether and become "proselytes by conviction"? Certainly they were not repelled by the rituals and ceremonies, and they were not in search of a "higher faith," purged of "works" and consisting wholly of creed, love, and ethics. It is generally agreed that the first gentile Christians came from among the judaizers and were by great majority of the lower classes. This fact, of itself, belies the view that it was its "ritualism" which stood in the way of the expansion of Judaism, and that the advantage of Christianity was its abrogation of the commandments. The judaizers observed commandments and practiced the customs of Judaism; they sent donations for the Temple, and to them as to the pagan world, generally, rituals were a natural form of religious expression, taken for granted. Of course, they were unable to observe all the commandments, even as the "am-ha-arez," the untutored among the Jews. But this was not a matter of principle, rather of practice, "technical" so to speak. Judaism was a characteristically communal religion, inclusive of a life pattern which could be realized fully only in communities. It encompassed every phase of life and could thrive only if it engendered communal institutions and an environment wherein its statutes and practices were the rule. The individual proselyte, therefore, was torn from his former society and domesticated in the Jewish community. Judaism was a way of life; it dominated the Jew's every act and permeated the whole of his being. Group rather than individual conversion, the proselytization of whole communities, was congenial to its social quality.

For the individual, on the other hand, acceptance of Judaism was difficult; conversion implied transition from one society to another. Judaism, as the religion of a people, could be received by communities more easily than by individual proselytes. Due, however, to its dispersion, it could no longer win communities; in the diaspora, individuals were won over, but not communities or nations. Many were spiritually close to Judaism and anxious to become sharers in its blessing, but were loath to sever all ties with their pagan backgrounds. In these circumstances, circumcision was a special obstacle, particularly difficult for the male adult. In the Graeco-Roman world, it was looked upon as altogether outlandish, and the proselyte who wanted to be circumcised had to surmount the prejudgment of his social environment. The judaizer, therefore, accepted Jewish beliefs and observed many Jewish practices, but found it too difficult to observe the whole of the Law, to enter the covenant and refashion his life. He did not deny the import of the commandments; they were not superfluous or unbecoming to a "purified" religion. But he was not brought to the point of accepting the whole of the Law; his status was transitional, its terminus in most cases final conversion.

The spiritual-emotional situation of these half-Jews was ideally suited to reception of the Christian "glad tidings." The judaizers were anxious to enter into the covenant but, by the circumstances of their daily lives, unprepared to become Jews, to accept in full the "yoke" of the commandments. They felt themselves inferior, Jews and not-Jews; a barrier remained between them and Israel's God. The "proselyte" is typically sensitive, and the judaizers felt that they could become really of "Israel" only if they observed the whole of the Law. It was incumbent upon them to be more rigorous in observance than Israel "of the flesh," the "cultivated olive."

Now came the baptism of Christianity offering them, as it were, the whole of "Israel" without further ado. By baptism the barriers were breached at one stroke; the Christian evangel promised the "kingdom of heaven," the supreme good, to all who would be baptized. The "kingdom of heaven" was not to every Israelite; even the observance of the commandments did not assure his entry. But now, by baptism the judaizer attained immediately the status of righteousness and piety which promised the "kingdom." This was the great attraction of the Christian message. The judaizers were not seeking to be rid in this way of the commandments, and they did not prefer Christianity because they thought it a "higher" or "purged" religion and, therefore, preferable to

Judaism. The abrogation of the Law according to the formula of Paul, that is, of all the commandments, was in fact a deterrent. Thus we observe (in particular, in the epistle to the Galatians) the gentile Christians disposed to retain at least some of the commandments and Paul's polemic against this. Although the abrogation of the total obligation, to observe the whole of the Law as a condition of entry into the covenant, was important to them, they would have preferred to observe the commandments voluntarily and to the extent possible. But the observance of all the commandments as a covenantal obligation was too much; and the Christian gospel bestowed the supreme status of piety without imposing the obligation of a system of commandments. For them, the Christian good news was "the giving of the Torah." Thereby, they entered the covenant with the God of Israel and became "Israel" and the heirs of the "kingdom" without being required to break with their society. In addition, the concept of "the Law" was not so dominant and firmly established among the judaizers as among the Jews. The judaizers were still beyond the precincts of the Law; they had not yet come within. In these circumstances, the "new testament" did not have to do battle with the "old." The judaizers were predisposed to receive a new way, more so than the Jews. Among them, Paul found ready listeners.

The beginning of gentile Christianity was before Paul; but Paul supplied a solid theoretical basis and thereby assured its survival. The gentile church of the apostles Peter and James was a strange, unviable Christianity, reflecting the ambiguity and obscurity of their views. There were, in fact, only two possibilities: for one, Christianity might have remained a sect within Jewry, a higher or supreme degree of piety which assured salvation. In that Christianity, Jew and gentile alike would have been obliged to the whole of the Law, which was, indeed, the position of Jesus. The other possibility was that the Law had been extinguished by the atonement of Jesus and was no longer requisite either for Jew or gentile; this the doctrine of Paul. As against this, the position of James, the brother of Jesus, to which Peter tended, and which was the basis of the "instruction" to the apostles (Acts 15:1–29), was weak and inconsistent. The Law bound Jews but not gentiles who became Christian, and James, who subscribed to the "instruction," or even wrote it, forbade Jewish Christians to eat with gentile Christians or to fraternize with them (Gal. 2:11f.). This halfway house was hopeless.

Christianity at the outset was a gospel of the pious and elect, threatening doom to all who would not "return" and did not practice extreme piety in addition to the observance of the Law. And now, the gentile Christianity of Peter and James, while denying salvation to Jews who obeyed the Law and were "pure," bestowed the highest reward of piety, the "kingdom of heaven," on men who had been considered "impure." Peter and James followed the trend in Jewry which tolerated various categories of "proselytes." Christianity, however, by reason of its sectarian-pietistic character, could not abide schismatic divisions of this sort. It required extreme piety, the indispensable key to salvation. It now remained for Paul to draw the logical consequence, the tendency implicit in the Christian mystery, that is, to create a new worship to replace the old. Paul sought out the essential meaning of the death of the Messiah: That God had offered a fearful sacrifice was of necessity a sign; it must be there was no salvation for mankind without that sacrifice. The Law given at Sinai could not save; the death of Jesus was become the way of salvation, of the "grace" which God had provided for man. The Law, therefore, was no longer obligatory. "For if uprightness could be secured through law, then Christ died for nothing" (Gal. 2:21). This is the essential of Paul's doctrine: The death of the Christ is the "end of the Law." Accordingly, all — whether Jew or Greek — who believe and are baptized are justified; they have no need of the Law.

Gentile Christianity, by its bestowal on the uncircumcised of the "kingdom of heaven" as reward of faith and baptism, could be justified only by this logic of Paul. Paul, of course, did not work out his doctrine in order to justify the new gentile Christianity;

and he certainly did not abrogate the Law in order to facilitate the expansion of Christianity. Rather, the Pauline doctrine is the adequate expression of the tendency endemic in Christianity to magnify the religious significance of the myth of Jesus, and to make attainment of the "kingdom of heaven" dependent on it. The perplexing problem of the death of Jesus was daringly re-solved in the Pauline system. It may be that the alighting of the "holy Spirit" on the uncircumcised was the germ of Paul's thought that faith in Jesus was the essential of salvation. In any event, it was the problem of gentile Christianity which inspired Paul to express his idea in such uncompromising language. And even though the extreme consequence of Paul's logic — the abrogation of the whole of the Law — was exceptionally unpalatable at a time when men, Jews and pagans alike, had no desire to do away with "ri-tualism," his schema was destined to carry the day in the Christian church. In this, Christianity chose the lesser horn of its dilemma: By reason of the Pauline doctrine, it escaped the confines of a sect of "inferior" gentile proselytes, the "unclean," separated from those of their faith who were Jews. To the proselyte, the advantage was that in Christianity he achieved the status of a full-fledged "citizen" in Israel without accepting the yoke of the command-ments. If, as in Judaism, he remained "unclean" even after baptism, what was his profit? In the church of Paul, he became a "citizen" by baptism in the "congregation of Israel"; he was wholly of "Is-rael."

Christianity — Nation versus Church

The origin, therefore, of gentile Christianity as a distinct entity was, as stated, not an innate spiritual propensity, not the negation of the significance of ethnic affiliation (beyond that of Judaism), nor "implied" by Jesus' ethical teachings. Rather, it was the out-growth of a movement which originated among judaizers anxious to be included in the "congregation of Israel." Christianity, even at that early date, was accomplishing among these judaizing groups its historic destiny: to propagate the religion of Israel by means of the "new testament," whereby the gentiles were received into the covenant. It was not the sectarian asceticism of Christianity which attracted the judaizers and made it seem preferable to Judaism. The baptism of Christianity was for them the way by which they could enter into the covenant of the faith of Israel and become fully accredited citizens within the "congregation of Israel."

Christianity had already ceased, so far as the judaizers were concerned, being essentially a mystery-faith and austere, mendicant way of life, of abstention, asceticism, and withdrawal from the world. It was now prepared to win converts for the faith of Israel; its adventitious superiority over Judaism was the greater ease with which individual converts could be received. Whether the political-exilic factor turned the scale in favor of Christianity in the initial rivalry of the two faiths for the souls of the judaizers may be questioned. But, certainly, it was a contributing factor. The political situation of Jewry stood in the way of winning communities and forced Judaism to be content with proselytization of individuals. Jewry's political disadvantage was probably more than merely a contributory factor. Many judaizers must have been unwilling to attach themselves to a nation living in exile, and many must have felt scorn and intense dislike of the Jews, even when they were drawn to Jewish religion. The "heathen" of Antioch of Pisidia were "delighted" by the stiff-neckedness of the Jews (Acts 13:48), and Paul felt compelled to warn them against their "looking down" on the Jews and thinking themselves better than them (Rom. 11: 17f.). The fierce hatred of Jewry which would soon break out among these gentile Christians must have been deeply rooted.

In any case, the decisive historical importance of the founding of the gentile Christian church was not the creation of a revised version of the faith of Israel without "commandments." The new religion, in its Catholic formulation, with its precise catechism and fasts, was not less demanding than Judaism with its detail of "commandments." Christianity's expansion dated from the time when it began to win whole communities. Expansion of that kind

167

was not precluded to Judaism so far as its societal structure was involved. The overwhelming significance of the founding of the Christian church was, as we have repeatedly said, that thereby a new vehicle for the propagation of the religion of Israel, which was completely detached from the fate of the nation Israel, came into being. The figure of Jesus could now be divested of its politically messianic garb, and belief in Jesus made the sole condition of faith, of receiving the religion of Israel. This new conversion did not associate the proselyte with the nation Israel. Jesus was no longer "the redeemer of Israel"; he had become the symbol of the "new covenant" between mankind and the God of Israel. Therewith, the nations were able to enter into the faith of Israel free of involvement with the messianic destiny of the nation Israel.

The universalism of the gentile Christian church was, therefore, not a new concept peculiar to Christianity. If we abstract from the differences between the old and the new conversion rites, there remains no theoretical difference in the universalist content of the two faiths; and it is evident that Jewry's propaganda could have resulted in the development of congregations of gentile proselytes. Judaism did, indeed, aspire to that and succeeded in certain instances. The phenomenon of active missionary proselytizing is, in fact, the outgrowth of the Pharisaic institution of religious conversion. The impression that the gentile Christian fathers surmounted a nationalistic or chauvinistic "stumbling block" and reached their decision to proselytize among the gentiles after they had breached a "barrier" and set aside the "boundary marker" of Judaism, is simply an illusion, a very interesting illusion at that. The early Christianity of Jesus and his disciples was more nationalistic than Pharisaic Judaism; and the origin of the illusion lies in the juxtaposition of the turning of the apostles to the gentiles with the "rebellion of Israel." To the church fathers, gentile proselytization was the obverse of the renunciation of "Israel" and the source of a new election, no longer the nations and Israel, but now the nations in place of Israel. God had chosen another "people" instead of "rebellious" Israel. Circumstances were really new: Israel had rejected the gospel which — as the evangelists believed — had been sent only to them; but the gentiles believed, and were entered into the covenant in place of Israel. Jewry also had aspired to win the gentiles to the faith of Israel; but it had never imagined this new election.

Here again, however, the origin was a new situation and not an aspiration or innate tendency. The early Christianity inclined in the direction of nationalistic limitation; and it was only Israel's "transgression" that forced the evangelists to the idea of the new election. That idea was, in fact, an outgrowth of the Jewish concept of religious conversion adapted now to the particular objective conditions in which the Christian gospel was operative. Jewry never believed in a new election accompanied by the rejection of Israel. But the theoretical possibility was implicit in the tendency within Judaism to stress the importance of religious over ethnic affiliation. The thought appears in Scripture in the form of warning and threat; God was ready to destroy Israel after the episode of the golden calf and to make "a great nation" of Moses (Exod. 32:10; Deut. 9:14). In Malachi, the message is even more comprehensive: "I have no pleasure in you, Saith the Lord of hosts.... For from the rising of the sun even unto the going down of the same My name is great among the nations.." (Mal. 1:10–11). Christian scholars use this passage as a kind of proof text, whereas in Judaism the idea was wholly abstract and its realization factually out of question. The prophets and the later Jewish sages anticipated the future redemption of Israel, and the salvation of the gentiles as their association in one way or another in the religion and the fate of Israel. The bond between the nation Israel and its religion might be weakened or broken by the later institution of religious conversion, but not by a new election. The idea of religious conversion implied renunciation of the significance of "the flesh," of race; it was wholly universalist. The thought, however, that Israel was rejected, which now took root in gentile Christianity, was the result of historic experience, not of more pronounced universalist orientation. The popular belief in Israel's preeminence had resulted from historic experience, that Jewry alone was devoted to the one God. The new Christian doctrine of Israel's default and the new election grew out of the historic circumstances of Christian proselytization. Missionary zeal among the gentiles had been a fact of life in Jewry for generations. But the circumstances which now turned the Christian evangelists to that same kind of missionary activity were the specific data of Jewish rejection and the positive response of the gentile judaizers to their message; for which reason their decision to proclaim the gospel also to the gentiles appeared to be something new. The appearance of novelty reflects, however, as stated, the extraordinary nationalistic restriction of Christian beginnings. If the Christian gospel had been universalist from the start — as universalist as the Pharisaic Judaism of the day — it would have been proclaimed from the beginning to Jew and gentile alike, even as Judaism. Proselytization of the gentiles would not have depended on the "rebellion of Israel" or been bound to the idea of the election of "Israel according to the spirit." It was only because Christianity, in its origins, was extremely restrictive and attained the thought of preaching the gospel to the gentiles by force of the "rebellion of Israel" that its message assumed the trenchant form of the renunciation of Israel.

And more, the idea of the new election, which evolved among the gentile church fathers, did not imply the annulment of the Jewish messianic judgment of the gentiles and a return to the "universalist concepts" of the prophets — their belief, that is, that the nations will repent. In the first place, the messianic concept of Christianity is that of later Judaism, not that of the prophets of Israel. The earlier, more universalistic prophecy envisioned the "end of days" as a new theophany of the God of Israel. In the end of days the peoples, when they beheld the miracles to be wrought at the time of Israel's redemption, would abandon their idols and come to serve the Lord. That is, the return of the gentiles would follow Israel's redemption. Postexilic Jewry, on the other hand, demanded repentance of the gentiles now, before the "days of the messiah." Only those gentiles who repented in time would share in the messianic bounty and become children of the most high. In the days of the messiah, those gentiles who delayed "return" would be left knocking "at the door." Thus, the days of the messiah are a time of judgment and retribution for the gentiles, not a new revelation which would cause them to repent. This is the view also of Christianity; there will be no repentance for the gentiles after the coming of the "Son of Man." Those who have not hearkened and have not, then, betimes — before the coming of the messiah — repented, will be lost on that day. Because of its sectarian origin, the judgment of Christianity was more rigorous than that of Judaism; there was no comfort for tardy proselytes of the time to come. The time for repentance was before the coming of the messiah; thereafter, there was no hope.

Moreover, when the apostles first turned to the gentiles they, like the Pharisees, did not think that the nations would return. In Christianity as in Israel, the traditional opposition, "Israel" versus the nations, remained in all vigor. The concept of a new election did not mean that pagan peoples were chosen now in place of the nation Israel. Here in particular, the equivocal use of the term nation (goiim, *etné*)[88] has been misleading and the source of confusion. The term is used in early Christian writings both with religious and with ethnic connotations; and also to denote individual gentiles and communities (nations, peoples) and specifically alien (gentile) nations and individuals ("idol worshipers"). Thus, also, the Greek-Hebrew *etné* as used in early Christian writings denotes both (heathen, gentile) nations and individuals.[89] When Paul and his companions speak of the repentance of the "heathen" (goiim, *etné*) and their salvation, the reference is always to individuals

---

88 Cf. above, p. 149 (*Golah ve-Nekhar*, I, 410).

89 Cf. Acts 10:45; 11:1, 18; 13:48; 14:2; 18:6; 21:11, *et passim*. The words, "gentiles, nations" and "Greeks" are used at times interchangeably. See I Cor. 1:22–23 (*etnesin, Ellénes*). In the third Epistle of John, v. 7 (variant version), *etnon* replacing *etnikon*, a usage found also in apocryphal literature, e.g., Hermae Pastor, *Similitudes*, parable 8, ch. 9, repeatedly.

and never to peoples, nations. The "heathen" of Paul who are saved are individual gentiles, the uncircumcised who have accepted the gospel and are rescued from the doom which is imminent. Paul does not use the word *etné* in the collective sense (other than in citations from Scripture); as he uses the term, it is a synonym for "uncircumcised" or "Greeks" or "aliens," gentiles. To be sure, Paul views his mission as the preaching of the gospel to "all the heathen" (Rom. 1:5, 16); those who are saved are not nations, rather "us whom he has called not only from among the Jews but from among the heathen" (ibid., 9:24). The false step of Israel is the "salvation" of "the heathen," Israel's defeat the enrichment of the world, of "the heathen" (ibid., 11:11–12). Paul does not imagine this "salvation" as the turning of nations to God. The "heathen" who repent are "cut from a wild olive," that is, from the nations, and "grafted upon a cultivated one," the "remnant of Israel" (ibid., 11:24). Paul's salvation is election of individuals, the breaking off of some of "the branches" of the "wild olive" through the grace of faith. He thinks that the salvation will come of itself, within his lifetime, to "the heathen," and he has been chosen to "win the heathen to obedience," which "Christ has accomplished through me" (ibid., 15:18). The congregations which have been formed are of "the heathen" who "have shared their spiritual blessings," that is, the blessings of "God's people in Jerusalem" (ibid., 15:26–27). The "heathen" who are saved by the stumbling of Israel are those who have attained "uprightness" (ibid., 9:30). The blessing of Abraham — "All the heathen will be blessed through you" — refers to the "men of faith," those of "the heathen" who believe in the messiah (Gal. 3:8–14).

The mood of the pristine church was eschatological: The day of the Messiah was nigh. In this frame of mind, the Christian fathers could not imagine that whole nations would accept the message. The first Christians believed that the end of this world and the kingdom of heaven would be within the lifetime of men then living. Their ministry was to proclaim the good news everywhere so that those who were "called" would hear and be saved. The world at that time, that is, before the return of whole nations, was ripe for the "kingdom of heaven." In this expectation, Christianity in its first three centuries recognized no ethnic or political attachment except to (the "true") Israel and Israel's holy places. Unlike Islam, which from the beginning was territorially and ethnically involved, Christianity was always a church in the fullest sense of the word.

The early gentile church did not encompass nations, nor did it anticipate that it would ever do so. Christians thought of themselves as a people apart, God's "own people," chosen from among the nations (Eph. 1:14; I Pet. 2:9; Titus 2:14; cf. Rom. 9:25; I Pet. 2:10 et al.). In that early period, Christianity possessed no sacred city or land other than the heavenly Jerusalem. Cities, lands, kingdoms, the world of the heathen were destined to destruction, "for we have no permanent city here on earth" (Heb. 13:14); this the temper of the early church. Rome was still "Babylon," symbol of pagan iniquity, not yet a holy city. The church had inherited the ancient antagonisms of Israel versus the nations. But the conflict was now of the sublimated "Israel" and "the heavenly Jerusalem" versus the pagan imperium. The same fate awaited the pagan nations in the Jewish and the early Christian eschatologies; the kingdom of heaven would be the end of pagan empire. Christian eschatology also took over the language and symbolism of Jewish eschatology. Jerusalem — at once the heavenly and the terrestrial Jerusalem — is the center of the universe. The church is a distinct entity, apart from the nations and unaffected by their fate. "Nation will rise in arms against nation, and kingdom against kingdom" in the end of days. The faithful "will be hated by all the heathen"; Jerusalem will be "surrounded by armies," and there will be "anger at this people," that is, Israel. "They will fall by the edge of the sword, and be carried off as prisoners among all nations, and Jerusalem will be trampled underfoot by the heathen, until the time of the heathen comes." Then "the Son of Man" will appear with his angels and "gather his chosen people from the four winds" (the vision of Jesus, Luke 21:8–36; Matt.

24:4–31; Mark 13:5–27). The days of the Messiah are the time of the fall of the nations and the ingathering of the elect from among the nations.

The eschatology of the Revelation of John is of particular interest. The "remnant of Israel," one hundred forty-four thousand, of all the tribes of Israel, occupy the head position in the kingdom of heaven; and with them the righteous-elect "from every nation, tribe, people, and language" (John 5: 9–10; 7:9f.). The condemned are still simply "the heathen," without qualification. The holy city and "the court outside the temple" have "been given up to the heathen" (John 11:2); and the "heathen" are enraged (ibid., 11:18). Babylon-Rome symbolized all the pagan nations; and the church has no "city" other than the heavenly Jerusalem. Babylon-Rome is destined to destruction; it will not repent. The "cities of the heathen" will fall with "Babylon" (ibid., 16:19), and the enemies of the elect are "peoples, multitudes, nations, and languages" (ibid., 17:15–16). "All the heathen" had "been led astray" by the "magic" of Babylon; in Babylon was "found the blood of prophets, God's people" (ibid., 18:23–24). From the mouth of the rider of the white horse "came a sharp sword ... to strike down the heathen" (bid., 19:15); the "kings of the earth ... gather to make war on him" (ibid., 19:19). Satan is bound, "to keep him from leading the heathen astray any longer, until the thousand years are over" (ibid., 20:2–3). Then he will be released and "go out to lead astray the heathen," and to muster "Gog and Magog" against the "beloved city" where the Messiah is enthroned (ibid., 20:7f.). In the description of the world after the second coming (wherein the author borrows from Deutero-Isaiah), "the heathen" are outside the precincts of the righteous.

The same point of view is to be found in the Christian apocryphal literature. Christians are a "people" apart, a "new people," [90] chosen from among the nations. In an early hymn, prayer is to God who "dost destroy the imaginings of nations"; God, who

90 Cf. Epistle to Diogenetus, beginning.

"dost multiply nations upon earth and hast chosen out from them those that love thee through Jesus Christ.... We beseech thee, Master, to be our help and succour ... turn again the wanderers of thy people ... let all 'nations know thee, that thou art God alone,' and that Jesus Christ is thy child, and that we are thy people and the sheep of thy pasture." [91] And further: "... cleanse us with the cleansing of thy truth, and 'guide our steps to walk in holiness of heart, to do the things which are good and pleasing before thee,' and before our rulers." [92] There is no expectation that the "rulers" will repent and be joined to the church; the earlier opposition between Israel and the worldly kingdom now prevails between the church and this world. The church is dispersed, the elect dwell among the heathen; they will be gathered in the time to come by the Messiah. Thus, the church's grace over the breaking of the bread: "As this broken bread was scattered upon the mountains, but was brought together and became one, so let thy church be gathered together from the ends of the earth into thy kingdom." [93] In this literature, the opposition to "the nations" is forcefully expressed; the church has inherited and carries on the struggle of Israel versus the nations.

The views of the church fathers concerning the eventual fate of the nations were essentially those of Jewry. In the end of days, the remnant of Israel would be saved, and of the gentiles the proselytes who had joined themselves to the remnant and been refined together with them into the true "Israel." The peoples, on the other hand, would perish on the Day of Judgment. Christianity, after it overcame the "chauvinism" of its beginnings, rose to the universalism of Judaism and, like Judaism, began to preach its gospel throughout the (Roman) world. But in the first centuries it, again like Judaism, did not anticipate that peoples as a whole, or even in masses, would be won. The two faiths, however, dif-

91 The first Epistle of Clement to the Corinthians, 59:3-4.
92 Ibid., 59:3.
93 The Didache, *Apostles' Manual,* 9.

fered in that in Judaism the heirs of the "kingdom" were Israel, that is, Israel "according to the flesh" together with those gentiles who had accepted Israel's faith; whereas in early Christianity, the heirs were the congregation of the "elect," that is, the remnant of Israel and the proselytes. Israel was, of course, the "spiritual" Israel; the people Israel had "sinned" and rejected the gospel.

Judaism was the faith of a people, and the nation's outlook was reflected in its messianic hopes. Christianity, on the other hand, was the faith of a congregation, of "proselytes" of various nations calling itself "Israel," but wholly apart from Israel "of the flesh." This Christian "Israel," however, like the nation Israel — Israel "of the flesh" — thought of itself as the few who were chosen from among the nations to be saved. There was a difference in the religious ground of the election. Israel's belief in its election, though it depended on the merit of the fathers, was not without conditions: the transgressors of Israel were excluded and the righteous proselytes included in the community of the chosen. In the Christian "Israel," which was essentially a congregation of proselytes, the election was by "grace." But neither Christianity nor Judaism believed in universal salvation, a salvation of the nations.

Moreover, in Paul, the "apostle to the gentiles," there is a uniquely ethnic belief which, to my knowledge, is without parallel in Judaism. Paul asks why Israel rejected the gospel, and finds answer in the concept of the "remnant of Israel." God's promise to Israel is yet valid, but "not everybody who is descended from Israel really belongs to Israel," and only those who believe are truly Israel (Rom. 9:6). Paul, however, is still not satisfied with this explanation. The doctrine of "election by grace," whereby he explains the conversion of the gentiles, troubles him: How can the fate of the transgressors of Israel be explained? They, too, were chosen from the beginning to be the recipients of God's mercy, and "to them belong the rights of sonship ... the divine agreements and legislation, the Temple service, the promises ..." (Rom. 9:4). Paul, therefore, as is his wont, appends a contradictory tenet to the doctrine of the remnant of Israel. The transgression of Israel is transitory. God hardened the heart of Israel in order to redeem the gentiles; and after "all the heathen have come in" — that is, after all those gentiles who have been appointed to salvation have come in —[94] then "all Israel" will be saved. This is the "secret" of the "false step" of Israel. All Israel, not just a remnant of Israel, will be saved, "for God does not change his mind about those to whom he gives his blessings or sends his call" (ibid., 11: 25–36). The false step of Israel is God's goodness, his salvation and mercy to the gentiles. But even now, in despite of its false step or even because of it, Israel occupies a special place in the divine counsel. Only the elect of the gentiles will be saved; but of Israel, all. God chooses among the gentiles according to his grace, but he has chosen Israel from of old to be his people; "they are dear to him because of their forefathers" (Rom. 11:28). God still intends to be "gracious to all of them," even as theirs is "the judgment of the sons" more favored than that of the nations. In this concept, the people Israel in their role as a nation are the subject of a future destiny. Aside from them, no people will be saved. There will be saved only "gentiles," "proselytes," who attach themselves to Israel. These are the elect of the rest of humanity, for whom there is no merit of the fathers. This idea conforms in a certain respect to the ideology of the Revelation of John. In the center of the kingdom of heaven, John envisions those "of the twelve tribes of Israel" who are "marked with the seal" and with them "a great crowd ... from every nation, tribe, people, and language" (ch. 7). The remnant of Israel are as a nation, the others a "great crowd."

Judaism and Christianity were alike in their efforts to spread the religion of Israel and to win converts and, also, in that they did not believe that peoples, the nations, could be won over. Chris-

94 Rom. 11:17–26. Paul does not say "all the heathen." Of the wild olive only (some) branches will be broken off and grafted to the cultivated olive. But the branches which were pruned from the cultivated olive, "if they do not cling to their unbelief," will be grafted (back) into the olive "to which they properly belong."

tianity's universal mission was accomplished by reason of specific historic circumstances and not according to any preconceived plan. With the gentile church, a new "nation" was born that had no part in the political aspirations of Jewry and its political struggle with the pagan world, and which was not burdened with the exile which grew out of that struggle.

The church also experienced hostility and persecution; indeed, the hostility was even greater than that toward Jewry. But it was hatred of a religious sect, not of an ethnic group, and it was not tied in with national antagonisms. From the point of view of paganism, Christianity might be a crime worthy of death; but the Christians were not "in exile," and their status in the periods of persecution was not the consequence of military disasters. Christianity did not aspire to found a terrestrial kingdom or to conquer lands and subjugate peoples. It was a congregation of "proselytes," separated from Israel and retaining only the apocalyptic anticipations of Jewry. Its messianic hope did not commence with wars among the nations and included no reverberations of defeat of a nation by its foes. Its "Messiah" was the apocalyptic "Redeemer" whose advent would mark the "end." The church had no thought of liberation by armed rebellion.

The signet of Jewish messianism was rebellion; that of Christian messianism, martyrdom, willingness to die for "the sanctification of God's name." To the Jews, degradation in this world, subjugation to the gentiles, was an abnormal state from which they sought to escape by force. Jewry dreamt of insurrection and the restoration of the throne of David. Christianity aspired to no kingdom or dominion; afflictions and tortures in this world were a token of grace. Apocalyptic tendencies never became completely dominant in Jewry; Jewish messianism always included political objectives centered in the restoration of Jerusalem, the holy city, and Israel, the promised land. And for all that they were basically religious, the messianic hopes took on the form of a nationalistic struggle. The messianism of Christianity, on the other hand, was altogether apocalyptic. It was only much later, in the period of the crusades, that Christianity set out to found a sacred kingdom in the Holy Land.

Thus, Christianity went its separate way. It had no part in the political and national aspirations of the Jews and was free of the stigma of exile which blocked the way of Jewish proselytization.

The gentile church, the Christianity of the judaizers, now took to itself the historic mission of Judaism: the battle against idolatry. In that mission, in the encounter with idolatry, Christianity triumphed. It did not overcome paganism by reason of its mythological content, not by the myth of the "Son of God" and the sacraments, and certainly not by its sectarian ethic and its negation of the world. It gained victory by the force of the monotheism inherited from Judaism. Christianity carried on the cause of monotheism and prevailed over idolatry; it triumphed, so to speak, by reason of its Jewish, not its "Christian," content. The importance of the specifically Christian elements of the new religion was that by them Paul created the gentile church. The new church, disjoined from the Jewish nation and not laden with its exilic degradation, was the bearer of a "new testament," a non-Israelite covenant. In the contest with paganism, it was the power of Israel's monotheism which prevailed; but the monotheistic doctrine had acquired a new formulation, the "new covenant," the covenant of the gentiles.[95]

It cannot be known how far Judaism might have spread if the judaizers had not been won over to the Christian gospel. The passion with which Jewry opposed the early Christian propaganda is evidence of the intensity of Judaism's universalistic aspirations, and of the grievous hurt caused by the rivalry of the daughter faith. With the realization that the judaizers were being drawn to Christianity, Jewry sensed that this would be the demise of its mission in the gentile world, and sought to suppress the new movement. It was a battle of despair, not that there was fear of the attraction of Christianity among Jews, but because Jewry would no longer be able to proselytize. Christian scholars are wont to

95 Cf. above, ch. 1 (= 7).

be perplexed by Jewry's opposition to the spread of Christianity among the pagans; they think that should have been of no concern to Judaism. The Jewish propaganda in the Hellenistic world suffices, it seems to me, to prove that the matter did affect Judaism very much. The spread of Christianity was of such concern to Jewry because Christianity meant the end of Jewish proselytization in the ancient world. The conversion of the "heathens" to a "heresy" was reckoned as one of the trials of the days of the messiah (Sotah 9:15). Jewry sensed that the "heresy" was destined to carry the faith of Israel to the gentiles, and that because of the "heresy," Jewry could not be the "witness-nation."

In Christianity, the religion of Israel was detached from the destiny of the nation Israel and therewith gained vigor above that of Judaism to defeat idolatry.

ISRAEL'S RELIGIOUS-RACIAL IDENTITY

Ethnic Disintegration

The argument of the two preceding chapters may be summarized as follows: The contention of Christianity and Islam versus the pagan religions of the gentiles parallels that of the religion of YWHW versus idolatry within Israel in the period of the first Temple to the Babylonian exile. The victories of Christianity and Islam were victories of Israel's monotheism over gentile polytheism. The two daughter faiths were accepted by the peoples because they fought the cause of Israel's monotheism; they fought idolatry. Theirs was the advantage, the superiority of Israel's monotheism over polytheism. Monotheism could not conquer pagan nations so long as it bore its original Jewish stamp. Jewry's exilic fate, its politico-ethnic defeat, stood in the way. Its monotheism could win the nations only after detachment from the nation Israel, and it was conveyed to the gentiles in new revelations, new covenants.

The new religions were accepted by the gentiles but not by the Jews; this because the battle against paganism had been fought and won in Israel long before the emergence of the new religions. The burden of the new faiths, their *raison d'être* in the gentile world, to eradicate idolatry, did not exist in Israel. The nations were prepared for "the giving of the Law," ready to receive it in new forms. Monotheism in Israel was encapsulated in fixed religious form which could not be altered by the younger faiths. But their superiority over paganism did not avail them in Israel, where paganism had long since expired. On the other hand, their advantage over Judaism in the gentile world, that is, their detachment from the fate of the nation Israel defeated and exiled, was no advantage in Jewish eyes. Jewry felt no need of a "new testament," and it was not prepared to accept a new revelation. Jewry was not swept along with the mighty currents of the religious revolutions which issued from within it to overwhelm and eradicate polytheism.

Thus, the historic bond of Israelite religion with the Jewish nation was made fast by a combination of factors. This connection was not natural or inherent, such as the tribal ties of primitive religions. Even as other higher religions, Judaism tended to transcend the ethnic limitations of its origins, to become the religion of alien peoples. It also was intrinsically universalistic, with innate tendency to transcend nationalistic limits. Why then did an inherently universal religion remain the inheritance of a single ethnic community; why did Judaism, of all the religions of Europe and the Near East, survive as a "national religion" — retaining, that is, its original tie to the ethnic community in which it originated? This in an age when other national religions were rooted out and disappeared. The cause of this unique phenomenon was, as indicated, not any innately nationalistic characteristic, rather extraneous factors which combined to determine its fate. Because of Jewry's historic political-ethnic situation the universalism which inhered in its religion could win converts among the gentiles only in distinct forms, when it was revealed anew — in new covenants. The religion of Israel in its original garb was confined within the Jewish nation. Jewry remained the sole votary of the religion of Israel in its original rendition, Judaism, specifically nontribal, remained, despite its urge to win converts among the peoples, a "national religion." Within this boundary, it revealed the universalistic impulse which was latent in it. It safeguarded the identity of the Jewish people even after the basis of their ethnic life had been destroyed; this because the people became the sole exponent of a faith which transcended national boundaries. Thus, Jewish religion revealed once more its essential nature. Extraneous circumstance prescribed an ethnic limit to broadly human tendencies; Jewish ethnicity was given universal basis. Religion was bound to the fate of Jewry and unable to transcend confinement within the nation. Political life, the historic catastrophe of Israel, put an ethnic limitation to Judaism against its intrinsic quality and aspiration. Though without natural social basis, the nation was able to preserve its identity; the nation itself would become, in a sense, universalistic even as its religion. But it was also, beyond a merely religious congregation, a tribal-racial entity, destined to distinct racial identity so long as its religious attachment did not fade.

The ability of religion to maintain the separate existence of the exilic nation was not the nationalistic element in it; indeed, both Christianity and Islam incorporated these strands. It was, rather, the religious core which had evolved and been concretized in specific historic circumstances. Jewry clung to its religion not insofar as it represented a national heritage; rather, indeed, because of the conviction that it was the true faith, the supreme religious belief. Thus the primary and decisive role of religion in Jewish history. Religion forged and strengthened the character of the people from earliest times. It struck ineradicable roots — the very basis of the nation's existence. By virtue of its religion, Israel became a solidly resistant entity insured against absorption into the religions of the gentiles. Jewry could not turn to other religions as did other peoples; this was the inner working of the religion. Jewry's inward direction, however, which was essentially religious, resulted also in ethnic-national consolidation because it failed to surmount the barrier, to win — in its original formulation — other nations. If Judaism had been able to do that, the Jews would certainly have been absorbed. In that case, the religion of Israel would not have been a barrier separating Israel from other peoples who accepted the faith. This characteristic operation of the Jewish religion — that it maintained the nation — was due, therefore, to the confluence of the two factors: religious universalism, which caused Israel to reject other faiths and held the people fast; and ethnic-national restriction — the result of Jewry's political situation which frustrated its tendency to expand — prevented its acceptance by gentile communities. The essential in Jewry's isolation was religious difference, the evolving differentiation of religious practice and traditions. Jewry remained a distinct religious entity. Because the Jewish community was also tribal-ethnic, its ethnic isolation and unity continued; and Jewish religion became the hallmark of a tribe-nation. Due to the historic linkage, religion with ethnicity, the historic tribal-national elements of Jewish religion retained their original vality; they did not become metamorphic-symbolic, as in Christianity and Islam. Nevertheless, it was religion which was the essential cause of the phenomenon: survival of the Jewish nation in diaspora.[1]

By virtue of the linkage, religion and nation, Jewry in exile withstood the disintegrating forces of cultural assimilation. The historic fate of exilic Jewry was determined by interaction of the two factors, religion and nation, which operated together to determine the relationship, Israel and the peoples.[2] It was, however, the religion alone which kept the Jews apart. Religion was an impassable barrier between Israel within and the peoples without, whereas other aspects of life in alien environments tended to erode Jewish separateness, to bring Jews and their neighbors together. The evolution of religious life stood as an iron wall between them. The operation of the nonreligious factors is given striking expression in the tendency of exilic Jewry to adapt culturally to its environment. Other influences, economic, national, political, which determine nationality, operated to erode Jewish solidarity and end isolation; they worked naturally within the Jewish soul to effect assimilation. However, these "metaphysical" factors were defective in one essential respect: They could not unite exilic Jews religiously with their neighbors. The assimilation which they effected was

1 Y. Kaufmann, *Golah ve-Nekhar,* I, ch. 10 (Exile and Ghetto).
2 Ibid.

secular-cultural and could not put an end to Jewry's religious, and therewith its ethnic, distinct identification. It was religion which maintained Jewry as a separate people after their dispersion and in despite of their incipient natural desire to be absorbed in their alien environments. Cultural assimilation could not raze the religious barrier.

The defeat of Jewry was cultural-ethnic as well as political. There had been emigration and founding of colonies abroad even in the period of the first Temple. Then, Assyrian rulers and the Babylonian kings exiled Israelites of the northern kingdom and — repeatedly — Judeans. Relatively few of the great Babylonian *golah* (dispersion, exile) returned in the days of Zerubbabel, Ezra, and Nehemiah; the greater number remained on foreign soil. Life among peoples of advanced civilization necessarily influenced the scattered exiles. Like all dispersed peoples, the Jews were subject to the assimilatory forces. Alien culture penetrated the Jewish ghettoes and gradually displaced their customary folkways. Within a few generations, Hebrew was supplanted by local vernaculars, and the exiles came to feel at home in their new homelands. They adopted the customs of their neighbors and in lands of developed civilization abandoned almost all their inherited secular Jewish culture, of which process the cultural assimilation of the Alexandrian Jewish community is a striking example. The Jews there became Hellenes linguistically, culturally, in all walks of life except the religious. The Bible had to be translated into Greek, lest it be forgotten, and even a devoted Jew such as Philo was not fluent in Hebrew. But it was not only in Alexandria; ethnic ruin proceeded apace in many precincts of the Greek-Roman world. Even in the ancient homeland, Hebrew was displaced. Linguistically, Palestinian Jewry became part of the Aramaic-Syrian population, and for them also the Bible had to be translated. In later times, the Bible would be translated into various tongues time and again lest it be forgotten; and the Talmud was written in alien vernacular (even though "close to the language of the Torah"). The language of the Zohar also and of the best of Jewish religious philosophy was not

185

Hebrew.[3] But linguistic defeat was only one indication of cultural-ethnic ruin and fragmentation. The natural process of assimilation operated among the scattered of Israel no less than among other diasporas — to assimilate and absorb them into the prevailing cultures.

Religion's Historical Effect on Judaism

There was, however, a limit to this natural process, the religious barrier. The natural tendency to ethnic change was checked by religious steadfastness. Religious life is a realm to itself with its own peculiar laws: specifically, that change of religion must be religiously motivated. We have observed that the tie which binds the individual to his religious values is unlike his relation to all other cultural values.[4] They — the religious values — are sacred to him; to abide by them is a duty which he is not free to deny. That is, he is bound to his religious convictions by the strongest of ties. The place of religion is unique among the values of human culture. Religion is a matter of belief, and honest change of religion can occur only by way of changes of conviction. Belief and nonbelief are irrelevant with respect to language, garb, nutrition, and personal ornamentation, and can be adapted readily under pressure of circumstances without soul-searching or fear of judgment in "the time to come."

Thus, religion is specifically a matter of faith to be changed only if belief is no longer the same. "Religious wars" are not uncommon in history. *Götterdämmerungen* have occurred more than once, gods demoted, their temples destroyed or devoted to other gods. Numberless religions have died natural deaths, of obsolescence or senility. Advances or changes in the intellectual and spiritual outlook have altered the sources of vitality and fostered or given birth to new creeds; or, again, these were vanquished and super-

3 Ibid.
4 Ibid., I, ch. 3 (Belief and Religion).

ceded by other faiths. But history records no instance of mass conversion which was not the consequence of modified religious conviction. Wherever men have forsaken their inherited faith *en masse*, it is because of the internal development of religious life. There have never been mass conversions due to factors other than the religious — with the exception, of course, of isolated instances of compulsory apostasy.

Certainly many peoples of antiquity who were absorbed culturally-nationally were also absorbed religiously. But this phenomenon was characteristic of religious beliefs at certain stages of their development. If religion is embedded in ethnicity, tied intrinsically or organically to ethnic ways, a change of ethnic-cultural life naturally involves religion. Ethnicity is itself a motivating religious factor. If the believer's attitude to his god(s) depends on his tribe or nation, any alteration of tribe results naturally in changed religious adherence. In antiquity, when religion was intrinsically ethnic-cultural, the sojourner, resident in alien land and social environment, accepted the (alien) god(s) along with the culture of his new homeland; this by inner compulsion. "Thy people shall by my people, and thy God my God" (Ruth 1:16) — the aspects bound together naturally and inherently. But when a religion breaches the ethnic-tribal bond, when it becomes universalistic, aspiring to win peoples and lands, change of ethnicity no longer implies change of religion. The cultural-ethnic factor no longer operates as a religious agent. Religious life transcends cultural-ethnic limitation; its values are independent of ethnic attachment, independence inherent in the nature of the "higher" religions.[5]

Thus it is that ethnic communities whose religion has evolved to a higher — universalistic — stage can with relative ease change their ethnic character, but not their religion. Residing in alien cultural environments, they are susceptible, with the passage of time, to the point of complete acculturation. But, since cultural assimila-

5 Ibid., I, ch. 5 (Jewish Universalism).

tion cannot of itself cause religious assimilation (that is, if a different religion prevails in the new environment), the newcomers (immigrants, "sojourners"), even though assimilated culturally, are likely to retain their separate religion. It is the specifics of the individual's life style — language and customs — ... which nourish and sustain his ethnic-national sense of belonging. All these are weakened or lost when he comes to live in an alien ethnic environment. With respect to religion, on the other hand, the basis of commitment, or continued commitment, is conviction. A religious man feels himself obliged to retain his faith wherever he resides and in whatever cultural clime. The tie can be broken only if the attraction of the new cultural environment is so strong that it effects a change in the religious beliefs of the stranger who comes under its influence. But since higher religions are not tied to ethnic cultures, they retain hold in despite of ethnic-cultural assimilation. Thus, the Germans who were absorbed in Russia retained in large part their Protestant faiths and the Poles their Catholicism.

This, the law of religious change, is due to the nature of belief — that change can come naturally only by reason of inner motivation. It follows that a true believer can accept a different faith (except for extraneous reasons) only if he is convinced of the truth of that other religion. This implies also that conversion to a creed (in which he does not believe) of an irreligious person is an unnatural act which is due to some combination of special (extraneous) circumstances. The disjunction, therefore, of ethnicity and belief of the "higher" religions implies that cultural-ethnic change does not result in change of faith except by reason of extraneous — nonreligious — circumstances.

This law — the law of religious change — is the great mystery, the basic factor [6] which has determined Israel's exilic fate. Differences of belief and practices between Jews and the gentile peoples

---

6 Re the idea of a basic or causal "law," see ibid., I, ch. 1 (Laws and Factors).

resulted in the confinement of Judaism within Jewry. There was no religious factor within Judaism or the gentile faiths which could bring Jews and the gentile peoples into religious communion. Thus, the societal assimilation, for all the havoc wrought in Jewish ethnic folkways, stopped short of religion and Jewry's racial-ethnic isolation which tied to its religious identity.

Even in the earliest periods of their dispersion, Jewry differed from other peoples. Cultural assimilation commenced with the destruction of the first Temple, but there was no religious assimilation. Pagan peoples, on the other hand, when they assimilated culturally, accepted the religion of their environment. This was a natural course in times of ethnically-territorially anchored, that is, nonuniversalistic, religions. The religion of Israel — of the Pentateuch and prophets — was already universalistic; Israel's God the one universal God whom the believer must worship wherever he might be. Idolatry was abomination; exilic Jewry could not deny God or give obeisance to idolatry even in the lands of its worshipers. Alien culture, even the highest, could not bring Jewish exiles to belief in pagan religions. Judaism had developed to the point that cultural assimilation was wholly secular. Jewish religion had shed the ethnic husk of its earthly origin, and cultural conversion was without effect on religious belief.

Subsequently, in Christianity and Islam, gentile religion also transcended ethnic bounds. National religions had given way to universalistic faiths, and the polemics of belief had become a world apart from the successions of national-ethnic culture: The rivalry between Judaism and the newer faiths would henceforth be fought out solely within the religious spheres. Jewish ethnic culture had long since succumbed; the secular cultures of Christian and Moslem peoples prevailed in the Jewish dispersions, even as in the earlier pagan cultures. Jewish ethnicity was without territorial base, but the cultural assimilation did not affect religious identity.

It was always the natural tendency and even the desire — though for the most part subconscious — of the dispersed Jewish communities to merge culturally into their surroundings. Moreover, in many lands through the long history of the diaspora, acculturation was in very large measure achieved. But because religion and secular culture were distinct domains, religious assimilation did not ensue. Attachment to the alien environments, their vernaculars, their customs and folkways, even complete cultural and political assimilation could not bring the Jews to belief in the gods of their neighbors. In Israel, unlike the pagan diasporas of antiquity, religious assimilation was not the natural, organic conclusion of acculturation. Jewish assimilation was wholly secular, with no effect on religious attitudes. Judaism as a religion might be forcefully suppressed by paganism or Christianity or Islam, but not as a natural sequence to immersion into the cultures of pagan, Christian, or Moslem nations.

It is true that Jewish religious life was affected by cultural assimilation. Acculturation tended to draw the Jew from his segregated Jewish way of life. Culturally assimilated Jews could not live wholly according to traditional practice; alien ways necessarily intruded. The ceremonial commandments whereby all aspects of Jewish life had been religiously determined could not be continued without some adaptation to the secular social environment, and alien religions and customs came to seem less bizarre or repulsive. In this way, assimilation might lead to indifference and disbelief. Religious indifference or disbelief, however, did not end the individual Jew's religious isolation; even in the ages of weakened faith, the power of Jewish religion continued. That power could live on the many ways, hidden in secret recesses of the soul, a spark alive amidst the ashes, an enduring barrier still. And more, indifference and disbelief might diminish the stature of religion and restrict its influence on Jewish life, but the Jew was not brought thereby to belief in another religion. He still could not accept the faith of his neighbors. Irreligion could not win Jews naturally — by conviction — to acceptance of alien faiths. Revolutionary religious change, such as occurred in pagan times or when Christianity and Islam were overcoming paganism, does not occur in periods when the hold of religion generally is weakened by external forces.

Rather, it occurs in times of religious exaltation when men are in need of faiths which are more satisfying to their spiritual needs than their traditional inherited beliefs.

Thus, we observe that at the close of the first period of Israel's religious development after the destruction of the first Temple — when rudimentary Israelite idolatry had been finally expunged — the alien religions found no popular response in Israel. This remarkable event is symbolized in the legend of the "slaughter" of the evil instinct of idolatry. The warfare of Israel's monotheism against polytheism was henceforth in the gentile world, outside the bounds of Israel. Individuals might stray, but the people Israel, in all its dispersions, remained forever faithful to its God. Even the "Hellenizers" and the "contumacious" of the Hasmonean period stopped short of religious assimilation. They were drawn to Greek culture, practiced Greek customs, were anxious to be as the surrounding peoples, and took various Jewish practices lightly. But they were not apostates; they did not voluntarily adopt Hellenistic religious practices, though they did not stand firm in the hour of persecution. The Hellenizing movement was cultural-political, without any tendency to bring Israel to idolatry; certainly there was no belief in the pagan gods. Paganism had no influence on Jewry. The situation was essentially the same in subsequent ages, in Christian and Moslem lands. From the beginning, few Jews were drawn to Moslem belief; Islam never found widespread response among Jews. Christianity also, even though born within Israel and in the beginning winning many Jews, attracted them only insofar as it remained a Jewish-sectarian, that is, "messianic," movement. Christian religious appeal to the congregation of Israel ceased with the passing of its messianic phase. When it made its way in the pagan world and became the religion of the gentiles, it was not longer a factor in Jewish religious life. Jesus the messiah was a problem within Judaism. Jesus, the "Son of God" in the Christian-pagan sense, was not a Jewish problem. The inroads of subsequent Christianity were conquests, not of the spirit, but of sword and fire. The only significant Christian religious movement

within Israel was that of the very early years; there was no reenact-
ment in any later period.

In sum, after the successful conclusion of the struggle against
idolatry within Israel, there was never again a popular religious
movement of mass conversion to another faith. This is the witness
of history, however it may be explained. Whether or not the explanation offered in the foregoing is accepted in all its detail, the
fact is that no positive religious influence ever operated within
Jewry to bring the Jews into religious association with their neighbors. In those periods and lands when the Jews of the diasporas
were given to the alien cultures, homelands, and languages, they
held fast to their separate religion. Can we, therefore, doubt that
here, in the realm of religious life, are the origin and explanation
of exilic Israel's nonabsorption? Anyone who seriously contemplates
this unique phenomenon must realize the extraordinary force and
value of religion in Jewish history. How, indeed, could there be
religious conversion without specifically religious motivation?
Therein, a boundary was fixed which Jewry could not surmount.
Jews could not believe in, they could not accept the alien faiths.
There was no positive religious force which could draw them from
the realm and influence of their traditional religion. For all their
cultural assimilation, the historic bond between religion and people
was never severed; so long as that bond remained, the tribal-ethnic
community of Jewry endured.

Just as acculturation could not take the place of religious motivation to bring Israel into religious union wtih their gentile neighbors, so also those extrinsic, artificial forces — the pressures and
tribulations of the *Galuth*, persecution, and forced apostasy. Even
in antiquity, Jewish religious separation and nonconformity were
met with hostility: pogroms and discriminatory decrees. Jewish
life in the diaspora is one long litany of bitter struggle, dating
back to pagan times. Persecutions, beginning some centuries after
Nebuchadnezzar, continued with increasing intensity into Christian-
Moslem times. There were, however, isolated periods of Jewish economic and social well-being. Were it not for their religious non-

conformity, the Jews, in those instances, might have merged into the surrounding population and become, for the most part, members of the upper classes. But, again, their religious-racial identification stood in the way. In those more favorable, more prosperous periods, the Jews still could not identify with their neighbors; they reamined a distinct society, hated and persecuted.

Persecution and suffering naturally roused hopes of escape from the isolation of the *Galuth*. The desire to advance in the social-economic scale, blocked by Jewish separatism, reacted against separatism. This was the social factor which, in its various phases, might have roused Jews to obliterate the religious barrier. It was the source of the phenomenon, apostasy, that is conversion motivated not religiously, rather the nonreligious ends. Jews throughout the generations, by thousands and tens of thousands, unable to withstand the trials of the diaspora, either its tribulations or the desire for social or economic advantage, sought, without conviction, refuge in the faiths of their neighbors.

Nonetheless, this apostasy originating in societal factors never attained the dimensions of mass conversion. Hope of social advancement could not alter religious belief; it could not imbue Jews with belief in their neighbors' religions. This "nonreligious" conversion generally meant absence of religious faith, in that the believer cannot change faith for the sake of material advantage. Moreover, besides lack of faith, the "apostates" were generally skeptical. Skepticism enabled them to move the more easily from religion to religion for extraneous reasons. Apostasy was the way out for individuals, many in various periods and places, but never to attain the magnitude of a mass movement.

Acculturation, on the other hand, encompassed the whole of Jewry. It was, in the exilic environment, natural; individuals might resist, but the masses adapted to their environments. Exilic Jewry, torn from the reality which maintained and preserved, endured in lands of alien cultures. The totality of the nation was subject to the influences of foreign environments. The realities of life, of strange lands, were as a melting pot by the nature of things, recast-

193

ing the physiognomy of the nation. The same occurs with sincere religious change; that is, conversion which is not forced or for extraneous reasons. When a people changes religion by conviction, the change is also societal. The movement may be slow, gradual, or sudden-revolutionary. But in either case, the great religious, movements which have encompassed tribes and nations were social, mighty currents which engulfed entire societies.

Apostasy is altogether different. It has always been sporadic, never of the scope of cultural adaptation or conversion by conviction. Religious change due to nonreligious motivation could not encompass whole communities in brief periods of time. Over longer periods — generations — large numbers were lost to Judaism, and probaly smaller, isolated Jewish communities have been absorbed through the centuries by attrition of this kind. But Israel, the nation, could not be absorbed by apostasy.[7]

And what apostasy — conversion for social, economic advancement — could not accomplish was also beyond the reach of political compulsion. Persecution obviously could not effect sincere conversion. Nonetheless, it could cause communities and even nations to accept dominant religions. Forced conversion plays a distinct role in religious history. Christianity and Islam were forced on various peoples by decree and war; idolatry was rooted out by fire and, sword. Changes of religion of peoples, nations — natural change evolved gradually over long periods; forced changes were sudden, revolutionary. Religious persecution engulfs communities, for all their differences, even as conversion by conviction. Persecution, indeed, might have forced all Israel to renounce Judaism, as in fact specific Jewish communities were compelled to do — if, that is, the whole of Jewry had been attacked at the same time. But such was never the case. Apostasy was forced always on some communities, never on the whole of Israel. It could not, therefore, stamp out Jewish faith. The single all-encompassing persecution of the pre-Christian ages, that of Antiochus Epiphanes, though it en-

7 Concerning contemporary apostasy, ibid., II, ch. 5.

dangered the core Jewish community, affected only a portion of the people. Moreover, it was of brief duration and without lasting result. The Maccabean revolt which it roused demonstrated the readiness of Jews to suffer martyrdom for their religion, that forcing apostasy on Israel was no light undertaking. Pagan rulers never again attempted to follow that path. The severe decrees of Hadrian and even those of the Sassanids were directed only at certain Jewish practices. They were not orders to renounce the faith. Christianity and Islam also did not proscribe Judaism as such. If they had judged Judaism as they did idolatry and decreed death on its followers, as they did for idolaters, Judaism — even as paganism — would have perished. The monotheistic peoples were inhibited from such extreme measures by religious-juridical scruples. The dominant faiths did not honor Judaism, but they did not judge it as idolatry. Jews were degraded and persecuted. Christianity and Islam used every means to woo the "chosen" people, including of course harsh persecution. But the practice of Judaism was not a sin deserving of death. The forced conversions of Christian and Islamic lands were not the consequence of any general condemnation, rather arbitrary enactments of fanatic rulers. Thus, they did not affect all Jewry. God, in his "compassion," had scattered his people among the nations.

Persecution and compulsion did not descend on Israel in all its diaspora at any one period. Thus Judaism, though decimated, was not obliterated. Jews retained their religious identity in pagan as well as in Christian and Moslem lands. They vanquished idolatry within; but in the victory over idolatry without — which they had initiated — they had no share. The younger religions rose to dominance in Europe and the Near East. Jewry stood firm amidst the tremendous religious storms which engulfed the gentile peoples. Jewry was isolated in its religio-ethnic identity; it alone stood guard over the religious legacy of its past.

Chapter 3

Judaism and Greek Culture

The fate of Jewry — its religious-ethnic isolation — was determined by its struggles first with paganism and subsequently with
Christianity and Islam. These were struggles among popular religious loyalties which are not to be confused, as is usually done,
with the literary polemics of later centuries of Jewish (and Christian and Moslem) scholars against Hellenistic philosophy and
culture. This was the clash between two world outlooks: on the
one hand, Greek conceptual science, natural-legalistic; and as
against this, popular religion with its mythic-legendary fundament.
It was a contrariety which Hellenistic philosophy had long since
sought to overcome. The philosophers tried to compromise; they
"interpreted" legends and elaborated "esoteric" meanings. From
the first contact with Hellenistic culture, Jewish intellectuals were
troubled by the same problem. They found support for Judaism's
principle of monotheism in the monotheistic tendencies of Greek
philosophy. But many specific Jewish beliefs could not be harmonized
with the spirit of Greek science; and, in particular, many religious
rites and practices could not be explained or justified "rationally."
Thus, Jewish scholars began to reinterpret Judaism to accord with
Greek philosophy and to counter arguments advanced by Hellenists. Of these early protagonists of Judaism in the world of
Hellenism, Philo Judaeus of Alexandria was the most prominent.
Jewish philosophy of the Middle Ages, and in part even to the
present, followed in his footsteps. In succeeding centuries, the difficulty of combining popular faith with Hellenistic science gave rise
to the "perplexed": Intellectuals, that is, who, though unwilling
to abandon the inherited religion, were yet keenly aware of the
challenges of rationalistic philosophy and science. Sages were concerned to give guidance to the "perplexed," instruction and argument whereby to strengthen their faltering faith.

The confrontations, Judaism versus science-philosophy, the en-
suing confusion, and the harmonizing exegeses of the Jewish philosophers of the mediaeval period were certainly of considerable worth.

196

Harmony between popular religion and Hellenistic science rein-forced belief, strengthening Judaism from within. With respect, however, to the fate of Jewry in relation to the rival religions — the popular faiths — literary argumentation was of no avail. It impinged in no way on the circumstances which determined Jewry's religious and ethnic isolation. The historic circumstances which prevented gentile acceptance of Judaism and Jewish association in the religious revolutions wrought by Christianity and Islam were of another realm altogether. Here, philosophic argumentation had no place; the battle line was between religions, not religion versus science-philosophy. Opposition to the world view of Hellenistic philosophy was common to the three monotheistic faiths, and the rivalry among them was not to be decided by philosophic disputa-tion. Philosophy in lesser or greater degree presented challenge to all popular faiths; and the religious philosophers sought com-promises, a "middle course." This had been the way also of pagan philosophy in earlier times, and the monotheists followed in well-trodden paths. Inasmuch as their midrashic exegeses were generally accepted, they brought no particular gain to any one of the mono-theistic faiths. Moreover, since paganism was closer to the philoso-phic point of view, the two being of a common root, Christianity and Judaism were forced into defensive positions, and the ultimate advantage of the confrontations accrued to pagan philosophy. Hel-lenistic philosophy had remained pagan to the end: Judaism and Christianity alike were barbarous superstitions. The apologetic writings of the Middle Ages sought to minimize the charge of irrationality. Christianity emerged triumphant. The mediaeval church fathers turned to attack: They considered Greek wisdom a satanic deception. Scholastics acclaimed Christianity's "absur-dity"; Greek academies were closed, and philosophy assigned the subordinate role of "handmaid" to theology.

Nonetheless, Judaism in the later Middle Ages was strongly in-fluenced by Hellenistic philosophy. Acquaintance with the Greek scriptures brought out resources which had remained incultivated. In the earlier days of the struggles among the four faiths (if "paganism" can be reckoned a faith), in the ages when Israel's unique fate in world history was being determined, the influence of philosophy was minimal, scarcely detectible. Within Judaism, Philo's thought was a passing phenomenon, without lasting influence. The Talmud, normative of the mainstream of Jewish life in the long centuries into the modern period, knew nothing of Greek thought; and on the whole, the influence of philosophy on Judaism generally was incomparably less than on Christianity. Christianity appropriated philosophic concepts and especially methodology and terminology. It endeavored to systematize its doctrines, to construct a rationalistic theology and structured credo. In Christianity, there were endless disputations, semiphilosophical debates on minute details of creed, and executions for trifling deviations.

Judaism, in contrast, accepting nothing of the forms and methods of philosophy, remained a religion of legend-midrash and Halakhic law. In Christianity, philosophic defense was very important. Whatever the role of philosophic reasoning in Judaism, it was at best subordinate and even essentially irrelevant. Christian apologetics was, as it were, spellbound by theoretical problems, whereas disputations with "philosophers" which are to be found in the Talmud are popular anecdotes which touch on abstract problems only incidentally. Incidents of "error" and the perplexity of those given to Greek learning and tending to wander from orthodoxy, as reported in Talmudic literature, are of popular-legendary genre, thus the account of Elisha ben Avuyah [8] and his companions. Hellenistic philosophy was tabu to "orthodox" Jewry. It is not without significance that no philosophic treatise in Hebrew or Aramaic, the two languages of popular and religious Judaism, has come down to us — and it appears none was written in all the generations of the sages of the Mishnah and the Talmud. Hellenistic-Jewish literature was completely forgotten; and even in Maimonides' lifetime, it was anathema to the very pious. Maimonides forcefully

8 Hagigah 14b, f.

introduced philosophic concepts into Judaism. But the more or-
tion. Philosophy in lesser centuries into the modern period, knew
nothing of Greek thought; and on the whole, the influence of
philosophy on Judaism generally was incomparably less than on
Christianity. Christianity appropriated philosophic concepts and especially methodology and terminology. It endeavored to systematize its doctrines, to construct a rationalistic theology and structured
credo. In Christianity, there were endless disputations, semiphilosophical debates on minute details of creed, and executions for trifling
deviations.

thodox always looked askance at any "compromise" with the
wisdom of Hellas and even ignored the "evil" so far as possible.
Whatever the merit, therefore, of mediaeval Jewish philosophy-
theology, it cannot be said that the fate of popular Judaism depended on the interpretations which the "perplexed" Jewish intellectual invented. The strength of Judaism was not due to whatever
philosophy was implicit in it. Belief in the revelation of Sinai, in the
absolute sanctity of Jewish tradition with all its symbols and values
was rooted in the Jewish soul and colored the Jew's daily existence.
This belief was the foundation and firm support of popular faith.
Thereby, the faith endured and, in the case of the intellectuals,
continued to give rise to the philosophers' "perplexity." Greek
science and philosophy challenged tradition. The faith in the sanctity of Judaism was troubled by opinions and views which to some
degree were incompatible with this faith. The "compromises" pro-
posed by the theologian-philosophers in order to remove or cover
over the contradictions represented, in fact, a triumph of the popular faith. The intellectuals were forced to find ways to retain their
belief.

In any event, the "perplexities" and the more or less successful
"compromises" with science and philosophy had no effect, as
stated above, on the confrontation Judaism versus Christianity and
Islam. Those religions also were beset with "perplexities" and
the effort to find reconciliations; the fate of Judaism would be
determined by the internecine warfare of popular religion.

Judaism's encounters with Greek culture, first in the Hellenistic period and subsequently in the Arab world, were, however, of particular significance because classical Greece was the birthplace of the first great secular culture in history. In all the highly developed societies of antiquity, other than the Greek, priests were the learned class and temples the seats of learning. Greek culture also was tied to religion and deeply rooted in it. But it was in Greece that separation began; learning and the arts tended to become independent. Scholars, poets, and artists, laymen, took over; science, philosophy, the arts developed and flourished in academies, in the market place, and in friendly intercourse. Science and philosophy were, for the first time, freed of religion's yoke, and even dared to attack religion. Secular literature appeared, wherewith the individual scholar could make his own special contribution. Religion itself was subjected to secular scrutiny, and art became secular. Homer, singing the annals of the gods, was neither prophet nor priest; his epics were not sacred in the essential meaning of the word. Greek sculpture, in great part, and the ornamentation of homes and public places were influenced more by aesthetic taste than religious considerations. Belles-lettres, the arts, theater, and certainly science and philosophy became independent disciplines tied loosely, if at all, to the religious soil in which they had sprouted.

Thus, in lands of Hellenistic culture, Judaism came for the first time into meaningful contact with the pagan world. What it would not and could not accept from priests in their temples it now learned from profane sources: from secular literature and lay teachers. For the first time literate Jews — reading Greek writings — became acquainted with paganism, what paganism really was. In consequence, the character of Jewish polemics against idolatry changed radically. Whereas previously it was content to belabor idolatry as worship of "wood and stone," it now attacked the reality of paganism with arguments based on Greek philosophy. On account of this secular basis, Judaism could and did accept much from Greece without being repelled by Greek religion — contamination with idolatry.

Nonetheless, the secular elements of Greek culture were after all "enlightenment," confined to an intellectual elite. Religion, pagan religion, was still the way of life in the pagan world, and no aspect of society or political government was free of religious influence or control. So far as the masses were concerned, the meeting of cultures was a religious confrontation. The demotic Greek, and certainly the ordinary Jew, made no distinction between the aesthetic-sacred and the truly religious aspect of Greek culture. The athletic contests, the gymnasia, theaters, circuses, and sodalities were viewed by Jews as tinged with idol worship; Jews sensed the pervasive pagan character of Greek society; to them, it was "abomination." Thus, Greek culture was rejected by Jewry, this in despite of the strong influence of its secular components on Jewish thought. Only in later times when the Greek spirit, after many metamorphoses, began to penetrate Europe, revolutionizing its thought and world outlook, only then, that is, in the period of the Haskalah, did it effect significant changes in Jewish intellectual life.[9]

The religion-oriented life of Israel and the peoples, whereby Israel became a distinct religious-racial entity, was such that the dispersed Jewish communities could not assimilate and be absorbed anywhere and at any time even to the present day. Certainly there have been scholars who, due to failure to realize the basic difference between cultural and religious assimilation, have challenged this datum. They have cited in particular Alexandrian Jewry as an instance of Jewish ethnic disintegration and decay to the point of complete loss of identity. Egypt of the first Christian century was a center of Hellenistic culture. The Egyptian-Jewish community of approximately a million souls played a significant role in Jewish life of that day. But there is no trace of Jewish presence in Egypt from the third to the tenth century. What happened to those great communities of Alexandria and Cyrene? It is generally

---

9 Y. Kaufmann, I, ch. 10 (Exile and Ghetto); II, ch. I (Collapse of Traditional Judaism).

assumed that the Jews of Egypt were absorbed in the course of a few generations, that they became Christians or pagans. This absorption was supposedly disintegration due to the influence of Hellenism. Under that influence Judaism, emptied of content, gave way to Hellenism. The Judaism which the Hellenistic thinkers, of whom Philo was the leading spirit, supposedly tried to bolster was not really Judaism, rather a construct of Greek philosophic concepts. These Hellenizers paved the way for the triumph of gentile Christianity and facilitated the turning of Egyptian Jewry to Christianity or paganism.[10]

This view is based on the erroneous assumption that there is no extant reference to the presence of Jews in Egypt during the period, third to tenth century of the Christian era. In fact, there were Jews in Egypt during those centuries, and there is evidence of that fact (see below). The confusion in this case, the jumbling of data which are essentially diverse, is characteristic of research into Jewish history. We must ask, however, how assimilation could have culminated in mass conversion to paganism or Christianity. Egyptian Jewry certainly assimilated culturally and even in Philo's time had reached the extreme limit of secular Hellenism. But scorn of and hostility to idolatry as religion did not diminish in the least. Even more, the "Greek enlightenment" of Philo and his intellectual followers could not sway the Jewish masses of Egypt toward paganism. In the first place, intellectual Helenism with its rarefied views was the property of a small elite, both of the Jewish and the Greek communities. Most Jews were not even aware of it; they followed traditional Jewish practice with full hearts. Their "cultural" assimilation stopped short of Greek philosophy, of Plato and Aristotle. It was run-of-the-mill conformation, Greek vernacular and ways of daily life, typical of mass adaptation to changed circumstances throughout history. But the Jewish intelligentsia also, though given

---

10 A. Ruppin, *Die Juden der Gegenwart*, 1911, 15f.; Ignaz Zollschan, *Das Rassenproblem*, 1910, end of book; W. Schubart, *Aegypten, von Alexander dem Grossen bis auf Mohamed*, 1922, 46. This view is expressed repeatedly in Hebrew writings.

to Greek philosophy and literature, were not thereby drawn closer to pagan religion, that is, the popular idolatry which, with its temples and sacrificial rites, was the only form which might have been "accepted." Indeed, Greek philosophy fought the popular beliefs. Certainly there were many efforts to find "compromises," various and sundry exegeses or interpretations of traditional beliefs. But many philosophers ridiculed and scorned them; thus Jewish intellectuals, heirs of a tradition of scorn, felt no need to "compromise" with idolatry. The "Greek" concepts with which they explicated Judaism were not pagan; they were applied by Greek philosophers also, thus the Stoics, to interpret the popular pagan religion. Both Jewish and Greek exegetes interpreted allegorically, and the latter were unable to win acceptance for their allegories.

The great influence of Greek culture on Jewry was due to its secular content, its rational quality referred to above. But Greek influence was limited to this aspect of Greek thought. Hellenistic influence on Israel, that is, was secular, never religious. Jewry's affinity for Greek secular culture did not, could not bring acceptance of idolatry. Indeed, paganism at that time was in the throes of decay, and there were many in the pagan world who, attracted to Jewish ways and values, abandoned idolatry.

Christianity and Islam — Persecution of Jews

So far as mass conversion to Christianity is concerned, it was much the same; Jewish intellectuals were not drawn to it. Certainly many Egyptian Jews, even as Jews elsewhere, accepted the gospel preached by Jesus' apostles. But Greek rationalism was totally absent in early Christianity; Christianity was, as emphasized above, the defeat of the Greek enlightenment. To the Greeks, Christianity was "foolishness"; to the Jews, "a stumbling block"; and to the Jewish intellectuals, both foolishness and stumbling block. Jews of Egypt, like other Jews, might, insofar as they were prepared to believe in its signs and wonders, accept Christianity as a development of their Judaism. But Hellenistic life styles could not make them, particularly those influenced by Greek philosophy, more receptive to Christianity than their more tradition-oriented brethren. Christian scholars made use of Philo's logos-doctrine in rather artificial manner to interpret Christian mythology rationally and give it philosophic formulation. But this is not to say that Philo paved the way for Christianity's triumph. The amalgamation of Christianity with the logos-doctrine — of which the apostles and even Paul knew nothing — was an event of little importance. Certainly, comparatively few Jews were acquainted with the logos-doctrine; and even if they knew of it, they could not thereby have been drawn to Christianity. There is, therefore, no historic basis for the opinion that the allegorizing exegeses of Hellenistic Judaism were conducive to Christian conversion.

There is, moreover, considerable historic evidence of the existence of Jewish communities in Egypt between the third and tenth centuries. Egyptian Jewry was impoverished, and dwindled rapidly after the great rebellion of the time of Trajan-Hadrian and the pogroms of the Roman general Martius Turbo and the Greek mobs. Only a small remnant of the great Jewish community of Egypt survived these disasters. Epiphanius of Alexandria says that Trajan destroyed the Jewish communities of Egypt.[11] A *baraita*, referring to this calamity, relates that at that time the strong arm of Israel was severed, and there was no hope of recovery until the advent of the messiah ben David (Jerus. Talmud, Succah 5:1). After these events, only a miserable remnant of the once great community remained in Egypt. Certainly, many of the survivors had found refuge in other lands. The community had not been decimated by apostasy, rather by violent upheavals to the point that it no longer played any part in the life of the diaspora. It vanished, as it were, for a time from history.

Nonetheless, there are isolated references to the continued existence of Jewish settlements in Egypt. Among the enactments of Theodosius the Great is a statute of the year 390 refering to a

11 *De bellis civilibus,* **II,** 90.

guild of Jewish sailors in Alexandria.[12] Synesius of Cyrene, in one of his epistles (evidently of the year 404), tells of his voyage from Alexandria to Cyrene in a ship of which the' skipper and most of the crew were Jews. He speaks of the Jews after the manner of Jew-haters of the period: "A cursed people who believe that they perform a worthy deed when they cause the greatest possible number of Greeks to die." The skipper does not work on the Sabbath; he sits reading "his book." He disregards the requests and warnings of the passengers and acts only if there is serious "danger to life." [13]

It is evident that the Alexandrian Jews of that time were not assimilated religiously. According to the church historian, Socrates, the Jews were banished about 415 from Alexandria by Bishop Cyril.[14] They returned, however, during the reign of Zeno at which time Domninus, a renowned Jewish physician, the teacher of Gesius, resided in Alexandria.[15] In the time of Anastasius I, emperor of the early sixth century, Urbib of Alexandria, a wealthy Jew (later converted to Christianity), supplied food in a year of famine.[16] Arabic historians tell that Amr Ibn Al-as, the army commander who conquered Egypt in 642, in a letter to the Caliph Omar, referred to the booty he found in Alexandria, including the tribute of 40,000 Jews of the city.[17] According to Johanan, Bishop of Nicaea, the Jews of Egypt fled in fear of the Moslems to Manuf and Alexandria.[18] Johanan also says that the Patriarch Cyrus, who

---

12 *Codex Theodos.* XIII, 5, 18.
13 Epistle 4, *Epistolographi Graeci,* ed. Hercher, 639f. *Patrolog, graeca,* ed. Migne, 1859, LXVI, 1327f. G. Grützmacher, *Synesios von Kyrene,* 1913.
14 Socrates, *Historia Ecclesiae,* 7, 13, 17. This banishment is reported also in other Christian writings.
15 Suidas, *Lexikon,* s. v. Thesios.
16 Eutychii Patriarchae Alexandrini (Ibn Batrik) *Annales,* Oxoniae, 1658 (Arabic, with Latin translation), part 2, 133.
17 Caetani, *Annali d'Islam,* year 20, paragraph 123. The letter is to be found also in the chronicle of Eutychius, part 2, 316f.
18 Chronicle of Johanan of Nicaea, chapter 112, translation by Zutenberg. See Caetani, year 19, paragraph 78.

came from Byzantium in order to negotiate with Amr after Amr's conquest of Alexandria, stipulated that the Jews be allowed to remain in Alexandria.[19] Although the accuracy of the foregoing report has been questioned, the fact that there were Jewish congregations in Egypt until and after the Arabic conquest is well-established.

The history of the Jews in Spain is in some respects similar to that of Hellenistic Jewry. In both instances, the basic and unmistakable contrast between cultural adaptation and religious nonconformity illustrates clearly the nature of Israel's religious-ethnic distinction. In both Arabic and Christian Spain, the Jews assimilated almost completely so far as secular life was concerned. In Moslem Spain, Jewry confronted Greek philosophy once more, this time in Arabic translation; and again, there were intellectual ferment and confusion. Jewish as well as Christian and Moslem scholars sought accommodation and synthesis between religious tradition and Plato or Aristotle. Here, again, the "perplexity" was confined to the thin upper crust of intellectuals. The mass and most of the religious leaders looked askance at the sophisticated reasoning of the synthesizers. Nonetheless, the encounter with alien culture tended to breach isolation, and among the intellectuals to cause religion to be taken less seriously. For all that, however, the intellectual acculturation did not diminish the contrast and opposition between Judaism and the dominant religions. There were those Jewish intellectuals who were weaned by Greek philosophy from the faith of their fathers. But, since that philosophy appeared in opposition to all traditional religions, the Jewish intellectuals were not drawn closer to Christianity or Islam. That is, there was nothing, in acculturation or in secular learning, to bring Jews by conviction and in truth to Christianity or Islam. The only way of conversion was still apostasy — the narrow path which only a few could travel — other than by compulsion. Thus, in despite of acculturation and the Greek-Arabic enlightenment of the time, Jewry as a religious

19 Ibid., chapter 120; see Caetani, year 20, paragraph 162.

community stood firm, of which the Marranos are reliable evidence. The Marranos were those Jews who succumbed. They accepted baptism without conviction. Rabbi Solomon Alami [20] testifies that most of the Jews — the common people — rather than accept Christianity, chose exile in 1492, whereas most of the intellectuals accepted baptism in the hour of trial.

The Marranos, therefore, were in part of the order of the assimilated intellectuals whose faith was weak. For all that, there were those apostate converts who continued secretly to practice their ancestral religion for generations even though they were subject to the Inquisition and death, of whom Solomon Molcho (1500–1532) is a striking example. Many attained high position, some even in the Roman Catholic hierarchy, and yet did not forget the religion of their forebears. In banishment, the exiles remembered their Spanish homeland. They held fast to their Spanish vernacular for generations, in some places even to this day, to the language, that is, of their earlier exilic homeland. Culturally assimilated, they were apostates by compulsion. They continued faithful to their inherited religion after generations of enforced nonobservance, a fact which highlights as nothing else the ambivalence of Jewish life in the diaspora. So far as secular culture went, Jews were subject to the assimilatory forces which blurred their image and tended to their absorption. But with respect to religion, they could not join with their neighbors. Jewry passed through every stage of cultural adaptation, but the ways of religious change was blocked.

---

20 *Epistle of Reproof and Faith*, published by A. Jellinek, Leipzig, 1854, p. 24f. The letter was addressed, in 1415, to his disciples in Portugal. R. Abraham ben Solomon of Torrutiel, in his "supplement to the Sefer haKabbalah of ibn David," part 3, says: "Most of the prominent Jews and their judges remained in their homes and abjured their religion ... And at the forefront were the skeptics ["Epikursim"], R. David Avraham Shneur ..." Also, in Spain "the Torah was neglected" ["almost forgotten"] in favor of "external learning." See Albert Harkavy, *Old and New* (Hebrew) in Graetz-Rabinowitz, *History of the Jews* (Hebrew). 8 vols., Warsaw, 1871-1890, part 8, supplement, p. 20.

Thus, assimilation could not be complete anywhere or at any time. In despite of cultural assimilation-adaptation through the whole long history of the diaspora, Israel remained apart, isolated, segregated, religiously and ethnically.

The origin of Jewry's religious-racial identity was its unique religious faith, rooted in ancient Israel, and to which it was given for the ages. From this perspective, its segregation-isolation was heart's desire, willing, intentional. Nonetheless, its historic destiny was the result of a combination of factors, not all of which were conscious and voluntary on its part. That is, Israel's historic fate was also objective-externally determined — necessity. Jewry's relationship with the peoples, even though its beginning was religion, was extraneous, determined objectively, and with consequences exceeding by far the realm of religion. The law of religious change barred the way of conversion to other faiths, this irrespective of continued conviction or nonbelief in the inherited faith. Factors, involuntary, largely unconscious, blocked — for the masses, the nation in exile — every avenue of escape. Only the possibility of apostasy remained. Individuals might tread the narrow path, conversion without conviction. But the nation, the Jewish people, was held fast, an enduring dilemma. The prophet Ezekiel expresses the despairing cry of the exiles in Babylon: "We will be as the nations, as the families of the countries, to serve wood and stone" (Ezek. 20:32). That is the enduring dilemma, from Babylon to the present day, Israel struggling with its unique fate, the isolation imposed upon it — to dwell alone, apart from all the families of the earth. In its confusion, Israel says: "to serve wood and stone," that is, to worship "gods" which are not God, this the very symbol of religious conversion without conviction, the barrier or gate of wood and stone through which the nation could not pass. Even against desire, Israel was forced to accept the yoke of the Kingdom, the rule which holds him "with a mighty hand, and with an outstretched arm and with fury poured out" (Ezek. 20:33).

INDEXES*

* Footnotes are listed in parentheses after page no. and only if page
is otherwise not listed.

NAME AND SUBJECT INDEX

Abraham — 42, 90, 91, 93, 94(53), 114, **128**, 151
    blessing of — 172
    children of — 46
    daughter of — 106
    descendant of — 42, 106
    faith of — 148
    kingdom of — 105, 107, 114
    seed of — 47(1), 147–149
    cf. God of Israel
Abraham ben Solomon of Tor-
    ratiel — 207(20)
Abraham ibn Daud — 64(20)
abrogation of Jewish law — **20–22,**
    40, 41, 43, **47–59**, 137(72), 138–
    146, 151, **161–167**
Adam — 31(37), 151
adultery — 14, 54, 55(11)
Ahura Mazda — 10
Akiba — 58, 60
Alami, R. Solomon — 207
Albo, Joseph — 31(37)
Aleinu (prayer) — 76(29)
Alexandria — 205, 206
allegorical interpretation — 7, 33
    (40), 138, 142, 203
Allah — 10(10), 11, 36, 44
am-ha-arez — 68, 80, 162
Amidah (prayer) — 77(29)
Amos — 82
Amr ibn Al-as — 205, **206**
Anastasius I — 205
anchorites — 82, 96

angels — 9, 19, 72, 78, 87, 88, 90,
    91, 93, 94, 98(56), 100, 105, 107–
    109, 115, 119, 130, 132(72)
    angelic status — 85
Antioch in Pisidia — 146, 152, 167
Antiochus Epiphanus — 194
Aphrodite — 9
apocalyptic —
    doctrine — 129–131
    kingdom — 89
    literature — 75–79, 87, 90
    messianism — 71–105, 129, 130,
    178
    redeemer — 74, 178
    seers — 75
Apocryphal literature —
    Christian — 138, 142, 171, 174,
    175
    Jewish — 58, 129
Apollonius of Tyana — 7
apologetic literature — 197, 198
apostasy — 187–208
Arabia — 10(10), 40, 146.
Arabs — 10(10), 40, 49
    conquests — 206
    historians — 205
    language — 206
    world — 199
Aramaic language — 61(15), 198
Aramaic-Syrian population of Pa-
    lestine — 185
Ares — 9
Aristole — 7, 202, 206

209

Arsacidae — 10
asceticism — 18, 37, 80, 82, 84, 94–
  96, 100, 105, 107, 135, 146, 154,
  167
Asia minor — 3
Assimilation, cultural and ethnic —
  181–208
Assyrian rulers — 185
Athenians, message to — 13
atonement — 108, 109, 134, 135(71),
  142, 145, 164
Augustine — 149(81)

Babylon — 173, 174, 208
  exile — 181, 185, 208
  kings — 185
baptism — 11, 81, 83, 84, 88, 112,
  120, 146, 150, 155–158, 160, 163,
  165–167
Barcelona — 23(22)
Bar-Kokba — 74, 121, 128
barbarians — 148
Barnabas — 152, 156
Basilides — 9
Beelzebub — 20, 102, 124(68)
Belial — 55(12)
Bethany — 99(57)
Bible, translations of — 185
blasphemy — 122–127, 137(72)
burial — 35, 99(57)
Byzantium — 206

cabalists — 18, 25
Cadiz — 7
Caesar — 115
Canaanite woman — 102, 153
canon — 104
Capernaum — 111
catechism — 167
Catholicism — 3, 4(3), 25, 41, 48,
  144, 151, 167, 175, 188, 207
charity — 82, 140
chosen people — 195
Christ, body and blood of — 142,
  145, 146

Christian Israel — 176
Christianity —
  apologetics — 20, 197, 198
  celebacy — 37, 41
  communism — 37, 95, 134
  converts and conversion — 42–
    47, 149–180, 202–204
  gentile Christians — 155–161,
    189–202
  and Hellenistic Philosophy —
    198–203
  homeletics — 139
  and idolatry (= paganism) —
    3, 4, 6, 7, 10–17, 13, 14, 26,
    37, 38, 41, 48, 137, 178–182,
    190, 195–198
  and Islam — 173
  jurisprudence — 144
  lands of — 1, 191, 195
  liberal theology — 35, 70, 138,
    151
  literature — 76, 138, 171, 205
  magic — 138
  Messiah — 23, 158, 171, 178 cf.
    Jesus
  messianism — 78–80, 105, 132,
    191
  missionaries — 2
  monotheism — 11, 41, 179
  as a mystery faith — 15, 167
  mythic elements — 15, 132, 138,
    142, 145, 150, 152, 154
  as a mythological cult — 145,
    150, 155
  nationalistic elements — 128–
    134, 154, 158, 168–170, 183
  pagan influence — 6, 145, 191
  Pauline — 42, 48–51, 55, 56,
    71, 72, 131, 137–146, 148, 153,
    155, 164–166
  persecution of by Pagans — 178
  philosophers — 141
  polemical literature — 17–26,
    189, 196
  polytheistic tendencies — 22, 23
  popular belief — 6

propaganda — 179
proselytization — 170
purity, ethical — 18
ritual — 41, 48, 132, 142, 151
ritualism — 48, 138 (73)
scholarship — 2-4, 17, 36, 48, 49, 51, 56, 60, 65, 67, 99, 108, 122, 141(74), 144, 147, 149(81), 155, 169, 179, 196, 206
sectarian-ascetic component — 14, 15, 37
theology — 197, 198
universalism — 14, 41-44, 47, 48, 147-154, 159, 168-170, 175, 189
cf. Catholicism, Covenant, eschatology, Jesus, Jewish Christians, priests, Protestantism, salvation, Scripture
Christus — 44
Chronos — 9, 11
church fathers, early — 19, 40, 168, 170, 175
   medieval — 197
circumcision — 41, 56, 150-152, 163
citizen — 166, 167
Clement — 175 (91, 92)
confession — 145
commandments, new — 37
commandments of the Torah — 13, 14, 19, 21, 32, 51-59, 132, 136, 138-146, 150, 153, 155, 158-167, 190
   according to Jesus — 53, 54, 67
   according to Pharasaic interpretation — 28(31), 47, 51-53, 67-69
   dependent on the Land — 21
   cf. abrogation, Law
conversion — 41-43, 46, 147-180, 192-208
   forced — 194, 195
   Halakhic — 151
   mass — 187, 192, 202, 203

cf. Christianity, Judaism, proselytization
converts — 10, 44, 47, 140, 167, 177
Corinth — 152
Corinthians — 140, 175
Cornelius — 155-158
covenant —
   in Christianity — 26, 27, 39, 41, 44, 47, 48, 118, 132, 158, 168, 169, 179, 181, 182
   in Islam — 27, 39, 41, 44
   and Jesus — 44, 118
   in Judaism — 27, 39, 41, 44, 49, 163, 164, 167
   new — 2, 39, 45, 47, 132, 158, 168, 169, 179, 181, 182
   at Sinai — 31(37)
creation — 28, 29, 34, 52, 55(12), 140, 151
Creator — 147
crucifixion — 36, 71, 108(60), 110, 117, 118, 122, 123, 127, 133, 140, 145
crusades — 179
cult of saints — 6
cults, mystery — 2
cup of affliction — 108
Cyrene — 201, 204
Cyril, Bishop of Alexandria — 205
Cyrus, Patriarch — 205

damnation — 17, 129
Deutero–Isaiah — 174
David — 54(6), 113
   crown of — 120
   heir of — 109(60), 111
   house of — 51(4), 77, 87
   kingdom of — 77, 78, 94, 107, 128
   line of — 108, 120
   messiah ben — 204
   monarchy of — 114
   scion of — 78
   seed of — 45
   son of — 74, 80, 85, 89, 106,

107, 113, 114, 120, 121, 123
(66), 130, 133
    throne of — 106, 115, 120, 178
Day of Atonement — 19
Day of Judgment — 13, 14, 35, 79–
83, 94, 119, 131, 154, 175
Day of the Lord — 80
Days of the Messiah — 94, 100,
170–174, 180
deification, of nature — 6
deities, western and eastern — 10
demigods, worship of — 5
demons — 4, 20, 73, 74, 84, 89, 102,
105, 108, 115, 119, 128, 151
determinism — 16
diaspora — 1, 157, 162, 184, 185,
190–193, 207
    Roman — 157
divination — 9
divine decree — 17
    intervention — 32
    salvation — 48
divinity — 7, 8, 10(10)
divorce — 54, 55(11), 62(16)
Domninus — 205
doomsday — 98
Duran, Profiat — 23(22), 28(31)
Duran, Simon ben Zemah — 28(31),
50(3), 56(13)

Edomites — 28
Egypt — 201, 205
    deliverance from — 28, 151
    exodus from — 151
Elazar, R. — 55(11)
election — 14, 15, 165, 168, 169,
170, 172, 174, 176, 177
Eliakim — 124(68)
Eliezer, R. — 66(25), 81(30)
Elijah the prophet — 5, 85–90, 100,
103, 119, 120
Elisha ben Avuyah — 198
Empedocles — 7
end of days — 170, 172, 175, 178,
cf. eschatology

Enoch — 85, 88, 100
Epicureans — 8
Epikursim — 207(20)
Epiphanius of Alexandria — 204
eschatology — 71–105, 129, 172–
175
esoteric rites — 8
Essenes — 49(3), 72, 78, 80, 82, 95,
103
    doctrine — 55(12)
eternal bliss — 8
eternal life — 9, 91, 147, 152
etne — 149, 171, 172
Eucharist — 142, 146
Europe — 182, 195, 201
Eutychios of Alexandria (ibn Batrik) — 205(16, 17)
evangelists — 66, 67, 69, 110, 169,
170
evil — 13, 14
    instinct — 54(11)
    spirits — 72
exegesis — 32, 33
exile — see Israel, Judaism
exiles, ingathering of — 94, 116–
118, 128, 129, 173, 174
exorcism of demons — 20, 35, 72,
102, 151
Ezra — 19, 150, 185

false messiah — 36, 120–127
false prophet — 30, 31(37), 122–
127
fasting — 73, 84, 95(55), 136, 167
Father, the — 11, 12, 143
father god — 3, 23
    in heaven — 13
festivals — 143
fetishism — 7
flood — 98, 103

Gabriel — 36
Galatians — 156
Galilee — 84, 89, 102(59)
galuth — see diaspora

Gamliel, R. — 121, 133, 137(72)
garden of Eden — 95(55)
Gehenna — 13, 69, 76, 91(35), 103, 104, 109, 113, 120, 154, 160
gentiles — 1, 13, 16, 36, 39–48, 60, 71, 72, 80, 94, 97, 105–107, 128–130, 132, 147–184, 189–192, 195, 197
Germans — 188
    Germanic tribes — 15, 40
Gesius — 205
Gnosis —
    doctrine — 8, 11
    pagan origins of — 8
    cf. salvation
God —
    the Father — 11, 12, 143
    fearers — 155–159, 161
    finger of — 152, 156
    glory of — 14
    hidden — 12
    of Israel (of Abraham, Isaac and Jacob) — 11, 12, 16, 26, 27, 37–39, 72, 78, 90, 105, 148, 164, 168, 170, 189
    as king in Judaism — 17
    kingdom of — 92(40, 49), 102–104, 112, 115, 118, 128
    the living — 122
    race of — 14
    throne of — 63
    unity of — 11
    word of — 38, 56, 60, 85
    worship of — 11, 35, 40, 160, 165
    wrath of — 14
gods — 3, 4, 6, 10, 16, 73, 79, 186, 187, 190, 200, 208
    of Rome — 161
Gog and Magog — 174
goi — 149, 171
golden calf — 169
Golgotha — 119, 132, 133, 146
gospels — 12, 50(3), 51, 61–63, 67, 68, 72, 77(29), 82–84, 93–101, 105,

107–113, 116, 117, 120–123, 128–180, 203
grace — 15, 16, 146, 159, 165, 172, 176–178
graven images — 9
Great Mother (of Asia Minor) — 3
Greek —
    — Arabic enlightenment — 206
    culture — 2, 191, 196–205
    — Hebrew — 171(89)
    Judeo (language) — 149
    literature — 200, 202
    mythology — 23, 196
    people — 28(32), 139, 140, 148, 153, 165, 171(89), 172, 203, 205
    philosophy — 2, 10, 139, 196–206
    and Roman world — 10, 12, 47, 140, 163, 185
    scholars — 199
    science — 196, 199, 200
    scriptures — 185, 197
    cf. Hellenism

Hadrian — 195, 204
Halevi, Judah — 23, 27, 28(21)
half-Jews — 155, 157–163
Hasdai Halevi Hasephardi — 32(38)
Hasidim — 36, 83
Haskalah — 201
Hasmonean period — 77, 191
heathens — 152, 153, 156, 171–177, 180
heaven — 14, 34, 63, 89, 92–94, 100, 102, 105, 113(62), 119, 120, 132, 134, 140, 151 cf. kingdom of heaven
    and earth — 4, 5, 64(20), 78, 79, 90, 103–105, 129
heavenly beings — 5, 106
    creatures — 85, 91
    messiah — 87
    Temple — 128
Hebrew — 185, 186, 198

hell — 100, 140
Hellas —
   pantheon of — 7
   wisdom of — 199
Hellenes — 185
Hellenism — 201, 202
   culture — 2, 196, 200, 201
   and Paganism — 7–10
   Persian influence — 10
   philosophy — 139–141, 196–
     199
   religious practices — 191
   science — 197
   world of — 15, 16, 180
Hellenists — 191
hereafter, the — 8
heresy — 180
heretics — 143
Hermas — 171(89)
Hermes — 9
Heroclitus — 7
Herod — 68
heroes, worship of — 5
Hillel — 58, 60
holy —
   city — 83, 173, 174, 178
   congregation — 32
   days — 143, 151
   Ghost — 140
   land — 179
   men — 5
   places — 173
Holy Spirit — 20, 24, 73, 102, 103,
   124, 126(70), 156–158, 166
Homer — 200
Hypolytus — 9

idol worship — 6–9, 161, 189, 200,
   208
   in Islam — 22, 201
idol worshipers — 149, 171
idolatry — 3–16, 23, 26, 27, 37–41,
   78–80, 108, 115, 128, 129, 154, 158,
   179–181, 189–195, 200–203

idols — 6, 63(18), 170
Idumean nation — 149(81)
India — 96
Inquisition — 207
Irenaeus — 9(8)
Islam —
   idol worship — 22
   lands of — 1, 4, 191, 195
   miracles — 25
   monotheism — 4, 11, 22, 38, 39,
     41
   nationalism — 183
   and paganism 10–17, 26, 37–
     41, 181, 182, 190, 194, 195,
     197, 198
   polemics — 17–19, 22, 24, 25,
     186, 189, 199
   popular belief — 6
   prayer — 40
   prohibition of alcohol — 40
   ritual — 41
   scholars — 196, 206
   universalism — 41–44, 189
   world — 11
   cf. covenant, Maimonides, Mu-
     hammad, Scripture

Israel —
   children of — 27
   congregation of — 46, 48, 80,
     166, 167, 191
   exile and dispersion — 1, 81, 83,
     129, 130, 167, 175–185, 188,
     192, 208
   house of — 106, 154
   and idolatry — 10, 11, 16, 191,
     192
   kingdom of — 100
   land of — 21, 40, 75
   messianism — 75
   northern kingdom of — 185
   rebellion of — 159, 168–170
   religion of — 28, 181–183, 189
   remnant of — 131, 174–177
   tribes of — 174
   cf. salvation

Index

Isaac — 91, 93, 94(53), 128, 151
  kingdom of — 105, 107, 114
  cf. God of Israel

Jacob (James the Just) — 36, 160, 164
Jacob (the patriarch) — 91, 93, 94(53), 128, 151
  kingdom of — 105, 107, 114
  cf. God of Israel
James son of Zebedee — 47, 111
Jeremiah — 82, 89
Jericho — 111, 112
Jerusalem — 19, 36, 40, 43, 44, 63, 64(19), 74, 83, 93, 94, 100, 107–128, 130–137, 143–146, 152(84), 156, 172, 174, 178
  heavenly — 172–174
  new — 94
  cf. Jesus, Temple
Jesse — 107
Jesus —
  apotheosis of — 6, 18, 50(3), 85, 88, 99, 101
  ascension to heaven — 151
  atonement in death of — 142, 145, 164
  authority of — 21
  baptism of — 84, 112
  birth of — 23
  blasphemy of — 122–127
  as bridegroom — 99, 131
  compared with Apolonius — 7
  Hillel and Akiba — 60
  Noah — 98
  crucifixion of — 36, 71, 89, 90, 108(60), 110, 117, 118, 122, 123, 127, 133, 140, 145
  death of — 61, 62, 71, 108–111, 114, 118–128, 132–140, 145–147, 159, 165, 166
  disappearance of body — 133
  divinity of — 24, 69, 71, 85, 140, 141(74)
  faith in — 98–105, 135, 136, 141, 146, 150, 157–161, 165, 166, 168, 172
  and the gentiles 39, 40, 60, 153
  healing — 20, 101, 102, 153, 157
  as heavenly being — 53, 72–74, 88, 99, 131
  as the hidden God — 12
  and idolatry — 37–39, 108
  in Jerusalem — 107–128
  as Jew — 18, 19, 49–70, 85, 94, 99, 117
  in Jewish polemics — 25, 49(3), 50(3)
  and John the Baptist — 80, 109
  and Judaism — 37, 42, 49–70
  as king of the Jews — 44, 68, 74, 107, 108, 120, 121, 127, 131
  kingdom of — 100
  as Mesiah — 20, 23, 24, 36, 60–71, 146
  lifetime — 61, 132, 136, 157
  as *Logos* — 85
  as Man of God — 88
  message to the Jews — 13
  as Messiah — 20, 23, 24, 36, 37, 44, 46(1), 50(3), 51, 62, 68–79, 84, 85, 89, 94, 99, 102–133, 141, 143, 152(85), 158, 160, 165, 172, 174, 175, 178, **191**
  miracles — 25, 50(3), 73, 89, 101, 104, 126(70), 157
  monotheism of — 38, 39
  mythological significance of — 131, 132, 136, 145, 161, 166
  not an ascetic — 94–96
  observance of the Commandments — 28, 34(45), 52, 58, 59, 160
  on marriage — 95(54)
  parables of — 36, 74, 92(38), 95–97, 109, 112, 113(62), 116, 117

as Pharisee — 69, 70
and the Pharisees — 47–77, 97,
99, 102–104, 120, 123(66),
124(68), 127
poverty of — 95, 96
as prophet — 27, 38, 39, 54, 58,
85, 88, 89, 94, 116, 121, 123
(67), 124
and Rabbinic literature — 70
as redeemer of Israel — 45, 69,
70, 74, 77, 78, 86, 87, 93, 99,
101, 103, 107, 109, 117, 124,
130, 132–136, 145, 160, 168
cf. apocalyptic redeemer
resurrection of — 20, 92(49),
110, 118, 119, 133–135, 137
(72), 140, 141, 145
as rival of Caesar — 115
as Son of God — 3, 11, 12, 16,
17, 19, 23, 24, 38, 48, 50(3),
52, 68, 69, 73, 84–89, 99, 122,
124, 125, 132, 140, 142, 145,
146, 179, 191
as Son of Man — 74, 84–89,
93, 99–110, 114, 119, 125(69),
128, 130, 137(72), 145, 171,
173
teachings of — 35, 47–60, 71–
76, 96, 99, 101, 105–107, 128,
146, 153, 166
trial of — 119–128
cf. Christianity, covenant, Scripture, signs
Jewish-Christians — 36, 37, 41, 147,
150, 157, 165
Jewry, Alexandrian — 142, 196,
204, 205
Egyptian — 201–206
Palestinian — 185
Spanish — 206–207
Joah — 124(68)
Job — 149(81)
Johanan, Bishop of Nicaea — 205
Johanan, R. — 55(11)
John son of Zebedee — 111

John the Baptist — 50(3), 60, 80–
84, 86, 88, 89, 94–97, 103–105,
109, 110, 117(64), 120, 141
Jonah — 96, 98, 99, 103, 104
Jordan (river) — 84
Josephus — 55(12), 36(47), 140
Joshua, R. — 81(30)
Judah Halevi — 23, 27, 28(31)
Judah, R. — 46(1), 64(19)
Judaism —

apologetics — 61
apostasy — 191–195, 207
assimilation — 181–208
cabalistic — 18, 25
converts and conversion — 11,
41–43, 140, 147–180, 182, 208
customs and practices — 26,
140, 162, 184, 185, 195
dispersion — 191, 201
Enlightenment — 33
eschatology — 71, 80, 129, 173
exile — 41–48, 167, 178–184,
189, 193, 208
gentiles — 11, 40, 147–180, 197
and Greek culture and philosophy — 196–206
Hasidic — 18
Hellenistic — 2, 138–142, 196–
206
historical beginnings — 26
holy days — 151
homeletics — 139
and idolatry (= paganism) —
26, 48, 106, 128, 129, 178,
181, 182, 189–191, 195–203
jurisprudence — 143–146
legendry — 151, 198
liberal theology — 35, 138
messiah — 31(77), 81(30), 87,
168, 170, 171, 178, 204
messianic expectation — 44, 45,
74, 176, 178
messianism — 128, 129, 135,
153, 154, 168, 170, 178, 191

monotheism — 2–17, 129, 138, 170, **179**, 181, 196
mysticism — 25, 88, 100
nationalism — 47–49, 51, 105–119, 128, 130, 148, 168, 178, 181–208
pagan syncretism in — 72
Pharisaic — 53, 60, 64, 96, 123 (*67*), 124, 149, 153, 154, 168, 170
philosophic — 18
and philosophy, medieval — 26–33, 185, 196, 197, 199
modern — 33–35, 196
polemics — 17–45, 49(3), 189, 196–200
propaganda — 180
proselytization — 42, 148–180
purity, physical — 17
religious persecution of — 192–195, 203–207
ritualism — 47, 48, 136, 145
scholars — 49, 61, 122, 124, 196, **206**
sectarianism — 80, 193
tribal ethnic character — 181–196
universalism — 41–44, 48, 139, 147–154, 182, 183, 189
world view — 11
cf. covenant, diaspora, Israel, Jesus, Jewry, priests, Scripture,
judaizers — 155–167, 170, 179
Judas Iscariot — 127
Judeans — 184
Judeo-Greek — 149
Justin Martyr — 23(18), 56(13), 125(69)

Ka'abah stone — 22
Kaddish — 76(29)
Khadijah — 19
Kingdom of heaven — 13, 15, 53, 60, 68, 74–78, 80, 81, 89–98, 100, 102, 104–115, 130–132, 136, 150, 151, 157, 158, 160, 163, 165, 166, 172–174, 177

Last Supper — 92, 118
Lat — 10
Law, the — 19–22, 27–34, 37, 42, 47–60, 100–104, 132, 136, 147, 154, 156, 160, 163–166, 181
canonical and secular — 144
divine origin of — 33
experts of — 103
Halakhic — 64, 198
Mosaic — 32(37), 48, 101, 146
old and new — 150, 151, 154
reformed — 37
ritual — 14, 58, 59, 61, 62, 132, 137, 138, 190
written and oral — 22, 56, 60, 61, 66, 131, 151
cf. abrogation, commandments, Jesus, Muhammad, Paul
Lazarus — 95(55)
Logos — 18, 85, 140, 141(74), 204
Lot — 98
Luke — 13, 137

Maccabean revolt — 195
Maimonides — 28–33, 54(11), 198
exegesis and midrash — 32, 33
and Islam — 32
Manuf — 205
Marianism — 4
marriage — 54, 95(54)
Marranos — 206, 207
Martius Turbo — 204
martyrdom — 178, 195
Mary — 3, 5, 44
Mecca — 22, 40
Mediterranean culture — 73
Meir, R. — 5
Menschenreligion — 33–35
Messiah —
messianic faith — 79, 80
hope — 176–178

judgment — 158, 170
   period — 69
   procession — 113–115, 118, 123(66)
   visions — 75
messianism — see Christianity, Israel, Judaism
Michael (the angel) — 75, 77, 87, 100
midrashic exegesis — 197, 198
   literature — 55, 81(30)
miracles — 25, 28, 29, 33(40), 35, 36, 50(3), 73, 101, 104, 116, 133, 134, 170
   cf. Jesus, Muhammad
Mithra — 12
Mithras, cult of — 10
mitzvah — 99, 135
Molcho, Solomon — 207
monarchy — 80
monogamy — 55
Moses — 25, 29, 30, 31(37), 33, 44, 52, 54, 60, 71, 85, 169
   covenant — 44
   seat of — 69
   cf. Law
mother of God — 3, 24
Muhammad —
   authority of — 21, 22
   and idolatry — 37–39
   Jewish followers of — 36
   and the Law — 40
   and monotheism — 38, 39
   as Prophet — 12, 19, 25, 27, 36–39, 43, 45
   rejected by Jews — 35–45
   sexual life of — 31
   teachings of — 11, 35
   cf. covenant, Islam, Scripture
murder — 57
mystery cults — 8, 15
   faiths — 8, 129
   prophets — 12
mystics — 72, 87, 100
mythology — 73

Naasenes — 9
Nachman, R. — 64(18)
Nachmanides — 23(22), 24(23)
nature — 6
Nazereth — 73
Nazarenes — 61, 71, 118, 119, 123 (66), 136, 137, 143, 145, 147, 150, 152, 157–160
   prayer — 92(38)
Nazerites — 97
   asceticism — 95
Near East — 182, 196
Nebuchadnezzar — 192
Nehemiah — 150, 185
New Testament — 24, 76, 94(53), 147–149
New Year — 76
Ninveh — 81, 98
Noah — 98
Nomos — 142

oaths — 62–67
Omar, Caliph — 205
Ophites — 9
Origenes — 65(21)

paganism — 1–16
   background of Judaizers — 163
   culture — 7, 189
   destruction of — 11, 37
   dominion — 82, 108, 129, 178, 180, 190, 191, 195, 200
   influence on Jewish Mysticism — 25
   lands of — 38, 78
   nations — 78, 106, 181
   philosophy — 7, 9, 197
   ritualism in — 166
   cf. Christianity, Islam, Judaism, priests
Papias — 93
paradise — 76
Parousia — 88
Paschal lamb — 92, 93

Index

Passover service — 5, 92, 108, 118, 127, 133, 151

patriarchs — 5, 11, 34, 78, 97, 105, 152

Paul —
  abrogation and nullification of the Law — 20, 21, 40, 47, 48, 56, 57, 136, 144–146, 164, 165
  address to the Athenians — 13, 135
  and Barnabas — 152
  and Catholic ritual — 48
  compared with Apollonius — 7
  Epistles — 47(1), 146
  as founder of gentile congregation — 44, 46, 49, 149(81), 152–155, 159, 164, 167, 171, 172, 177(94), 179
  as a Jew — 148, 159
  and the Jews — 167
  and keeping the Law — 137, 160
  and the Last Supper — 118
  on marriage — 95(54)
  and the Messiah — 165
  and the murder of Stephen — 137(72)
  as a Pharisee — 137(72)
  preaching in the Synagogue — 20
  and the rejection of Jesus — 36, 123(66)
  as Saul — 137(72)
  sermon at Antioch — 146, 152
  and the teachings of Jesus — 45, 56, 58, 59, 130, 131, 136, 145, 166
  cf. Christianity, Jesus, Scripture

Pentecost — 133

Pentateuch — 22, 44, 51, 53, 55, 66, 124, 125(68), 127, 142, 189

perdition — 9, 158

Perseus — 23

Persian religion and culture — 10, 12, 28(32)

Peter — 47, 134, 148, 155, 160, 164, 165

Pharisees — 28(31), 36, 96, 97, 134, 137, 170, 171
  and Jesus — 47–77, 102–104, 120, 123(66), 124(68), 125, 127

Philo — 140, 142, 185, 196, 198, 202, 204

piety — 135, 154, 164, 165

Pilate — 94(53), 97, 117(64), 124 (68), 125(68), 126, 127

pilgrimage — 5

Pisidia — 146, 165

Plato — 7, 202, 206

pogroms — 192, 204

Poles, the — 188

polytheism — 3–8, 10(10), 12, 27, 181, 182, 191

Portugal — 207(20)

poverty — 95, 135

prayer — 35, 40, 73, 81(30), 84, 132, 136, 174

priests,
  Amalekite — 31(37)
  chief — 120
  high — 121, 122, 125
  Christian — 14
  Jewish — 5, 11
  Levite — 31(37)
  pagan — 199, 200

prophet and prophecy — 32, 33, 36–45, 54, 83–88, 95(55), 102(59), 103, 105, 106, 108(60), 110, 116, 117, 124, 125, 157, 200
  false — 30, 31(37)

Prophetic literature — 20, 52, 53, 57, 87

prophets, Israelite — 20, 54, 57, 59, 75, 76, 82–91, 94(53), 96, 99, 101(58), 105, 110, 116, 142, 146, 160, 169, 170, 174, 189

proselytism — 9

219

proselytization — 147–180 cf. conversion
prostitution rites — 13
Protestant scholars — 3
Protestantism — 41, 88
providence, divine — 34
purification — 7

Queen of Heaven — 3, 5

Rab-shakeh — 124(68)
Rabbah — 64
Red Sea — 104
redeemer — 2, 9, 15, 36, 52 cf. Jesus, apocalyptic
redemption — 2, 12, 78–81, 85, 87, 96, 98, 106–109, 129–131, 135, 146, 150, 154, 155, 159, 169, 170, 171
Reformation — 4
religions, higher — 182, 187, 188
repentance — 13, 17, 58, 78–82, 84, 91(35), 96, 98, 106, 109, 111, 114, 127, 131, 132, 135, 145, 158, 170, 171, 173, 175
resurrection of the dead — 20, 31 (37), 35, 54, 75–79, 91, 92(49), 94, 100, 107, 128, 132(72), 140, 141, 151
retribution, divine — 80–83, 171
revelation — 2, 7, 25–33, 39–44, 48, 71, 104, 124, 132, 158, 160, 161, 171, 181, 182, 199, cf. Sinai
Rex Judaeorum — 117
righteous the — 83, 88, 91(35), 93–96, 105, 140, 154, 158, 174
ritus — 132
Roman world — 175
Romans — 120–123, 126, 139, 140
Rome — 107, 108, 114, 115, 127, 144, 161, 173, 174
Russia — 5, 188

Saadia — 23(22), 27
Sabbath — 53(6), 54(6), 62, 118, 143, 151, 205

sacrifices — 7, 8, 44, 58, 64, 65, 136, 138, 142, 143, 203
    abolition of — 21
sacrament — 179
Sadducees — 60, 61, 66, 81(32), 120, 123, 125, 134, 137
sages — 169, 198
saintly, the — 8, 78, 83, 98, 104
saints — 2, 4, 5, 14, 105, 107, 149
salvation — 17, 109, 119, 129, 146, 150, 152–154, 159, 161, 164–166, 169, 171, 172, 176, 177
    in Christianity — 17, 109, 119, 146, 150, 152–154, 159, 161, 164, 166, 171, 172, 176, 177
    in Gnosis — 9
    in Israel — 16, 109, 150, 169
    in Judaism — 176
    universal — 176
Samaritans — 42, 46, 96, 106, 153
Samuel, R. — 81(30)
sanctification — 146
    of God's name — 178
sanctuary — 62–64
Sanhedrin — 20, 119, 124–127, 134
Sassanids — 10, 195
Satan — 16, 52, 54, 61, 72, 78, 84, 89, 91, 102, 105, 108, 110, 115, 119, 128, 130, 131, 135, 140, 151, 174
savior — 11, 87, 128
Scholastics — 197
scribes — 60, 61(15), 69, 97, 120, 137(72)
Scripture —
    anthropomorphism — 7, 25, 141, 142
    in Christianity — 28, 35, 42, 43, 46(1), 93, 143, 145
    evidence of Jesus — 20–26, 134, 143, 145, 160
    evidence of Muhammad — 19, 22
    Greek — 185, 197
    in Islam — 28, 35, 43

and Jesus — 54, 55, 62, 107, 110
in Judaism — 26, 42, 43, 139, 143, 169
and Paul — 172
reinterpretation in Christianity and Islam — 35
Scythians — 148
seers — 36, 75
Septuagint — 63(17), 185
Sermon on the Mount — 53, 54, 56 (13), 143
Servant of the Lord — 79
seventy-two, the — 102
Shabbetai-Zevi — 74, 128
Shammai — 55(11)
Shammaites — 62(16)
Shebna — 124(68)
Shekhinah — 18
Sheol — 75, 130
Shneur, R. David Abraham — 207 (20)
shrines — 4, 6, 7
signs —
of God of Israel — 27, 29, 30, 34
of Jesus — 19, 20, 31, 98, 100, 103, 104, 120, 122, 125–128, 134, 157
of Muhammad — 19, 31, 34
and wonders — 27, 29, 30, 31, 33, 156–158, 203
Simon Cephas — 50(3)
Simon the Leper — 99(57)
Sinai —
covenant at — 30(37)
miracles at — 28, 104
revelation at — 2, 27–33, 48, 161, 165, 199
theophany at — 29, 34, 132, 146, 160
slavery — 145
Slavic tribes — 15, 40
Socrates (chuch historian) — 205
Sodom — 98, 103, 109, 115

Solomon — 31(37), 99
Son of Man — 78 cf. Jesus
Spain — 206
Spanish —
language — 207
Stephen — 124(68), 125(69), 137 (72)
Stoa — 2
Stoics — 7, 203
Suidas — 205(15)
superstition — 70, 142
supreme good — 7
synagogue of Satan — 61
synagogues — 20, 62(16)
syncretism — 9, 10
Synesius of Cyrene — 205

Tacitus — 140
Talmudic literature — 59, 62, 65, 80, 81, 126(70), 185, 198
eschatology — 77(29)
Targumim — 76(29)
Temple, the (of Jerusalem) — 44, 50(3), 79, 83, 93, 99, 114, 120, 136–138, 142, 143, 146, 162, 174, 176
first, destruction of — 79, 189, 191
heavenly — 128
period of — 181, 185
second, destruction of — 83, 143
temples —
destruction of — 11
new — 137(72)
pagan — 13, 186, 199, 200, 203
testament, new — 48, 167, 179, 182
Theodosius the great — 204
theophany — 29, 34, 132, 146, 160, 170
time to come — 21, 93, 140, 171, 175, 186
Torah — 13, 14, 18, 21, 25–30, 32, 34, 44, 45, 50(3), 54, 55(11), 56–

60, 71, 124, 131, 150–153, 160, 164, 185

Trajan — 204

trinity — 3, 18, 23–25, 141(74)

Trypho the Jew — 23(18), 53(13), 125(69)

twelve apostles — 93, 100, 104, 111, 112, 118
    thrones — 91, 100, 104
    tribes — 45, 91, 100, 104, 106, 177

uncircumcised, the — 155, 158, 165, 166

universe, center of — 173

Urbib of Alexandria — 205

visions — 35, 157
    of God — 85

vows — 62–67, 73

war, religious — 186, 194

wealth — 95

wicked, the — 83, 88, 91

wine — 5, 92, 93, 118

wisdom — 141
    esoteric — 16
    pagan — 16

word of the Lord — 88

world to come — 90, 94, 95(55), 103, 106

worship — cf. God, heroes, idol

YHWH, religion of — 181

Zebedee, sons of — 111, 112

Zeno — 205

Zeus — 9–11, 23

Zerubbabel — 185

Zohar — 25(25), 185

INDEXES OF SOURCES

** *Hebrew Bible*

Genesis — 151:
  2:24 — 54, 55

Exodus
  32:10 — 169

Leviticus
  19:12 — 63(17)

Numbers
  23:7 — 50(3)

Deuteronomy — 143
  9:14 — 169
  11:19 — 54(7)
  13:1 — 30
    2 — 126(70)
    2–4 — 125
  13f. — 32(37)
  18:20 — 126(70)
    20–22 — 125
    20–26 — 122
  21:11f. — 54
  23:22 — 63

2 Kings
  18:37 — 124(68)

Isaiah
  11:1f. — 87
  53 — 135(71)
  66:1–2 — 137

Ezekiel
  20:32, 33 — 208

Hosea
  6:6 — 57(14)

Zephania
  3:12 — 95(55)

Haggai
  1:12, 14 — 79
  2:2 — 79

Zechariah
  8:6, 11, 12 — 79
  9:9 — 113

Malachi
  1:10–12 — 169
  3:23 — 87

Ruth
  1:16 — 187

Daniel — 75, 77
  7:13 — 92(41)
    13–14 — 88
  12 — 75
  12:1 — 87
    3 — 92(48)

Ezra
  9:8, 13, 15 — 79

Nehemiah
  1:3 — 79

** *New Testament*

Matthew — 102(59)
  3:1–4 — 80
    2 — 81(31)
    7, 8 — 81
    9 — 97
    13 — 84
  4:1–10 — 72
    1–11 — 54(10), 84
    1–14 — 89
    12 — 84
    17 — 76(29), 77(29), 84
  5:3 — 95(55)
    17–18 — 52, 53
    19 — 21, 52
    19f. — 97
    31–32 — 55(11)
    31–33 — 62(16)
    32 — 54

33 — 63
34–36 — 64(20)
6:5f. — 84
24–33 — 96
7:12 — 54(9)
13–14 — 97
21f. — 101(58)
29 — 52
33 — 89
8:11f. — 91(35)
9.2f. — 102
3 — 124(68)
15 — 99
21f. — 101
34 — 20
10:1f. — 102
5–6 — 153
6 — 44
23 — 93, 89, 102(59)
56 — 106
11:18 — 84
19 — 95(55)
25 — 103
29 — 98
12:1f. — 62(16)
1–7 — 54(6)
6 — 99
9–14 — 62(16)
11 — 62(16)
11f. — 54(6)
24 — 20
24–29 — 102
31–32 — 103, 124(68), 126(70)
38–40 — 98
39 — 98
41–42 — 99
13:11–15 — 97
17 — 99
34 — 97
36–49 — 92(46)
39f. — 92(38)
43 — 92(48)
14:1f. — 89
15:1f. — 62(16)
3f. — 64

3–5 — 54(6)
5 — 62(16), 65(21, 23), 66(24)
19 — 58
21–27 — 106
24 — 102, 153
26 — 153
16:3–14 — 89
13f. — 20
23 — 110
28 — 89
17:12 — 57
18:8–9 — 92(37, 40)
17 — 106
19:3 — 62(16)
3f. — 55(11)
4f. — 54
12 — 95(54)
16 — 100
16–29 — 97
17 — 72
17–18 — 54(8)
18–19 — 57
21 — 100
27 — 101
28 — 92(39, 43)
29 — 92(37), 94, 101
30 — 104
20:16 — 104
22–28 — 111
21:1–9 — 113
15–16 — 114
23 — 120
31–32 — 103
22:14 — 97
21 — 114
22–32 — 60
29–32 — 141
30 — 92(47)
31–32 — 54(7)
35–40 — 54(9), 57
41–45 — 85
23:1–2 — 60
3–5 — 69
14 — 104
16f. — 62

16–21 — 54(6)
16–22 — 63
22 — 64
23f. — 57
29–31 — 105
37 — 93
37–39 — 116
38 — 117*
24:3 — 92(38)
4–31 — 173
30 — 92(41)
37–39 — 98(56)
25 — 113(62)
14–30 — 112
31 — 92(42)
32 — 92(44)
46 — 92(45)
26:6–13 — 99(57)
12 — 99(57)
29 — 93(51), 118
38 — 19
63 — 122
64 — 92(41), 119
65 — 122, 123
67–68 — 121
27:37 — 117(64)
41–43 — 122

Mark
1:2–3 — 81(31)
4, 6 — 80
12–14 — 84
24 — 72
27 — 72, 101
28, 34 — 72
2:15–19 — 95(55)
21 — 62(16)
23–28 — 54(6)
3:2–6 — 62(16)
4 — 54(6)
21 — 73
22 — 20
4:11–12 — 97
34 — 97
6:7–13 — 102

7:1f. — 62(16)
8 — 65(21)
10–12 — 54(6)
12 — 66
27 — 153
27–28 — 106
8:27f. — 20
38 — 9
9:1 — 93, 110
29 — 73
31, 32 — 110
33–37 — 111(61)
38 — 73
43 — 92(37)
43–47 — 92(40)
45 — 92(37)
10:2–12 — 54
17f. — 54(8)
17–30 — 97
18 — 72
19 — 57
28–31 — 94
31 — 104
33–34 — 110
35f. — 111
42–45 — 112
11:1–10 — 113
12:1–11 — 116
28, 31 — 57
32f. — 58
13:5–27 — 174
7 — 92(38)
26 — 92(41)
30 — 93
14:3–9 — 99(57)
25 — 118
34 — 119
58 — 93
61 — 20
62 — 119
63 — 119, 122
65 — 121
15:26–27 — 117
31–32 — 122
16:38 — 112

Luke

2:25 — 78
3:3 — 81(31)
 7, 8, 10–14 — 81
4:1–13 — 54(10)
6:1–5 — 54(6)
 6–11 — 62(16)
 20 — 95(55)
 31 — 57
 46 — 101(58)
7:29–30 — 103
 33 — 84
 34 — 95(55)
 36 — 68
 36–48 — 99
8:10 — 97
9:1–6 — 102
 18f. — 20
 27 — 110
 46–48 — 111(61)
10:1f. — 102(59)
 17, 18 — 102
 21 — 103
 24 — 99
 25–28 — 57
11:1 — 84
 29–30 — 98
 31–32 — 99
 39f. — 57
 46 — 69
 46–48 — 105
 52 — 104
12:32 — 97, 104
13:1–5 — 97
 15–17 — 54(6)
 16 — 106
 23f. — 97
 28–29 — 91(35)
 30 — 104
 31 — 68
 34 — 93
 34–35 — 116
 35 — 117*
14:5 — 54(6)
 14 — 91(36)

15 — 92(49)
 16f. — 91(35)
16:17 — 52
 18 — 54
 19f. — 95(55)
 31 — 52
17:27 — 98
18:18f. — 54(8)
 18–30 — 97
 20 — 57
 28–30 — 94
 32–34 — 110
19:9 — 106
 11–27 — 112
 12 — 113(62)
 38 — 113
 38–40 — 114
21:8–36 — 173
 9 — 92(38)
 27f. — 92(41)
22:14–30 — 118
 16 — 92(50)
 30 — 92(49)
 31–32 — 119
 36–38 — 114
 63–65 — 121
 70 — 119
24:21 — 74
 30f. — 92(49)
27:37 — 117(64)

John

1:47 — 106
5:9–10 — 174
7:9f. — 174
11:2, 18 — 174
16:19 — 174
17:15–16 — 174
18:23–24 — 174
 36 — 94(53)
19:15, 19 — 174
 21 — 117(64)
20:2, 3, 7f. — 174

Acts — 138, 152
1:3 — 134

6 — 40, 118, 134
16 — 74
2:36 — 134(71), 135
42 — 118
44f. — 133, 134
3:1–11 — 134
15, 18, 21 — 134(71)
4:1–2 — 137(72)
10–12 — 134(71)
14 — 101
5:12–16 — 134
30–31 — 134(71)
34–39 — 121, 134
6:8–7:60 — 124(68)
11, 14 — 137(72)
7:47–50 — 137(72)
52 — 135(71)
53, 56 — 137(72)
56–57 — 125(69)
8:32–35 — 135(71)
10–11 — 155
10:34–35 — 148
41 — 49
42–48 — 156
43 — 135, 136
45 — 171(89)
11:1 — 171(89)
17–18 — 156
18 — 158, 171(89)
13:16–41 — 146
22f. — 45
46 — 152(85)
48 — 167, 171(89)
14:2 — 171(89)
15:1–29 — 165
8–9 — 156
17:16f. — 13
31 — 135(71)
31–32 — 140
18:1–6 — 152(85)
6 — 171(89)
18 — 20
24–25 — 84
20:16 — 20
21:11 — 171(89)

17f. — 137
20 — 134
26 — 137
22:17 — 136, 146
18 — 136
23:6, 9 — 137(72)
26:6–7 — 45
28:20 — 45
25–28 — 152(85)

Romans
1 — 13, 14
1:5, 16 — 172
2:11 — 148(76)
3:29 — 148
4 — 148(78)
4:16–17 — 46(1)
9:4, 6 — 176
7f. — 148(78)
24 — 172
25 — 173
30 — 172
10:12 — 148(77)
11 — 148(79)
11:11 — 152(82)
11–12 — 172
17 — 167
17f. — 46
17–26 — 177(94)
24 — 172
25–26 — 152(83)
25–36 — 177
28 — 177
15:8f. — 152(84)
18 — 172
26–27 — 152(84), 172

1 Corinthians
1–2 — 141
1:22 — 123(66), 171
23 — 139, 171
6:1f. — 144
7:1f. — 95(54)
12:13 — 148(77)
15:3 — 146
17–18, 32 — 141

Galatians — 164
  1:17–18 — 146
  2:11f. — 165
    21 — 165
  3f. — 47(1)
  3:2–5 — 157
    8–14 — 172
    14–29 — 148(79)
    28 — 148(77)
  4:4f — 56
  5:3 — 56

Ephesians
  1:12f. — 148(80)
    13 — 157
    14 — 173
  2:11f. — 148(80)
    12 — 46(1)

1 Thessalonians
  4:15f. — 141

Titus
  2:14 — 173

Hebrews
  13:14 — 173

1 Peter
  2:9,10 — 173

3 John
  7 — 174(89)

Revelation
  7f. — 177

** *Apocrypha and Pseudepigrapha*

Ascent of Moses — 76(29)

1 Enoch — 75, 82, 87(33), 92(48)
  45f. — 88
  46:1–6 — 88(34)
  48:2 — 88(34)
    2–6 — 88
  52:1–16 — 88(34)
  59:24–29 — 88(34)
  62:13–14 — 92(49)
  71:14–17 — 87, 88(34)

  94:6f. — 95(55)
  94f. — 58
  108:8–10 — 95(55)

2 Esdras (4th Ezra) — 129

Psalms of Solomon
  5:18f. — 76(29)
  17:3 — 76(29)

Sibyllines
  3:46f. — 76(29)

** *Rabbinic Sources*

Bereshit Rabbah 24 — 58

Mishnah — 63, 123(67), 124, 125, 198
  Nedarim 1:3 — 63, 64(19)
    2:1 — 63(18)
    2:2 — 67(26)
    3:2 — 66(25)
    9:1, 4 — 66(25)
  Sanhedrin 7:5 — 123(67), 124
  Shevuot 4:13 — 64(20)
  Sotah 3:4 — 61(15)
    9:15 — 180

Talmud, Bab.
  Gittin 9–10 — 55(11)
    56–57 — 50(3)
    90b — 55(11)
  Kiddushin 21b — 54(11)
  Nedarim 14a — 63(18)
  Niddah 61b — 21(13)
  Sanhedrin 43a — 50(3)
    60a — 124(68)
    90b — 54(7)
    92a — 54(7)
    97b–98a — 81(30)
    101a — 62(16)
    107b — 50(3)
  Shabbat 31a — 58
    128b — 62(16)
  Shevuot 35 — 64(20)
  Sottah 47b — 50(3)
  Yoma 86b — 81(30)

Talmud, Jer.
  Bikkurim 1:4 — 46
  Hagigah 22 — 50(3)
  Succah 5:1 — 204

Yalkut Shimoni, part 1, 771 — 50
  (3); 798 — 50(3)

** *Other Primary Sources*

Adversis haereses (Irenaeus), I c.
  224 — 9(8)
Analles (Eutychios of Alexandria)
  — 205(16, 17)
Antiquities of the Jews (Josephus),
  18:1:5 — 55(12); 20:9:1 — 36
  (47)
Apostles Manuel, *(the Didache)* IX,
  3 — 175(93); X, 7 — 92(38)
Be Not Like Thy Fathers (Duran,
  P.) — 23(22), 28(31)
Beliefs and Opinions (Saadai), Preface, 5, 6 — 27(26); Part 2, chaps.
  4f, 7 — 23(22); Part 3, ch. 6f —
  27(27)
De Bellis Civilibus (Epiphanius of
  Alexandria), II, 90 — 204(11)
Book of Principles (Albo), Part 3,
  chaps. 14f., 20 — 31(37)
Chronicle of Johanan of Nicaea, ch.
  112 — 205(18)
Civitus Dei (Augustine), Book 18,
  ch. 47 — 149(8)
Codex Theodosianus, XIII, 5, 18 —
  205(12)
Dialogue with Trypho the Jew
  (Justin Martyr), ch. 8 — 23(19),
  57(13); ch. 38 — 125(69); chaps
  38f. — 23(20); chaps. 55f. —
  23(18), 125(69); chaps. 66f. —
  23(18); ch. 67; — 23(21); ch.
  68 — 125(69); chaps. 68f. —
  23(20); ch. 74 — 125(69)
Didache — see *Apostles Manuel*
Epistle of Barnabas — 138(73)
Epistle of Diogenetus — 174(90)

Epistle of Reproof and Faith (Alami) — 207(20)
Epistle of Synesius of Cyrene, 4 —
  205(13)
Epistle to Yemen (Maimonides) —
  22(16), 24(24), 28(32), 31(37),
  32(38)
First Epistle to the Corinthians
  (Clement) 59:3 — 175(92); 59:
  3-4 — 175(91)
Guide to the Perplexed (Maimo-
  nides) 2:16 — 29(33); 2:25 —
  29(33), 33(40); 2:33 — 30(35);
  2:39 — 31(37); 2:40 — 31(37)
Hermae Pastor (Hermas' *The She-
  pherds*) — 171(89)
Historia Ecclesiae (Socrates), 7, 13,
  17 — 205(14)
Koran — 22
Kuzari (Judah Halevy), 1:11f. —
  27(28)
Lexicon (Suidas), s.v. "Thesios" —
  205(15)
Life of Jesus (Toledoth Yeshu) —
  50(3)
Milhemet Hobah (anthology) —
  28(31), 50(3)
Mishne Torah (Maimonides),
  Melahim 11:3 — 31(37)
  Nedarim 1:27 — 64(18); 3:1,
    6f. — 64(20)
  Shevuot 8:35 — 64(18); 12:
    3-4 — 64(20)
  Teshuvah 9:12 — 31(37)
  Yesoday haTorah 8:1 — 30(34);
    8:2-3 — 30(35); 9:1 — 30
    (36)

Pistis Sophia — 7; sec. 136 — 9(6)
Prayer Book (Jewish) — 76(29)
Refutation of Christianity (Duran,
  S.) — 28(31), 50(3)
*Responsa and Letters of Maimo-
  nides* — 22(15), 32(38)
Story of Simon Cephas (Otzar ha-
  Midrashim) — 50(3)

Supplement to Sepher Hakabbalah of ibn David (Abraham of Torutiel) — 207(20)

Zohar — 25(25), 185

** *Modern Authors*

Arkish, I. — 23(22)
Billerbeck, P. — 65(22), 76(29), 77(29), 123(66)
Blau, J. — 22(15)
Bousset, W. — 3(1), 9(9), 51(4), 123(67)
Buechler, A. — 61(15), 62(16), 65 (21, 23)
Caetani, L. — 205(17, 18)
Chamberlain, J. — 4
Chwolsohn, D. — 61(15), 62(16), 65(23), 123(67), 125(70), 126(70)
Delitsch, F. — 6(24)
Geiger, A. — 49
Goodspeed, E.J. — 117*
Graetz, H. — 49, 56, 113(63), 207 (20)
Gruetzmacher, G. — 205(13)
Gunkel, H. — 3(1)
Halkin, A. S. — 22(16)
Harkavy, A. — 207(20)
Harnack, A. — 3(1), 4(3), 49(3), 148
Harvey — 9(8)
Havet, E. — 140(74)
Hennecke, E. — 57(14)
Hercher, R. — 205(13)
Herford, R. T. — 50(3)
Hertz, J. — 76(29)
Hirschfeld, H. — 27(28)
Husband, R. W. — 123(67)
Jellinek, A. — 50(3), 207(20)
Kaufmann, Y. — 48(2), 113(62),

137*, 153(86), 154(87), 184(1, 2) 186(3, 4), 201(9)
Kalthoff, J.A. — 3(1)
Klausner, J. — 50(3), 51(5), 54(6, 11), 61(15), 62(16), 65(23), 66 (25), 70(28), 93(52), 94(53), 108(60), 109(60), 123(67), 125 (70)
Krauss, S. — 126(70)
Lichtenberg, E.L. — 32(38)
Liechtenhan, R. — 9(7)
Luther, M. — 65(21)
Mendelssohn, M. — 33
Migne, J.P. — 149(8), 50(3)
Meyer, E. — 3, 49(3), 51(4, 5), 65 (21), 124(68), 147–148
Norden, E. — 3(1), 7(4)
Pfleiderer, O. — 3(1)
Rabinowitz, S.P. — 207(20)
Reimarus, H.S. — 51, 110
Reitzenstein, R. — 3(1)
Renan, E. — 12, 89
Rousseau, J.J. — 51
Ruppin, A. — 202(10)
Schechter, S. — 55(12)
Schmidt, K. — 9(6)
Schubart, J.H.C. — 202(10)
Spengler, O. — 4(3)
Steinschneider, M. — 22(17), 23(22), 25(25)
Strack, H. — 65(22), 76(29), 77 (29), 123(66)
Usener, H. — 3(1)
Weinel, H. — 57(14)
Wellhausen, J. — 10(10), 51(4), 82, 122(66), 144
Wendland, P. — 3(1). 8(5)
Wuensche, A. — 65(23)
Zahn, T. — 65(21)
Zelinski — 3(1)
Zollschan, I. — 202(10)
Zutenberg — 205(18)